CW00456967

M. G. Flowers

THE
FIGHTER
PILOT'S
HANDBOOK

Overleaf: The tail-end of an F-16C, with speed brakes open, frames the 'macho' image of the combat-ready fighter pilot.
(David Rothenanger)

THE
FIGHTER PILOT'S
HANDBOOK

JOHN ROBERTS

ARMS AND
ARMOUR

Arms & Armour Press
A Cassell Imprint

Villiers House, 41–47 Strand, London WC2N 5JE.

Distributed in Australia by Capricorn Link (Australia) Pty.
Ltd., P.O. Box 665, Lane Cove, New South Wales 2066

British Library Cataloguing in Publication data:
Roberts, John
The fighter pilot's handbook
I. Title
623.74609

ISBN 1845090933

Edited and designed by Roger Chesneau.
Typeset by Ronset Typesetters Ltd, Darwen, Lancashire.
Monochrome reproduction by M&E Reproductions,
North Fambridge, Essex.
Printed and bound in Great Britain by
Mackays of Chatham PLC, Chatham, Kent

CONTENTS

HIGH FLIGHT

Oh, I have slipped the surly bonds of Earth
And danced the skies on laughter-silvered wings;
Sunward I've climbed and joined the tumbling mirth
Of sun-split clouds – and done a hundred things
You have not dreamed of – wheeled and soared and swung
High in the sunlit silence. Hovering there
I've chased the shouting wind along and flung
My eager craft through footless halls of air.
Up up the long delirious, burning blue
I've topped the wind-swept heights with easy grace.
Where never lark, or even eagle, flew;
And, while with silent, lifting mind I've trod
The high untrespassed sanctity of space,
Put out my hand, and touched the face of God.

John Gillespie Magee Jr

Foreword

Wing Commander Mal Prissick RAF

Being a fighter pilot means having extreme pride in being a member of an élite team of thoroughly professional individuals who devote their whole existence to the pursuit of excellence in the demanding and occasionally unforgiving world of fast-jet flying. These are people who exude a total confidence in their own ability, learned over many years of hard training, to fly their machines to the limits and to win through no matter the difficulty of the circumstances. They never accept second best, and the words 'defeat', 'failure' or 'losing' are not in their vocabulary. In short, flying fighters is the 'sport of kings'. No other occupaton can compare with the challenge, excitement and sense of achievement.

I will treasure this book in the years to come because *The Fighter Pilot's Handbook* provides an articulate, insider's expression of what my profession is all about. This book isn't just for fighter pilots – it's for everyone who wants to understand them, and to understand why they are important to our nation.

THE AUTHOR

John Roberts was a USAF fighter pilot. He taught USAF
Combat Operations and Tactics at the US Air Force Academy
and was Aide and Executive Officer to the Vice Commander of
US Air Forces in Vietnam, where he flew 134 combat missions
in the F-4 Phantom. Later he was an Air Combat Tactics
Instructor Pilot and the Operations Officer of a NATO fighter
squadron. He is a graduate of the US Armed Forces Staff
College and holds an MBA degree from New York University.
He is now the editor of *Air Forces International*.

*This book is for just a few of the great fighter pilots I flew with
in peace and war who gave me their help, encouragement,
friendship and, most of all, their fighter pilot attitude, along
the way:*

General Robert Dixon	*Colonel Al Lambert*
Brigadier General Robin	*Colonel Don Creighton*
Olds	*Lt Colonel Bob Delaney*
Colonel Doyle Ruff	*Art Chase*
Colonel Al Bache	*Joe Bailey*
Colonel Ken Coffee	*Sam Planck*

Colonel Bill Hubbell

and for all of you who share the fighter pilot spirit.

*One crowded hour of glorious life
is worth an age without a name.*
Mourdant

Introduction

As with every profession, the fraternity of fighter pilots has its own special history, character, literature, ideology, standards, ideals, procedures, equipment and heroes. This collection is a sampling from that body of writings and illustrations – a flavour of pages, pictures and thoughts from a vast encyclopaedia which grows ever larger.

Above all, it is a book for fighter pilots. It is a compilation of a few of the things that I wish had been collected in one place when I was in the profession. And now that I am not, this is a book that I will always enjoy picking up. You could say that I put it together as much for myself as for anyone else, for this represents the life and ideals which were once my guiding force.

And it is, of course, not just a book for fighter pilots, but for all those who enjoy their story, admire their lives and respect their profession. For simple adventure and interest, there are few better images.

If you have known a fighter pilot, the chances are you knew someone with spirit, who approached the world positively and who was comfortable with himself. The man who masters himself and his aeroplane does not always master the other elements of his life, perhaps because he devotes himself so singlemindedly to his flying. Sometimes the drive and exuberance needed by his profession are out of place in the mortal world and outsiders find him a bit odd. Whatever the case, this book may help you to understand him.

But, no matter who you are, this book will tell you something about one of mankind's most admirable defenders, one who has been given a romantic role and a separate place in the pantheon of good, brave men.

NOTE TO THE READER

There is so much material of interest on this subject that I hope to compile a second volume. I therefore solicit suggestions, submissions and any writing, information or photographs suitable for a similar book. Everything will be acknowledged, and returned if requested (although copies of original material are preferable). In particular, I would welcome first-person accounts and photographs of both historical and current fighter operations. Active-duty personnel should clear submissions through their Public Affairs Office using this book as a reference. Address everything to the author, care of the publisher.

ACKNOWLEDGEMENTS

I am particularly grateful to McDonnell Douglas for their extensive assistance, and to the other manufacturers and individuals for their photographs. Because of the Gulf War, budget cuts and policies in general, USN and USAF agencies in the United States and USAF bases in Europe did not provide the assistance and contacts requested, thus leaving some obvious gaps in the coverage that I hope will be filled in a future volume. An exception was Major Carolyn Hodge, Public Affairs officer at my former base, RAF Bentwaters, who, with USAFE Public Affairs approval, gave me a day to tour my former squadron – a real pleasure. The other exceptions were the Tactical Air Warfare Center and the USAF Thunderbirds, who, by the nature of their missions, are PR organizations and enjoy having their story told.

John Roberts

I

FIGHTER TRAINING

Great fighter pilots are made not born . . . A man may possess good eyesight, sensitive hands and perfect co-ordination, but the end product is only fashioned by steady coaching, much practice, and experience. – Air Vice Marshal J. E. 'Johnnie' Johnson RAF

IT HAS BEEN reported that it requires an expenditure of over $6 million to convert a college graduate into a combat-ready fighter pilot, at which point he is still no more than the least experienced member of a squadron of 30 or 40 pilots. He will continue to train and practise his skills as long as he flies. Consider some of the training a typical USAF fighter pilot experiences:

1. Preflight Training
2. Pilot Aptitude Selection
3. Primary Pilot Training
4. Basic Pilot Training
5. Academic Pilot Training
6. Physical Training
7. Survival Training
8. Resistance, Escape and Evasion Training
9. Basic Fighter Training
10. Combat Ready Training
11. Weapon Delivery Training
12. Air Combat Tactics Training
13. Annual Instrument Training
14. Advanced Combat Training
15. Flight Lead Training
16. Intelligence Training
17. Nuclear Weapons Training
18. Physiological Training

Switching to a different aircraft repeats many of the above, as does a return to flying following a desk job. In addition, there are many kinds of Officer and Military Training.

In essence, the few precious hours' training in flight simulate the real thing – combat, the purpose of existence. It is always a

11

compromise: if you don't train like you fight, you won't get the job done when the time comes; but if you train too realistically, the accident rate goes up to unacceptable levels. Only great commanders know how to walk this fine line.

A combat-ready fighter pilot flies about 20 hours a month. The rest of his job is to spend ten times that on the ground, training and learning things so that each expensive hour in flight will be worth while. The best fighter pilots are those who train themselves. You're a big boy and you are expected to do your job without a lot of supervision, but the evaluation is frequent and serious, just to make sure and to improve performance.

Every fighter pilot is also a teacher. Soon he will lead flights, and every flight briefing and debriefing is a training experience, with no mercy for mistakes, no respect for rank. That is the way we learn. No pilot is ever perfect: there is always something more to absorb. Except for combat itself, training is everything. A fighter pilot may train for up to 20 years and never see combat. It must be done. There is no other way.

THE US AIR FORCE ACADEMY AIRMANSHIP PROGRAM

As AFA cadets move through four years of tough academic, military and athletic education, they also experience a wide variety of aviation programmes designed to give them a head start in an Air Force career. Seventy per cent of graduates go on to flying programmes, and the remainder will support flying operations in some way, so this is considered an essential part of their preparation. Seventeen different courses offer basic and advanced instruction in gliders, aircraft and parachuting. They offer selected cadets the opportunity to qualify for commercial and flight instructor glider ratings, private, commercial, instrument and flight instructor aircraft ratings and parachute ratings.

When I was instructing at the Academy, I flew many cadets in both gliders and the T-33 jet trainer — a most rewarding duty when working with highly motivated young students. Two experiences stand out; I once soloed a student in a glider after just two hours of flying time, and he could barely believe he was doing something he had dreamed of for several years in such a short time. Yet he had the self-confidence to go up and do it without hesitation. I hope he became a fighter pilot. In another example, I once taught a young cadet the basics of instrument flight on his first flight in a T-33 to another base. He picked it up quickly, so on the return flight, at night, I got him to fly the aircraft all the way back home until I took it for let-down and landing. He was so incredulous that he had been

T-41 (Cessna 172) over the Air Force Academy. Thousands of Air Force pilots have received their first flying training in this popular little aeroplane. A great many others were eliminated from the programme at this early stage because they could not demonstrate the necessary co-ordination and aptitude soon enough. (US National Archives)

able to perform this mysterious skill that he thought was years ahead, and had done something only his heroes could do, that he was a bundle of excitement and plans when he got out of the jet, already thinking of his pilot career and knowing that he was probably going to be able to fulfil his ambition. In all my years of teaching, I never had more rewarding experiences. I also led 300 cadets through Fort Benning, Georgia, one summer, where every one of us without exception performed five parachute jumps and received our Army parachute wings. I think I was more proud than the youngsters 15 years my junior. The Academy has always believed that cadets should have a chance to challenge themselves, to build confidence in, and knowledge of, exciting things away from the classroom. The fighter pilot begins to learn courage and self-discipline long before he ever touches an aircraft.

Since almost the very beginning in gilders, and since 1968 in T-41s, the Academy has offered flying programmes in which cadets learn to fly and solo small aircraft. Cadets aiming at pilot training fly over 20 hours in the T-41, including a solo and check ride. Navigator indoctrination is provided in two T-43s (Boeing 737s) of the Colorado Air National Guard, which have 12 state-of-the-art nav stations. Nine motor-gliders, and other sailplanes, give flying and advanced soaring experience. The Academy also maintains two Twin Otters for parachute training, supporting about 13,000 jumps a year. In addition, cadets visit Air Force bases during summer training and have the opportunity to fly in operational USAF aircraft. There are, of course, extensive ground schools in support of all these flying activities.

The result of all these programmes is a corps of cadets that is

13

strongly motivated and informed about flying. As a result, the retention and success rates in USAF flying programmes and careers are higher than those in other sources. Young men and women seek appointment to the Air Force Academy because they know they will begin immediately to immerse themselves in their aviation career.

SIMULATOR TRAINING

Since the earliest days, pilots have practised flying procedures on the ground before flying. From the manoeuvrable Link trainers of the Second World War, we now have developed complicated, computer-based simulators that accurately reproduce many of the sensations and conditions of flight. These enable the pilot to practise on the ground, in safety and in a teaching environment, much of what he will do in flight. It is, of course, true that some things simply cannot be simulated, and there are limitations on the realism, and the education, that can result.

The basic simulator is little more than a procedures trainer. It allows the pilot, especially the beginner, to practise the basic routine and emergency procedures for flying the aeroplane. In the next stage, simulators tie in radar and weapon systems in order to enable more complex operations to be practised.

New simulators have motion and sounds that try to convey to the pilot what the aircraft is doing, the instruments acting almost exactly as they do in the real thing. In front of the pilot, on a screen surrounding the cockpit, the world can be projected and changed by computer in response to the movements and actions of the pilot. Thus even air-to-air combat against another fighter on the screen can be practised.

F-16 simulator. Complete combat missions can be flown in the simulator. Note the location of the stick on the right console, the realistic computer graphics and image generator and the screen outside the cockpit. (Evans and Sutherland)

14

F-16 simulator. The Link Tactical Flight Simulator is a complex system that provides complete combat simulation, including air-to-air and LANTIRN missions. (Link)

The instructor, of course, has a console outside the cockpit where the crew's actions can be monitored. Action may be frozen so that a situation can be discussed. The position of the aircraft can be run forwards or backwards to save time. If the aeroplane 'crashes', the reset button solves everything. When the lesson is done, the pilot or crew and instructor can go over all the actions and improve the learning.

Simulators allow a pilot to practise dangerous situations that cannot be practised safely in real flight. The cost of simulator training is obviously a fraction of the real thing. While every pilot knows the value of simulations, it is also possible to say that almost every pilot hates them. Flying, like sex, is not so much fun when simulated – just too boring to really enjoy.

In a modern extension of the flight simulator, there now exist in various places around the world much more complex systems – combat simulators. Real aircraft fly in real airspace, carrying pods and sensors and recorders, transmitting information to ground receivers. Simulated 'kills' can be accomplished and weapons fired. When the flying is done, the entire battle is recreated in a theatre on the ground, allowing the combatants to learn from their victories and defeats. The regular Red Flag exercises in Nevada make full use of this modern electronic form of warfare.

TRAINING AIRCRAFT

There exist in the air forces around the world a great variety of aircraft for training fighter pilots. Some of them are generations old and others are the latest state of the art. Smaller air forces naturally tend to use older, less expensive and less sophisticated aircraft, some of which have been retired from the larger air forces. Although the Iraqi Air Force consisted of nearly 800 aircraft before the Gulf War, a large number of them were training aircraft, such as the hundred Tucano propeller-driven aircraft, ancient MiG-15s and other types useless in modern combat. This fact was generally ignored by the media, giving the IAF a greater importance than it deserved. On the other hand, training aircraft with limited weapons can be used in some lower-intensity conflicts, especially by smaller nations who cannot afford advanced machines. Many trainers, such as the T-38, T-37, Jet Provost and Hawk, have fighter versions. The F-5 (T-38), an economical aircraft with a high performance, was the most successful aircraft ever produced for Third World nations. Some trainers, such as the Tucano, are licenced for manufacture in other countries. There is an obvious advantage for the student who flies a trainer which can be used for both pilot training and fighter training – such as the Hawk.

USAF PILOT TRAINING

*The greatest ace was once a dumb student who could
not even hold an airplane straight and level. – J. R.*

In the days following the Second World War, students were separated into two tracks, for bombers and fighters; after primary flight training, fighter students went to the Lockheed T-33, the trainer version of the F-80 early jet fighter, while bomber students learned their trade elsewhere. When I went to pilot training in 1959, I already had 30 hours in a Piper Cub in an AFROTC training programme which was designed to filter out those without aptitude. I then received 30 hours in a T-34. With that 60 hours under my belt, my first flight in a T-37 was a shock: I did not see how I

T-37 'Tweety Bird'. The side-by-side Cessna has been training USAF and other pilots for over 30 years. A modified version with larger engines became a nimble fighter-bomber that was used in Vietnam. Even today it is flown by the Portuguese aerobatic team. (US National Archives)

WORLD TRAINERS

UNITED STATES

T-41 Mescalero	Cessna (172)	USAF light prop
T-37 Tweet	Cessna	USAF primary jet
T-38 Talon	Northrop	USAF basic jet
T-45 Goshawk	British Aerospace	USN primary jet

GREAT BRITAIN

Bulldog	British Aerospace	RAF light prop
Jet Provost	British Aerospace	RAF primary jet
Tucano	Short Brothers	RAF primary prop
Hawk	British Aerospace	RAF advanced jet

OTHER SUCCESSFUL TRAINERS

PC-7, PC-9	Pilatus (Switzerland)
Alpha Jet	Dassault/Dornier (France/Germany)
Magister	Aérospatiale (France)
MB-326, MB-339	Aermacchi (Italy)
T-2, T-4	Mitsubishi, Kawasaki (Japan)
Tucano	Embraer (Brazil)

A massive study is currently under way in the United States to provide a new trainer to replace the three USAF trainers and the Navy T-34. The Joint Primary Aircraft Training System (JPATS) will replace the T-37 and T-34 around 1997 and the Bomber/Fighter Training System (BFTS) will replace the T-38 around 2005 but in the meantime the two jets, which came into service in the early 1960s, have undergone major life-extension programmes. The BFTS will have a somewhat higher performance than the T-38, with lower operating costs, and a modern cockpit which will provide a springboard to the Advanced Tactical Fighter. In the RAF, the Tucano is replacing the JP. The RAF believes that the high-performance turboprop can do the job of the older jet. The cockpit has been designed to provide a smooth transition to the Hawk.

could ever keep up with the zippy little jet. But I caught up quickly and soloed it in about eight hours, receiving 90 hours of total training in it. Others on my base were still flying the old T-28 in primary. I then flew 120 hours in the T-33, which I found easy to fly after the T-37.

I then became an instructor in the new all-jet Undergraduate Pilot Training programme. The T-34 was eliminated and students went directly to the T-37, even if they had no previous flying experience. We soloed them in around 12–15 hours, but many had trouble with this sudden introduction to high-speed flight. So, around 1965, the Air Training Command introduced the T-41, a slightly modified Cessna 172, and returned to the concept of slower and less expensive lead-in training and selection. At the same time, the T-38 was replacing the T-33. This primary–basic training system has continued to this day.

The Northrop T-38 Talon, a supersonic basic trainer which has trained thousands of USAF and Allied pilots for nearly 20 years. This is the author during his tour as an Instructor Pilot. (Author)

Now, however, with a smaller Air Force and new aircraft entering the inventory, the US has decided to return to the split-track concept. By 1992 it will buy 125 special training aircraft for the Enhanced Flight Selection programme. This aircraft, far superior in performance to the little T-41, will be used for an aggressive, aerobatic programme designed to eliminate unsuitable students and select those who will go on to T-37s and then split into the T-38 fighter/bomber or T-1 tanker-transport tracks. The flight selection programme will be conducted at Hondo Air Force Base near San Antonio, Texas, and at the US Air Force Academy in Colorado.

Tanker/transport students are now flying the T-1A Jayhawk, a modified twin-engine business jet, instead of the T-38. Because bombers like the B-1 and B-2 are so fast and complex, students heading in that direction will fly the T-38 along with the potential fighter pilots. In another innovation, students will be carefully evaluated after the flight selection programme and split into the two tracks even before flying the T-37. In this way, the entire pilot training programme can be designed to prepare the student for the kind of aircraft he or she will later fly. The aspiring fighter pilot may be severely disappointed if he is assigned to tanker/transport before he gets a chance to show his stuff, but the flight selection

Hunting (BAe) Jet Provost. The primary jet trainer in the RAF for several decades, the JP is now being replaced by the Tucano. (Author)

programme and other methods of selection based on extensive testing and interviews will try to place the student where he belongs.

RAF PILOT TRAINING

Training is designed to eliminate the weak and build the strong. – J. R.

The RAF student pilot usually has some flying time acquired in the Bulldogs of the University Air Squadrons, the Chipmunks of the Air Training Corps or privately. Candidates must first go through the Officers' and Aircrew Selection Centre, soon to be moved from Biggin Hill to Cranwell. Here they will undergo thorough evaluation and testing to determine officer and flying aptitude. An evaluator there stated: 'Our standards are high and we apply them strictly. We make no apology for that. We are in the business of selecting the next generation of officers for a high-technology fighting service, ready to defend Britain in the event of war. The men and women we select will be given a long and expensive training, leading to a very demanding job; they are likely to be responsible not only for millions of pounds' worth of sophisticated equipment, but for the well-being – maybe the lives – of others. Wrong choices on our part would be costly in more ways than one, and we cannot take chances.'*

From here, flying students move to 18 weeks of Initial Officer Training at RAF Cranwell and then on to Basic Flying Training at one of several bases. As the venerable Jet Provost is phased out, they will receive approximately 165 hours in the Shorts Tucano, a turboprop aircraft which has been redesigned from the original Brazilian machine to foster a smooth lead-in to the Hawk and Tornado. Although propeller-driven, it can outperform the JP in most respects, especially on longer, combined training missions. Some students, who do not have previous flying time, go through the long course which includes time in the Chipmunk, while others with at least 30 hours' previous experience will take a shorter course. Near the end of this course, after thorough evaluation which also considers their own desires and the needs of the service, students are separated into one of three streams, Helicopters, Tanker/Transport or Fast Jets.

Fighter students then move to RAF Valley for about 85 hours of Hawk training. Royal Navy students aimed at the Sea Harrier also attend this course. With the nimble, operationally oriented Hawk

---

*This quotation, and additional information on the fighter training process, can be found in *RAF Fighter Pilot*, by Tim Laming (London: W. H. Allen, 1991).

Above: The Shorts Tucano is the RAF's primary trainer. It has a redesigned cockpit for smooth transition to the Hawk and Tornado. Right: Hawk T.1A trainers and fighters. The Hawk, also flown by the Red Arrows, has been modified to carry Sidewinders. Teamed with RAF Tornados and Phantoms, the aircraft are part of the Mixed Fighter Force for Britain's air defence. (British Aerospace)

(there is, remember, a fighter version), the student begins to think and act like a fighter pilot, even to the point of leading some flights and operating the aircraft at maximum performance. At completion the students receive the Wings of an RAF pilot, on what is probably the most satisfying day in their lives.

Next, they move to the Tactical Weapons Unit at RAF Brawdy to learn to deliver basic weapons. They will receive about 74 hours' training, including more lead experience and a balance of ground attack and air-to-air experience. Following this, they are assigned to an Operational Conversion Unit for the fighter they will fly. After about 70 more hours of training in the Tornado, Jaguar or Phantom, they are considered 'limited combat ready'. Another 50 or so hours in the squadron and they will be fully combat ready, prepared to go to war and fly the toughest missions, just as new members of Tornado and Jaguar squadrons did in the Gulf.

NATO PILOT TRAINING

Rather than operate their own expensive pilot training establishments, most NATO and other Allied nations send their students to a combined Euro-NATO Joint Jet Pilot Training Program in the 80th Flying Training Wing at Sheppard AFB, Texas. The British, feeling that the course is not up to their standards or aims, send a token group but operate their own programme. Graduating students going on to fighters may remain in the USA to check out in the F-15 or F-16 at Luke etc.

This programme, very similar to the USAF programme, consists of about 135 hours in the T-37 and 135 hours in the T-38. From there, RAF fighter students return to Britain to fly the Hawk for another 140 hours of advanced training before moving on to the Tornado, Phantom or Jaguar.

Another important NATO flying operation is at Florennes, Belgium – the Tactical Leadership School. Here, experienced flight leaders and crews from various nations learn the more advanced elements of leading combat missions and co-ordinating with each other in the Allied Tactical Air Force operations that NATO would conduct.

USAF FIGHTER TRAINING

With his Wings and his fighter assignment in hand, the prospective fighter pilot moves to Holloman AFB, New Mexico, for Lead-In Fighter Training (LIFT). Since he is already familiar with the T-38, the student will find it easy to fly the AT-38, the same aircraft with the addition of a few switches, bomb racks and gun pod. Here, fighter pilot instructors will teach him the basics of weapons delivery. The student discipline and wash-out potential of pilot training are replaced by the more relaxed camaraderie of fighter

Convair F-102 trainer and fighter. The side-by-side trainer lacked the performance of the single-seater. With a bigger engine and advanced electronics, the F-106 delta wing was a major improvement. Its trainer had tandem seating. (General Dynamics)

THE FIGHTER MISSION CARD

Every fighter pilot fills out a mission card before and during the flight briefing. It contains the essential information he needs to fly the mission in the proper way and sequence. These cards are typical: they were used by Captain David 'R-10' Rothenanger, a highly experienced Instructor Pilot in the F-16 Replacement Training Unit at Luke AFB, Arizona. The mission is BFM 3, Basic Flight Manoeuvres, and the student has an IP in the back seat of his D model who will talk him through the manoeuvres and demonstrate when necessary. The back of the card shows Rothenanger's artwork that reminds him of the individual manoeuvres to be briefed and practised. Flying time is critical, and every moment of air time must be used to good effect.

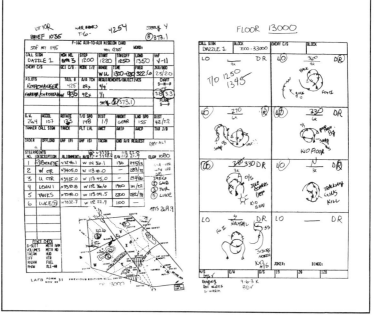

pilots, and the young pilots experience the most enjoyable flying of their brief careers. This training is to be phased out as the F-117 Stealth Fighter moves from Nevada to Holloman and students once again move directly from pilot training to the operational fighter.

Luke Air Force Base, just outside Phoenix, Arizona, is the largest fighter training base in the world, with two separate training wings for, primarily, F-15s and F-16s. F-111, A-10 and other training takes place at other bases. At Luke, students receive about four months and 65 hours of training, depending on the aircraft and their experience. Pilots returning from staff jobs or other aircraft to fighters will also upgrade their skills here.

THE FIGHTER GRADE SHEET

From his first flight in pilot training to frequent combat-ready flight checks and his annual instrument check, the fighter pilot is constantly being evaluated by Instructor Pilots and Stan/Eval (Standardization/Evaluation Section in each Wing) check pilots. These grade sheets are used to evaluate student pilots in the F-16 RTU at Luke. At the end of the mission, the IP will debrief the student item by item and try to correct any deficiencies. Failed rides are repeated, and the student must be careful not to start the slide toward elimination. The sheet on the left is for BFM, or Basic Flight Manoeuvres, the one on the right for more advanced Air Combat Tactics (ACT) training.

These units are called Replacement Training Units (RTU), as they send replacements to operational squadrons. The student receives the full range of fighter training so that, when he arrives at his squadron, local training and familiarization will make him combat ready in a month or two.

RAF TORNADO WEAPONS TRAINING

The Tornado Tactical Weapons Conversion Unit at RAF Honington takes the student from the Tri-National checkout programme at

RAF Cottesmore where he learns how to fly the aircraft and teaches him to employ his weapons. The phases of this programme are:

1. Ground School – 1 week.
2. Familiarization phase – 2–3 flights.
3. Lay-down and loft bombing – several flights.
4. Dive and strafe – several flights (3 and 4 add in formation and low-level, some leading).
5. Night – 2–3 flights (includes low-level on terrain-following radar at 500ft, followed by loft delivery).
6. Check ride – qualification and instrument, no weapons.
7. Air combat tactics – several flights.
8. Operations – several flights.

The final Operations Phase ties it all together and is the most important. The student crew will brief an instructor crew and lead a two-ship mission on a low-level and simulated weapon delivery on three targets. Along the way, they will be bounced by another Tornado about three times and have to use Air Combat Tactics to evade. To lead such flights so early in their RAF fighter training is extremely difficult, something the USAF does not do to this extent, and prepares them for being both good wingmen and good leaders.

After three months (about 45 hours) at Cottesmore and three more months (30–45 hours) at Honington, the crew then report to their operational squadron for additional training before becoming combat ready.

TORNADO INTERCEPT/AIR COMBAT TRAINING*

'The ability of the Tornado to intercept and track-while-scan a lot of targets means that we can be very flexible in air combat. You never fight fair in air defence. You never accept a one-on-one fight, so if there's three of them and two of you, you run away. Or maybe you try to make sure they don't know you're there, and you creep up on them . . . it's not a polite game. So while you might sometimes fly as a singleton, on your own holding Combat Air Patrol, going after whatever target you're directed to, generally you would fly as a pair or two pairs, if you can. Consequently we would fly a four-ship on occasion . . .

'The Basic Intercept Phase. They'll get airborne, go out about a hundred and fifty miles over the North Sea to get away from the airways and all the other traffic, and at fifteen thousand feet or

---

* This section, by a Tornado Instructor Pilot, is reproduced, with permission, from *RAF Fighter Pilot*, by Tim Laming (London: W. H. Allen, 1991).

Tornado/Hawk. This Hawk
weapons trainer from
No. 234 Squadron at RAF
Brawdy becomes an
operational fighter when
working with the
radar-equipped Tornado as
an air defence team in the
Mixed Fighter Force.
(British Aerospace)

above they will split by fifty miles, and one guy runs in while the
other learns how to pick him up on radar, understanding the
geometry of how to put your aircraft in the right place. We normally
operate on an attack, re-attack basis, where if the target is judged
to be hostile, the pilot will fire head-on a Sky Flash missile when
he's up to about fifteen miles, but assuming that it will miss the
target he then does a re-attack, coming around the target to fire off
a Sidewinder heat-seeking missile from the rear. The pilot will be
taught the rudiments of doing the intercept, although it's the
navigator who is the tactical commander and he really controls the
attack . . . they will start off flying one-versus-one without flying
any evasion manoeuvres. Then one-versus-one with evasion, with
the target aircraft trying not to be caught, but within limitations,
nothing really serious. We then move down to low level and do the
same thing with the target at two hundred and fifty feet, so that
they're using the radar in a look-down mode . . .

'The Combat Phase . . . We will remind them of some of the things
they've already seen, the heavy manoeuvring, the high-g or low
speed and high angle-of-attack combat manoeuvring, learning how
to get the best out of the aeroplane . . . what happens if they get a
nose-high attitude, with the speed getting very low. In certain
circumstances you could do what is known as a loaded pull back on
the guy who is attacking you, but if the speed gets really low, well
you're probably going to die in combat anyway. We'll look at high
angle-of-attack manoeuvring, that's the scissors, flat scissors and
rolling scissors . . .

'They will also look at maximum rate turning, a fighter pilot's
bread and butter; how to get the maximum performance in the
horizontal, vertical or oblique planes. You don't bother with the
sixty-seven degrees wing setting, as that's essentially a go-faster
position, a run-away wing, an attack-at-high-speed wing. So you'll
turn with a forty-five degrees wing setting, with six to seven g, and

that's quite severe, more than even the spacemen ever used, although not quite as much as the F-16 for example, which can pull about nine g, but then Tornado is an interceptor, not an air superiority fighter. Then we'll try to do the same turn but without as much energy, which is a situation you might find yourself in, so we'll try a twenty-five degrees wing, and about two hundred and ninety knots, which comes out at about four and a half g. If you're in that low-energy situation we then look at the bug-out, basically reducing all of the drag on the airframe, unloading the turn, getting your speed back as quickly as possible, and then you either want to run away because you don't like what you see, or you're getting energy back before you pitch back into the fight again . . .

'They'll practise the various manoeuvres, for example the high yo-yo, pulling up from the turn, the low yo-yo, losing height, then pulling up back into the turn, and then a lesson in how you often don't need that kind of manoeuvre in this aircraft as it can almost turn square corners. If you're fighting a Phantom you don't have much of a problem, but with two aircraft of similar performance as in this situation, or if you're up against something like the F-15, you might have to employ moves like that to gain an advantage. They will look at flat and rolling scissors on the next sortie, and then they will start what we call neutral splits, using the radar. So they'll split at about forty miles, come in towards each other, ideally supersonic, and then try to get the head-on missiles, the Sky Flash, off against each other; and then as they cross on the merge, go into the close-in dogfighting. Although if we were doing this for real, we teach them that they should fire off their missiles and just blow through and disappear, if they don't like what they see. He who turns and runs away, lives to fight another day.

'Eventually they will reach a stage where they can fly dissimilar air combat, flying two-versus-two or two-versus-four, often against Hawks, when we get a detachment from one of the TWUs. Although the Hawks aren't supersonic they are very capable little fighters and they will come over to Coningsby and act as our targets. So a Tornado can take on two Hawks, head-on, combat and so on. The Hawks don't have radar, but they are given control by the ground-based radar stations, whereas the Tornado crew won't be given that information so they have to use the aircraft's radar. Then two-versus-two, then two-versus-four. This will be against Hawks, F-16s, or indeed anybody we can find.

'The Tornado was never designed to be an air superiority fighter, so, for example, I would never want to mix it with a Fulcrum or an F-15, but at the same time would fight with them more happily than I would have done with a Phantom. From the point of view of its manoeuvrability, at low level it is very good; its turning rate is very close to that of an F-15, up to about ten thousand feet or so. It is the fastest aeroplane around. It will be cleared to eight hundred and fifty knots, and you have to throttle back at seven hundred and fifty knots, so that's very, very fast. There's absolutely nothing that can run away from us.

'Supersonic at high level, it is also very good. Everybody waxes lyrical about the Lightning: well, I flew Lightnings, and the Tornado will fly just as fast, and having gone that fast, and manoeuvred just as hard, it will have more fuel, and what's more, it carries eight weapons. Where it is possibly weak is at a medium level at lower speeds, and at high levels at lower speed. Although it is a swing-wing design, it doesn't have enough wing basically, until you go supersonic with the wings swept back, when it's like a Lightning. It's disappointing in heavy manoeuvring at medium and high level until you get supersonic.'

SURVIVAL AND RESISTANCE TRAINING

In the First World War, the fighter pilot who was shot down and survived was often picked up immediately and taken to the enemy mess for a drink and a chat. Even in the Second World War, Douglas Bader was treated with great respect, allowed to sit in the cockpit of a German fighter and discuss its capabilities. Not so in most other situations. Wars take place in strange parts of the world. The pilot must be able to survive in hostile environments. Everything is done to try to help him.

First, he is given a proper kit, in most cases a flotation device to keep him upright in the sea and a life raft attached to his ejection seat, and to him, which deploys below him for a water landing. He finds in it, and in his harness, various items to help him stay alive and draw rescue. He may have a survival radio in combat, over

The author in the survival situation. Realistic training gives the crew member confidence in unfamiliar and difficult conditions. (Author)

which he can talk to the fighters and rescue helicopters. His system will have a 'beeper' which activates on ejection, allowing the rescuers to home in on his location. In Vietnam, flying over the high-canopy jungle, we even had a tree-lowering device, which allowed us to escape the ignominious fate of hanging until death or capture 100ft above the jungle floor. And the fighter pilot usually carries a pistol, since some captors take no prisoners.

Second, the fighter pilot receives specialized training, in sea and land survival schools, which teach him to stay alive, to live off the land and to assist in his own rescue. He learns how to find food, how to build a shelter, how to navigate and how to treat wounds. He becomes an outdoorsman.

And, finally, he learns how to deal with the enemy, the cold-hearted, inhuman enemy who will beat and torture him in search of information or propaganda. He learns how to resist, to escape, to evade. He gives strength and definition to his bravery and self-control and love of country, the things he has learned as a youth and which will be needed if he is captured. Men have lived lifetimes in prison in appalling conditions, but, among the fighter pilots, the great heroes were those who survived up to eight years in the torture and deprivation of the prisons of North Vietnam.

The Geneva Convention tries to protect these people against maltreatment, against being exposed to further danger, against being used by the enemy. It often fails, because modern war is frequently just as brutal as the ancient style. The fighter pilot can be made to say things valuable to the enemy in a world in which propaganda and political objectives can be more important than military victory.

USAF fighter pilots learn the Code of Conduct. Americans captured in Korea were not prepared for capture and the mental torture they experienced. They had no guidelines. So the Code was created and taught to every man who was captured in Vietnam. Some of them fought their captors fiercely, and suffered grave damage to their mental and physical systems. The Code was therefore modified, and men were given more leeway to make statements under force, knowing that the outside world was more mature, more able to realize that what they said under duress was not believable. It is a fine guide for men in battle.

TOP GUN

The US Navy Fighter Weapons School is located at Naval Air Station Miramar, San Diego, California. In Vietnam, it became apparent that US pilots lacked certain advanced skills in flying air-to-air combat and that they were not using their weapons effectively. Air-to-air missiles, in particular, were not being used properly. It was clear that the normal training given to each pilot should be supplemented by extraordinary, graduate-level training for special or more experienced pilots. Not only would this provide a nuclear force of super-fighters for combat, but the improved training would filter down to the rest of the pilots as these 'top guns' were spread through the force.

The first class entered training in March 1969. One of the early graduates of the programme was Lt Randy Cunningham. The Top Gun command was created in 1972. The present course lasts just five weeks, much shorter than that at the USAF Fighter Weapons School, which is broader in scope and places more emphasis on individual weapons. Five classes of experienced Navy and Marine pilots each year study fighter tactics, techniques, procedures and doctrine. The course includes 75 hours of lectures and a rigorous flight syllabus during which student crews fly against F-16 and A-4 adversary aircraft flown by Top Gun instructor pilots.

The school conducts a separate adversary instructor course twice a year, designed to create pilots similar to the USAF Aggressors. The three Aggressor squadrons have been disbanded in an economy move, although a condensed force at Nellis is still maintained in order to preserve the knowledge and study the subject for weapons school training.

RED FLAG*

General Robert Dixon, the dynamic commander of Tactical Air Command in the early 1970s, created Red Flag as a new way to train fighter pilots. Prior to that time, training had been concentrated in small units, with some occasional mass gaggles. Dixon, a Spitfire reconnaissance pilot during the Second World War, had flown wing to Ralph Parr, the Korean ace, and been General George Brown's deputy in Saigon, where I served as his humble aide in between flying tours. Dixon knew combat, and he knew how to forge ahead and get things done. He recognized the need for more complex combat training as a result of the electronic revolution that had overtaken the fighter business and the increasing need to co-ordinate the many different kinds of aircraft and weapons in an air battle. Not only were the defensive and offensive weapons, and their co-ordination, much more complex, but the ability to monitor

---

* This information was largely collected by reporters for *Aviation Week and Space Technology*.

and evaluate training had also improved. Red Flag, a highly realistic combat training exercise at Nellis AFB, Nevada, was the result. In a way, Bob Dixon did a lot to cause the overwhelming victory in the air war in the Gulf fifteen years later.

The 440th Tactical Fighter Training Group runs several Red Flags a year, with some special exercises thrown in. Desert Flag, in response to the Gulf War, is one of them. Over a period of six weeks, about 90 aircraft from fifteen units fly into Nellis, with about 20 pilots and 75 maintenance personnel from each unit. The experience is highly valued, not only by USAF fighter pilots but also by those of other nations. Desert Flag in 1990 had pilots from Britain, Italy, Germany and Singapore. US Navy, Marine and Army personnel also take part. Pilots fly once a day for a week on large-scale attack exercises. Perhaps 45 aircraft will fly on a typical mission, with a Blue Force of 'friendlies' and a Red Force of enemy fighters. The full range of combat aircraft takes part in a simulated wartime strike. The Nellis ramp in full swing is an exciting collection of modern fighter technology.

The Nellis Red Flag range, a huge area, larger than Kuwait, contains 1400 ground targets, including simulated airfields, aircraft, buildings, petrol tanks, missile sites and industrial complexes. Aircraft launch a mass attack and must fight their way through jamming, enemy fighters and heavy simulated missile and gun fire. Video cameras on the ground combine with various kinds of radar and telemetry monitors to track the action of every aircraft in the exercise, providing a realistic picture of the battle which is replayed back at Nellis during the extensive debriefing. This is as important as the flying itself in teaching better ways to fight in the modern environment. The Red Flag Measurement and Debriefing System is the most advanced of several similar systems in the world, such as those over the North Sea and in Sardinia. It is similar to the Fallon Range in northern Nevada used by the US Navy and it will be connected to the Army National Training Center at Fort Irwin, California, in 1992. Large-view screens at Nellis show every aircraft, with colour-coding and symbology to show aircraft altitude, heading, speed and location and gun and missile firing. The range can also accommodate night air-to-air exercises, LANTIRN and Stealth operations and many other kinds of flying operations. RAF pilots have told me that it is the best training they have ever had. USAF pilots love the experience, saying it is the closest thing to combat there is.

II

FIGHTER AIRCRAFT

THE MODERN FIGHTER aircraft is the most dangerous and complicated machine operated by man. No other machine is as quick to penalize a mistake, as quick to convert a routine, enjoyable condition into sudden death. No other machine requires such a combination of mental and physical skill to use it at maximum performance. No other machine becomes such a part of the man who operates it. Formula One cars are taken to the edge of performance, but a crash is usually not fatal, thanks to new safety design. No design can survive the high-speed crash of a fighter against the Earth. The Space Shuttle is a complicated machine, but it is flown largely by computers. No, the fighter aircraft is unique among man's greatest machines.

The fighter has evolved from the wood, wire and wind of 1914 to the electronic rocket of today. It seems to come in endless varieties, consisting of strange shapes with mysterious missions that only the shadowy pilot understands. Yet its duty is still the same: to deliver weapons on target and to deny the use of air to the enemy.

When you walk through cavernous factories, looking at pieces and shells being wired and welded together by hundreds of skilled men and women, the fighter seems to be a complicated, miraculous animal waiting to be given life; but when you crawl into a mountain valley and see those thousands of pieces smashed and tumbled over the rocks, it becomes a fragile, unrecognizable junkyard, a terrible tumulus for the bodies of its crew bored into the Earth: friends are suddenly no longer alive, but not so dead as the machine, deprived even of its individuality.

Imagine – with one machine, one man can kill millions of people, or he can enter single, personal combat, like a knight on horseback, but out of sight of the fair princess. He can sit restless on the runway, and a minute later float 10 miles above the Earth, where there is no sensation of speed, no connection to the five billion people below. He can slip through the air, edging into space, trapped in his tiny cockpit, wired into the machine so completely that it is part of his body, and be totally alone.

The fighter aircraft is one of man's most beautiful and terrible

THE AUTHOR'S TOP 15

Every fighter pilot or enthusiast has his own list of favourite fighters. Mine, I suppose, is based on my own reading of history mixed with personal desires about which ones I wish I could have flown. Some have a special beauty, like the slim F-104; some have a tremendous performance, like the Lightning; some have a stirring history, like the Spitfire; and some have a personal attachment, like my Phantom. So please don't take offence if I have ignored your favourite fighter. Make your own list and dream!

1. Fokker DVII
2. P-51 Mustang
3. Spitfire
4. Bf 109
5. F-86 Sabre
6. Lightning
7. F-104 Starfighter
8. F-4 Phantom
9. F-105 'Thud'
10. F-14 Tomcat
11. F-15 Eagle
12. F-16 Falcon
13. MiG-21 Fishbed
14. MiG-29 Fulcrum
15. F-22 Advanced Tactical Fighter

creations. The cost of the latest fighter now approaches fifty million dollars, the cost of training the pilot six million dollars. All over the world, people throng to air shows to watch these amazing machines perform their high-speed dashes, loops and formations. Most major air forces have aerial demonstration teams, a good way of showing the flag and recruiting people to fly and support the aircraft.

Yet the fighter is no more than a killing machine, a modern version of a sword and a shield, for use in war. In the hands of a larger, responsible government, it is an essential element of national defence. Some say we should not glamorize machines of death, but most of us cannot help admire this dashing example of man's advanced technology, the extension of a single man's verve and desire to soar.

FIGHTER AIRCRAFT MARKINGS

All fighters have some kind of painted marking, ranging from discreet little numbers in grey camouflage to the bright skin of the Red Arrows. Each is appropriate to its mission: the combat aircraft does not want to be seen, the display aircraft does. Just that one little flash of colour in the murk could be the target of the gunner or the signal to break away from an air attack. Yet morale has its place, and a little squadron colour along a fin, a small unit insignia or a funny bit of nose art are tolerated. In some units, only the Commander's aircraft is decorated beyond combat grey. Even in combat, nose art, often featuring sexy women with little or no clothing, is accepted for a time.

Gone are Richthofen's red Fokker Triplane and the painted prop cowlings of the Bf 109s of the Abbeville Boys, designed to let the enemy know they were risking a fight with the best. Now the Stealth fighter has moved the nose art to the inside of the weapons bay doors.

If you know the numbers, you can tell a lot about an aircraft. The spotters, with their little notebooks and sharp eyes, keep track of serial numbers and specific planes, as though they were movie stars, each with its own personality and need to be recognized. There is a worldwide army of amateur aircraft watchers hanging

---

USAF TAIL CODES

Perhaps the most interesting marking is seen on USAF fighters, where units are identified by a two-letter tail code that is visible on most aircraft. Sometimes they relate to base, state or city locations, and sometimes they mean nothing at all. Here are some typical USAF tail codes:

AK	F-15C	21 TFW	Elmendorf AFB, Alaska
AL	F-16A	187 TFG	Alabama Air Guard
BT	F-15C	36 TFW	Bitburg AB, Germany
CC	F-111D	27 TFW	Cannon AFB, New Mexico
CR	F-15C	32 TFG	Soesterberg AB, Netherlands
DC	F-16A	113 TFW	Andrews AFB, Maryland
ED	Various	USAF Flight Test Center	Edwards AFB, California
FF	F-15C	1 TFW	Langley AFB, Virginia
HL	F-16C	388 TFW	Hill AFB, Utah
HO	F-15A	49 TFW	Holloman AFB, New Mexico
HS	F-16A	31 TTW	Homestead AFB, Florida
IS	F-15C	57 FIS	NAS Keflavik, Iceland
LA	F-16	58 TTW	Luke AFB, Arizona
MC	F-16A	56 TTW	MacDill AFB, Florida
MJ	F-16C	432 TFW	Misawa AB, Japan
NJ	F-4E	108 TFW	New Jersey Air Guard
OT	Various	USAF Tactical Air Warfare Center	Eglin AFB, Florida
RS	F-16C	86 TFW	Ramstein AB, Germany
SJ	F-15E	4 TFW	Seymour Johnson AFB, North Carolina
SP	F-4G/ F-16C	52 TFW	Spabgdahlen AB, Germany
TJ	F-16C	401 TFW	Torrejon AB, Spain
UH	F-111E	20 TFW	RAF Upper Heyford, England
WA	Various	USAF Tactical Fighter Weapons Center	Nellis AFB, Nevada
WP	F-16C	8 TFW	Kunsan AB, Korean ('Wolfpack')
WR	A-10	81 TFW	RAF Bentwaters, England
ZZ	F-15C	18 TFW	Kadena AB, Okinawa

Tailcode 'Whisky Romeo':
'WR' represents RAF
Bentwaters, England. The
yellow flash on the A-10
represents the 92nd
Tactical Fighter Squadron.
(Author)

around the airfield fences, more powerful than any intelligence agency, who delight in spotting aeroplanes, collecting numbers, building the squadrons of air power, admiring the machines they wish they could fly. Air forces have been known to paint different numbers on the same aircraft to try to confuse or frighten enemy intelligence. If you see '79-064' on the tail of a USAF F-15, you know it was the 64th plane built in 1979. The three digits on the tail of a Tucano tell you when it was built, and for whom, if you have the right guide book. The letter or letters on the tail of an RAF Tornado or Phantom, such as 'AY' or 'C', tell you which of the squadron's aircraft it is, and the pilots may refer affectionately to 'Charlie' or 'Mike'.

THE MODERN FIGHTERS

In 1992, there are perhaps seven comparable air superiority fighters:

1. MiG-29 Fulcrum
2. Su-27 Flanker
3. F-15C Eagle
4. F-16C Falcon
5. F/A-18 Hornet
6. Mirage 2000
7. F-14 Tomcat

Pit them against one another, one-on-one, and the result would depend more on the pilot, and the luck of the situation, than the aircraft. They are surprisingly close in their ability to perform in a dogfight, although the MiG has proved to be superior in practice close-in engagements where its ability to manoeuvre at high angles of attack gives it an advantage. The Sukhoi is comparable. Some

Above: Su-27 Flanker – a powerful, manoeuvrable Soviet fighter which may be the best dogfighter in the world. This one flew at the Farnborough Air Show in 1990. It is much larger than, but very similar to, the MiG-29. A carrier version is in testing. (Author)

Right: Mirage 2000 pair. The leader carries a fuel tank and heat missiles. Interceptor or dogfight teams rarely fly in close formation. They remain in wide extended positions for mutual support and manoeuvring flexibility. (Armée de L'Air)

35

would question whether the F-18 and Mirage are quite in the same league as the other four. The F-14 is clearly weaker in close-in fighting.

In a few years, the interim generation of super-fighters will go into production, if they can still be afforded:

1. The Swedish Gripen
2. The French Rafale
3. The Eurofighter (somewhat later)

A few years after that the next generation of super-fighters will become operational:

1. The American F-22 Advanced Tactical Fighter
2. The Soviet advanced fighter.

Outstanding examples of current aircraft for various missions are:

Air Superiority: MiG-29 Fulcrum, F-16C Falcon
Long-Range Interceptor: Tornado F.3, F-15C Eagle
Interdiction/strike: Tornado GR.1, F-15E Strike Eagle
Close Air Support: F/A-18 Hornet, F/A-16 Falcon
Tank-Buster: A-10 Warthog
Fleet Defence: F-14 Tomcat
All-Purpose Fighter: F-16C Falcon
Wild Weasel: F-4G Phantom

THE F-14 TOMCAT

The F-14 first flew over 20 years ago but, like a few other classic aircraft, it is so well designed that it remains a top-line fighter.

Left: Saab JAS.39 Gripen, the latest in a long line of distinguished aircraft built in Sweden primarily for self-defence. The first Gripen crashed because of fly-by-wire problems, but the difficulties were corrected. (Saab)
Right: F-16 flight demonstration take-off. The major aircraft manufacturers show their aircraft's capabilities at the alternating Farnborough and Paris Air Shows. (Author)

Upgraded versions will fly for the United States Navy well into the next century.

In the middle of the Vietnam War, the Navy was forced by the Pentagon to accept the F-111B version of the swing-wing fighter-bomber being developed for the Air Force. But it was seriously overweight and unsuitable for carrier operations, so the project was cancelled. Grumman, which had been part of the General Dynamics team, developed the F-14 using much of the technology from the F-111 plus new weight-saving techniques.

Central to the aircraft's air-to-air operations has been the large, long-range Hughes AIM-54 Phoenix radar missile and powerful AWG-9 radar/fire control, enabling the F-14 to engage six targets simultaneously and track up to 24 more. The radar can see out to 200 miles and the missile, using high-altitude cruise, can reach out to well over 100 miles, diving on its target at Mach 5 with considerable ECM capability. Alternatively, the F-14 can carry a mixture of Sparrow and Sidewinder missiles. With its swing-wing loiter capability, excellent dogfighting performance and the new AIM-120 AMRAAM, the Tomcat remains the ideal fleet defence aircraft.

Other features of the aircraft are a chin-mounted FLIR (Forward-Looking Infra-Red) sensor, automatic carrier landing system, automatic wing sweep according to Mach speed and the typical M-61 20mm Gatling gun. Another unique item is the TV Camera System that magnifies images from beyond visual range for target identification.

The Tomcat has demonstrated its air-to-air capability in head-line-making combat, destroying a pair of Libyan MiGs over the Mediterranean Sea on two separate occasions in the 1980s. The flights made full use of radar and modern air combat tactics to destroy their opponents. The F-14 also saw service in the Gulf War, although its primary role was fleet defence and it did not have the opportunity to 'mix it' up with Iraqi fighters as USAF F-15s did.

THE F-15E STRIKE EAGLE

The most advanced fighter in the world today is the E model of the F-15. It may look a lot like its older brother, but inside it is a totally different aeroplane. At 81,000lb, the maximum gross weight for take-off is roughly twice that of the original F-15. All that extra weight and weapons capacity means that, even though it can pull 9g, it cannot always accelerate, climb or turn the way the air-to-air fighter can. It is, however, equipped with all the necessary air-to-air eqiupment along with all the new air-to-ground systems it carries. It is, in other words, a dual-role fighter.

Central to the aircraft is the back-seat Weapons System Operator and the Martin Marietta LANTIRN (Low Altitude Navigation and Targeting Infra-Red for Night) system that he operates. In essence, the aircraft can navigate at low altitude on automatic terrain-following radar, with an improved Hughes APG-70 multi-purpose radar, infra-red mapping and a superior, new Honeywell ringed-laser INS for guidance. The aircraft is also capable of carrying all the new 'smart' weapons that can be delivered by these systems in any weather. The cockpits have seven Sperry multi-purpose mono-chrome and colour displays, four in the rear and three in the front, plus, of course, a new Kaiser wide-angle HUD upon which daylight-quality IR video images are projected. A sophisticated internal ECM system protects the aircraft.

In addition to the training aircraft at Luke, the 4th Tactical Fighter Wing at Seymour Johnson AFB, North Carolina, was the

F-15E Strike Eagle – the most capable fighter aircraft in the world. Much heavier than the original single-seat air-superiority fighter, it won't dogfight as well, but it will put a bomb through a window in the worst weather. (McDonnell Douglas)

first operational Wing, and it served in the Gulf. The second Wing of aircraft will replace the 48th TFW F-111s at RAF Lakenheath. No other purchases are planned.

THE F-16 FIGHTING FALCON

The F-16 Fighting Falcon is a compact, multi-role fighter aircraft. Its highly manoeuvrable design has proven itself in air-to-air combat and air-to-surface attack. This aircraft provides a relatively low-cost, high-performance weapon system for the air forces of the United States and allied nations.

In an air combat role, the F-16's manoeuvrability and combat radius (distance it can fly to enter air combat, stay and fight, and return) exceed those of potential threat fighter aircraft. It can locate targets under all weather conditions and detect low-flying aircraft in radar ground clutter.

While operating in an air-to-surface role, the F-16 can fly more than 500 miles (800km), deliver its weapons with superior accuracy, defend itself against enemy aircraft and return to its starting point. An all-weather capability allows it accurately to deliver ordnance during non-visual bombing conditions.

The F-16 has excellent self-defence. Because the Fighting Falcon is small and has a smokeless engine, it is difficult to detect, visually or with radar, and hard to hit. Its 360-degree threat-warning system and excellent visibility from its bubble canopy reduce the chances that the pilot will be caught off-guard. Moreover, the F-16's manoeuvrability makes it harder for enemy aircraft and surface-to-air missiles to hit. The F-16 weapon system has many features that increase its ability to survive if hit. The aircraft structure is simple and rugged. Metal alloys for lower wing panels were selected for strength and damage tolerance. Hydraulic, electrical and fuel feed systems are redundant and separated. It has an explosion suppression system for fuel tanks.

In designing the F-16, advanced aerospace science and proven reliable systems were selected from other aircraft such as the F-15 and F-111. These were combined to simplify the aircraft and reduce its size, purchase price, maintenance costs and weight. The light weight of the fuselage is achieved without reducing its strength. The F-16 can withstand up to 9g (nine times the force of gravity) with internal fuel tanks filled — greater than any other current fighter aircraft. The blended body and wing design increases lift at high angles of attack and decreases drag. It also adds internal space for fuel and essential equipment. The wings have leading-edge flaps that automatically change their contour to suit the angle of attack

39

or flight and speed of the aircraft. This gives the plane maximum lift-to-drag ratio and minimum buffet throughout all flight modes.

The cockpit and its bubble canopy are designed to give the pilot almost unlimited visibility. The pilot has almost unobstructed forward and upward vision, and greatly improved vision over the side and to the rear. The seat-back angle is changed from the usual 13 degrees to 30 degrees and the height of the heel rest is greater. This increases the pilot's comfort and g-force tolerance. The air-conditioned cockpit has an escape system capable of safely ejecting the pilot even at zero-altitude and zero-airspeed. Emergency canopy jettison is provided by explosive unlatching devices and two forward-mounted rockets.

The pilot has excellent flight control of the F-16 through its fly-by-wire system. Electrical wire carry commands, replacing the usual cables and linkage controls. A side-stick controller is used instead of the conventional centre-mounted stick for easy and accurate control of the aircraft during g-force combat manoeuvres. Hand pressure on the side stick controller sends electrical signals to the actuators of flight control surfaces such as ailerons and rudder.

Advance design combines the fire control system with the radar, head-up display and hands-on controls to eliminate any need for the pilot to look away from the target. Using the throttle, side-stick controller and stores management system, the pilot has quick-reaction, fingertip control of displays and weapons.

A broad selection of external ordnance can be carried on the F-16's nine ordnance stations or pylons – one under the fuselage, six under the wings and one on each wing tip.

Avionics systems include a highly accurate inertial navigation system in which a computer provides steering information to the pilot. The plane has UHF and VHF radios plus an instrument landing system. It also has a warning system and modular

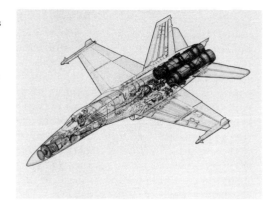

Hornet x-ray view. The F/A-18 (Fighter/Attack) was developed as a competitor to the F-16. It is flown by the US Marines, USN, Blue Angels and countries such as Australia and Spain. It is well designed for both air-to-air combat and ground-attack missions. (McDonnell Douglas)

F-16C Fighting Falcon. With the addition of better engines, LANTIRN to USAF Europe birds and then the AIM-120 AMRAAM, the F-16C continues to hold its reputation as the most versatile first-line aircraft in the world. (USAF: 86 TFW)

countermeasure pods to be used against airborne or surface electronic threats. The fuselage has growth space for additional avionics systems.

Maintenance has been made easier by the use of hinged or removable panels for easy access to all components, and by built-in tests and fault and condition indicators. A maintenance fault table stores data to be used to locate problem areas. When a faulty unit is replaced, an automatic self-test shows whether the system is operating. These features reduce the time required to find system failures and replace units. They also reduce the number of flight line maintenance personnel and skill levels required.

The F-16 costs less to build and uses less fuel than any other current US Air Force fighter and attack aircraft and has a significantly increased combat capability. For example, when performing the same mission, it uses 50 per cent less fuel than an F-4 Phantom.

The F-16A, a single-seat model, first flew in December 1976. The first operational F-16A was delivered in January 1979 to the 388th Tactical Fighter Wing at Hill Air Force Base, Utah. A two-seat model, the F-16B, features an extended canopy to cover the second cockpit. To make room for the second cockpit, the forward fuselage fuel tank and avionics growth space were reduced. During training the forward cockpit is used by the student pilot, with an instructor pilot in the rear cockpit.

The F-16C and F-16D are the improved single- and two-place counterparts of the F-16A and B and incorporate the latest cockpit control and display technology for maximum mission flexibility. All F-16s delivered since November 1981 have built-in structural and wiring provisions and systems architecture that permit expansion of the multi-role flexibility to perform precision strike, night attack and beyond-visual-range interception missions.

Externally, the F-16C is difficult to distinguish from an F-16A. Internally, however, there are major differences, which include an

APG-68 Multimode Radar with increased range, sharper resolution and expanded operating modes; an increased maximum take-off gross weight and an increase in gross weight limitations; and an advanced, versatile cockpit with improved pilot-vehicle interface features.

THE A-10 WARTHOG (THUNDERBOLT II)

The A-10 Thunderbolt II is the first US Air Force aircraft especially designed for the close air support of ground forces. It is deployed to Europe to help equal the imbalance of armoured forces between the Warsaw Pact and NATO countries.

The A-10 is a single place, twin-turbofan aircraft designed to be simple, effective and survivable in the demanding close air support mission, with a particular emphasis on the anti-armour role. All of the attributes necessary to perform the close air support mission have been built into the A-10. The versatility and flexibility of the A-10 are best displayed by its large-payload, long-loiter, wide-radius capabilities. Its ability to loiter for hours within the battle area where it can operate under 1,000ft ceilings with less than two miles' visibility makes the A-10 highly responsive to the immediate needs of the Army combat commander.

The A-10 can carry up to 16,000lb with a mixed load of ordnance and fuel on ten underwing pylon stations or nearly 11,000lb with full internal fuel. Ordnance includes both conventional and laser-guided weapons, electro-optically guided bombs, cluster bomb munitions, Maverick missiles and electronic countermeasures. Mounted internally along the aircraft's centreline is a seven-barrel 30mm cannon capable of firing at 4,200 rounds a minute. The GAU-8/A Avenger gun, designed specifically to arm the A-10 in its anti-armour close support role, ensures a high probability of a tank kill in a single strafing pass. In tests, the gun has demonstrated its tank killing ability by destroying tanks with one- and two-second 30mm bursts. In addition to the armour-piercing projectile which is capable of penetrating medium and heavy tanks, the gun can also fire high-explosive ammunition which is extremely effective against a wide variety of other targets such as trucks, armoured personnel carriers and other vehicles. The manoeuvrability of the A-10, combined with the gun's inherent accuracy, allows the pilot to deliver his ordnance quickly on targets, even in adverse weather and poor visibility.

The A-10 is powered by two quiet and smokeless General Electric TF34-100 turbofan engines, each generating 9,065lb (4,082kg) of thrust.

Ruggedness, reliability and ease of maintenance have been the primary considerations in the A-10's design. Its structure is conventional, with approximately 95 per cent of the airframe constructed from aluminium. Numerous aircraft parts are interchangeable left and right, including the engines, main landing gear and vertical stabilizers.

The A-10 achieves its survivability both by having a high manoeuvrability at low airspeeds and altitudes and by being a 'hard' aircraft. The pilot is encircled by a titanium armourplate 'bathtub' which also protects the vital elements of the flight control system. Redundant primary structural elements can survive major damage; self-sealing fuel cells are protected with internal and external foam; and the A-10's primary hydraulic flight control system is further enhanced by a backup 'manual reversion' system which permits the pilot to fly and land the aircraft when all hydraulics are lost.

The A-10 first flew on 10 May 1972 and following a competitive evaluation with another aircraft was selected for production in January 1973. Deliveries began to Tactical Air Command in 1976. A total of 713 A-10s were delivered to the Air Force before production ended in 1982.

THE F-15C EAGLE

The F-15 Eagle is an advanced tactical fighter aircraft, designed to excel in air-to-air combat and used by the US Air Force for the air defence superiority mission. Simply stated, the F-15 is designed to out-perform, out-fly, and out-fight any enemy aircraft in the forseeable future. It is a single-seat aircraft in the 45,000lb weight class, powered by two Pratt and Whitney F-100 advanced technology turbofan afterburning engines. Each engine is in the 25,000lb thrust class and together they provide a thrust-to-weight ratio considerably greater than 1:1. This extraordinary power enables the Eagle to accelerate in the pure vertical and sustain high-g turns.

The enormous power of the F-100 engine, in combination with low wing loading, gives the pilot the ability to outmanoeuvre opposing fighters, especially in a close-in fighting environment. The optimized aerodynamics provide for excellent speed, in excess of Mach 2, and for very stable flight characteristics at all angles of attack and g-loadings. The F-15C model incorporates increased internal fuel capacity, an additional UHF radio transmitter, an improved pilot ejection seat, improved landing gear, and advances in the aircraft radar and electronic warfare capabilities.

THE WORLD'S TIME-TO-CLIMB RECORDS

The most spectacular display of jet fighter performance is the time-to-climb record. Nothing better illustrates the tremendous power of the modern, afterburning turbojet engine, and the kind of performance the pilot must manage in air-to-air combat. The F-15, in an operation known as 'Streak Eagle', set all the major world time-to-climb records in early 1975. The aircraft was one of the early, pre-production models, and after being stripped of non-essential items, including even its paintwork, it weighed 2,800lb less than the normal aircraft. The fuel load was just enough to fly the carefully designed profile, a restraining device held the aircraft until full power was reached, and the flights took place from Grand Forks, North Dakota in winter, when the air was thickest, giving the most thrust.

Major Roger Smith below describes the flight profile of the attempt on the 30,000m (98,425ft) record. Weight was 32,000lb, the take-off roll was only 500ft and the peak altitude reached was 102,400ft:

Release from the holdback cable at full afterburner with 7,000 pounds of fuel. Gear up and rotate for takeoff at the first indication of airspeed, about seventy knots. Watch the gear unsafe light and hope it goes out by 350 knots. If not, abort, fast. Look for .65 Mach – about 420 knots. Rotate vertically into an Immelmann and hold 2.65 Gs. Expect to arrive level upside down at 32,000 feet at 1.1 Mach. Roll 180 degrees to right side up and accelerate to 600 knots. Climb at eight degrees to 36,000 feet and 600 knots. Hold 36,000, accelerate to 2.25 Mach, pull four Gs to 55 degrees. Look for four degrees' angle of attack. Hold four degrees until mission control calls to recover (passing record altitude). Shut down afterburners when they blow out. Shut down engines when they quit. At the 'recover' call, try to hold zero angle of attack to minimize any tendency for control or gyroscopic unknowns to the flight path in the rare atmosphere. Ride ballistically to a 55 degree dive angle. Look for 100 knots airspeed and start turning for home. At 55,000 feet or below, look for four green lights on the instrument panel to indicate the boost pump is on. Try to start both engines at once when above 350 knots and 12% rpm. If at least one starts and you have radio contact with mission control, talk about coming home to Grand Forks, depending on fuel remaining. If there is no start or no contact on radio, think about Fargo or ejection.

Altitude (ft/m)	Time (sec)	Previous (sec)	Pilot	Margin (%)
3,000/9,843	27.5	34.5 (F-4)	Smith	20
6,000/19,685	39.3	48.8 (F-4)	Macfarlane	19
9,000/29,528	48.9	61.7 (F-4)	Macfarlane	21
12,000/39,370	59.4	77.1 (F-4)	Macfarlane	23
15,000/49,212	77.0	114.5 (F-4)	Peterson	33
20,000/65,617	122.9	169.8 (MiG-25)	Smith	28
25,000/82,021	161.0	192.6 (MiG-25)	Peterson	16
30,000/98,425	207.8	243.9 (MiG-25)	Smith	15

A few months later the Russians claimed that an experimental version of the MiG-25, the E266, broke the following records (Western experts believe that the aircraft was rocket-assisted, and not an operational aircraft like the F-15): 82,000ft – 154sec; 98,400ft – 190sec; 114,800ft – 251sec.

The standard armament for the Eagle is an internal, wing-mounted, cannon, four AIM-9 Sidewinder missiles and four AIM-7 Advanced Sparrow missiles. Both missiles are greatly improved versions of proven weapons. With its advanced radar and fire control system, coupled with a sophisticated communications system, the Eagle is able to provide an extremely flexible and highly self-sufficient weapons system which can be used effectively in any weather. The AIM-9 missile has a vastly improved seeker head, giving the Eagle the ability to shoot down targets from all angles using a heat-seeking missile.

The radar in the F-15 gives the pilot the capability to locate, track and fire against both high- and low-flying aircraft at great distances with extraordinary accuracy. The 'lookdown/shoot-down' capability avoids the ground clutter that appears on other radars and permits the pilot to see only moving targets and, with his radar missiles, shoot down these very low-flying aircraft. The head-up display and visual situation display combine to provide the pilot with the flying, target and armament information needed to fly the aircraft and engage the target.

The radar allows the pilot to lock on to targets at distances well

Bitburg Eagles. F-15s typically fly in two- or four-ship formations, sometimes larger, depending on the threat. Complex tactics using four or more aircraft have been devised for various air combat situations. (USAF: 36 TFW)

beyond 50 miles. Once targets are located, it provides him with information concerning the target's aspect angle, heading, speed, range and altitude. The pilot will then know where the target is, where it is going and what must be done to manoeuvre into the most advantageous position to fight it. The radar and HUD displays tell the pilot when he is in range to fire the various types of armament carried and even help him visually locate and identify the target by encircling it in a target designator box.

To increase the F-15's survivability in combat, redundancy is incorporated into its structure. For example, one vertical tail, or one of its three wing spars, can be severed without causing the loss of the aircraft. Redundancy is also inherent in the F-15's twin engines, and its fuel system incorporates self-sealing features and foam to inhibit fires and explosions. The combined hydraulic and mechanical flight control system is backed up by a fly-by-wire capability to increase survivability.

The F-15 is an aircraft designed and built with maintenance in mind. When a component of the aircraft needs repair, specialists remove it quickly, replace it with a spare and repair the broken part in specially designed maintenance areas. Even the F-100 engine is composed of five modules, each being interchangeable from one engine to another.

THE MiG-29 FULCRUM*

To many US fighter pilots the name 'MiG' had come to be almost synonymous with the words 'bandit', 'enemy', and even 'target'. Many of those lucky and determined high achievers who have chosen the cockpit of an F-15 or F-16 regard a MiG as little more than a slightly enhanced type of flying target, perhaps more difficult to shoot down than a QF-106 drone, but inferior technology, flown by an inadequate opponent. Such views have only been strengthened by the poor showing of MiGs in Korea and subsequent disastrous performances in the Middle East. A claimed 82–0 performance by Israeli fighter pilots against Syrian MiGs made a much greater impression on NATO fighter pilots than the less comfortable results recorded when Indian MiG-21s met Pakistani F-104s, Mirages and Sabres.

---

* By Jon Lake (copyright; reproduced with permission). I have included this rather lengthy analysis of the MiG-29 because it counters the conventional wisdom and well illustrates the central problem of air power – designing modern aircraft in a rapidly changing, high-tech world and enabling fighter pilots to compete against the best aircraft the enemy has. Jon Lake probably knows more about the MiG-29 than any other journalist, having talked to many Western and Soviet pilots who have flown it and having written a book about it.

The emergence of the MiG-29 did little to shake the fundament-ally (and hitherto justifiably) complacent attitude of many Western fighter jocks. Fine, so its airshow performances were spectacular enough, but what about that primitive cockpit, the agricultural finish, the radar, the weapons, and above all the pilot? Remember who built it, remember who's flying it. It's no match for an F-15 or F-16, right? The only people claiming it's any good are non-flying journalists seduced by having an airplane with red stars on it to watch, and impressed by airshow manoeuvres like the tailslide and Cobra, right? And the kill statistics in Desert Storm tell the whole story, right?

Wrong! The MiG-29 is the Soviet answer to the West's super-fighters, and in many ways it's a superior fighter airplane. Who says so? It's not just the eager-for-sensation, non-pilot journalists and Design Bureau pilots and engineers. There are plenty of well-qualified and impartial witnesses, too. There are the Western pilots who have actually flown it, men like Major Bob Wade, a Canadian CF-18 Hornet pilot with some 6000 hours of fighter time, and John Farley, former British Aerospace Harrier Chief Test Pilot, to say nothing of the pilots who've flown or flown against the ex-East German MiG-29s. These are hardly Soviet 'salesmen', and their opinions are likely to be more objective than those of Western fighter pilots who haven't experienced the MiG-29 at first hand. Every front-line pilot loves his own aircraft type, and will be difficult to convince that another aircraft is superior. Try telling a Hurricane pilot that the Spitfire was better, or a Crusader pilot that the Phantom was superior!

Nor should we be too scathing about Soviet technology. The first nation into space has also demonstrated its ability to build the world's first SST, the world's largest transport plane, and the world's largest helicopter, while a Soviet fighter had shattered the time-to-height records set by the Streak Eagle. A world class fighter aircraft is easily achievable. The US Government's own *Soviet Military Power 1989* had something to say on the subject: 'Moscow's willingness to invest in R&D has gained the Soviet Union technological advantages in certain key areas . . . they are now, in some cases, fielding more technologically advanced systems than those of the United States'. I suggest that the Soviets enjoy such a lead in the field of fighter aerodynamics, and perhaps also in the field of passive target detection and acquisition systems. Soviet-built needn't mean second-best, and both of the American Ad-vanced Tactical Fighter evaluation teams have described the MiG-29 and Su-27 together as the world's best dogfighters.

Unlike many lightweight fighters (most notably the F-16), the MiG-29 does have a genuine beyond-visual-range (BVR) capability.

While BVR combat is inherently less glamorous than a dogfight, it should not be forgotten that the job of the fighter pilot is to destroy his opponent with as little risk to himself as possible. Ideally, the aim should be to smack the enemy in the teeth from maximum range, since a turning fight will always be unpredictable, and therefore risky, even when your aircraft enjoys an advantage. The MiG-29 can detect, engage and destroy its target from beyond BVR, and beyond the range of the F-16's radar and weapons, using its NO-193 radar. This has been confirmed as being closely equivalent to the West's most widely respected fighter radar, the Hughes AN-APG-65, as used by the F/A-18. This should not be surprising, since the USSR devoted considerable time, money and effort to obtaining technical documents relating to this radar through espionage, and a Hughes employee was prosecuted for passing information to the Russians. Having stolen the technology, it's quite possible the Soviets have improved the radar, making it more powerful, and more able to burn through hostile jamming.

By using its Infra-Red Search and Track system in conjunction with a long-range IR-homing version of the AA-10 'Alamo', the MiG-29 can engage a target without alerting the RHAW gear of its target. Anyone who doubts the tactical utility of the IRST should remember that similar equipment is being fitted to the West's latest fighters, including the F-14D, EFA and ATF.

In a close-in, turning fight, the MiG-29 also enjoys some advantages. These can broadly be summarized as superior handling characteristics, especially at low speed and high angle of attack, a wider aerodynamic and structural envelope, and superior turn performance. The MiG-29 also enjoys an outstanding power-plant, which performs well throughout the envelope.

As fighter development has progressed over the years, the job of the aerodynamicist has become more and more difficult. He has had to come up with a shape optimized for a wide range of different parameters — absolute performance, slow-speed capability, good handling and manoeuvrability throughout the envelope, high life, low drag, etc. — some of which are incompatible. In the West, we handed the problem to the fly-by-wire control system, which used high-speed digital computers to provide acceptable handling for aircraft which were inherently too unstable to be flown by an unaided human pilot. The computers were also programmed to keep the aircraft within certain hard limits, to prevent the pilot from going into areas of the envelope where he risked overstressing or departing his aircraft. Control systems were designed to the lowest common denominator, making the aircraft safe for the weakest pilots. Inevitably this meant that some capability which might be used by the best pilots was sacrificed. The F-16 pilot can demand full up elevator, but he will only be given this if the computer determines that it will not cause him to depart or to exceed 9g, even if to do so would let him evade a missile, or clear the top of a hill, and even if to do so would only entail pulling 9½g.

The Soviets have chosen soft inner limits. These warn the pilot when he is approaching departure from normal flight or where he might overstress the aircraft, but they do not prevent him from making brief excursions into these areas to seize a tactical advantage, out-turn a missile or avoid hitting the ground. So, the Soviet fighter can fly slower, or at higher angle of attack, or at higher g than the F-16, even without reaching the soft limits of the flight controls, which are defined by stick stops, but which can be pulled through when desired. It does, however, require some experience to know when and where you can exceed the limits without losing control of the airplane.

In a close-in, turning fight, the ability to fly at high angle of attack can mean the difference between winning and losing. If you can point the nose of your aircraft away from the direction of flight at the target, you may be able to gain a temporary gun or missile 'snap' shot. The MiG can sustain 30 degrees angle of attack without departing, and can achieve 50 degrees for up to 15 seconds and 80 degrees for a brief moment. The MiG also has a helmet-mounted sight that enables him to launch weapons at targets well off the nose. To launch a missile at a target at 3 or 9 o'clock may reduce its kill probability, but it is a useful option that could win a fight.

The MiG-29's higher g limit (9½ in service, 10½ in air shows, 14 in combat) can be important because it can give greater turn performance at similar airspeeds. So, the F-16 has a smaller manoeuvring environment. The MiG's higher thrust-to-weight ratio and lower induced drag will allow a smaller radius or higher rate of turn.

The MiG has twin, widely separated, engines, which give it an advantage in terms of battle damage or back-up reliability. It can also operate from very short dirt strips by using the engine inlets above the wing, which can give it a capability for hidden location and post-strike or operational surprise.

The MiG is not perfect. It lacks range and endurance and a Western pilot would initially find the cockpit and weapons switch-ology primitive and hard to use. It lacks the flexibility of the F-16, is inferior in ground attack, has much more limited visibility and isn't as reliable in constant operation.

At the bottom line, the equation still comes down to pilot quality, and at squadron level, and in terms of realistic air combat training, NATO probably still has the edge. Soviet pilots are learning to 'push' the envelope and use the full capabilities of the airplane to seize tactical advantage. Tactical flexibility in Soviet units still needs to be improved. The MiG-29, however, is a superb aircraft; it has already demonstrated in tests against the F-15 and F-16 with the Luftwaffe MiGs that it can win dogfights by using its advantages.

Author's Comment: I have changed my mind somewhat about the MiG after exchanging several letters with Jon Lake and hearing the indisputable results of the dogfight tests against the Luftwaffe MiGs, which won consistently in the close-in fights. However, without going into all the individual comparisons, which I have discussed in other articles, my main view, after discussing the situation with F-16 Instructor Pilots, is that the F-16 has a great superiority which would take effect if the F-16 pilot manages to avoid, as he should, certain situations where the MiG is superior as Jon has pointed out. One F-16 IP said: 'You'll never get me to turn in a phone booth with a MiG. If you slow to zippo, you better have a good jink game plan. You have to fight your own smart fight.'

The essential advantage of the F-16 pilot is simply that his cockpit is superior: he can see better out of it, he has modern instruments and switches instead of the MiG's obsolete steam gauges, he has a superior HOTAS switchology capability, and, in general, in a high-pressure, frantic air battle, he can gather, process and implement information much faster and more correctly than the busy MiG pilot. Any F-16 pilot will tell you how very long it takes to get really good at 'piccolo playing,' using all the switches and systems correctly and swiftly against realistic, multiple threats at high speed with a lot to think about and do in a short time.

The answer, I think, is that Jon and I are both right. It depends on the situation and on the pilot. Dogfights are rarely textbook, one-versus-one engagements between equal pilots, so I don't

This MiG-29 has air-to-air radar and a heat-seeking missile armament, and the air intakes close to the ground have inbuilt protection against foreign object damage with back-up intakes also on the top of the wing. When first seen at Farnborough in 1988, the 29 gave a flight demonstration of high manoeuvrability and great power. (Jon Lake)

want to go too far in accepting the Luftwaffe MiG victories. Each aircraft has areas where it will be superior. Right now, I believe USAF pilots and USAF air battle command, control and intelligence capabilities are superior and would, as in the Gulf, win any air war the US chose to enter. Replace the Iraqi control system and pilots with Soviet ones, and I believe the result would have been much the same, although with more fighting and more US air losses. Soviet generals were disappointed, if not shocked, at the US ability to use ECM, Wild Weasel and other methods to win the air battle before aircraft-to-aircraft engagements even began. The Gulf War was not a fair test, and, in a straightforward comparison, it is clear that the MiG-29 is one hell of an aeroplane that, in the hands of a good pilot, would be very dangerous in the same sky as an F-15 or F-16.

THE TORNADO*

Tornado is a two-seat twin-engine variable-geometry aircraft capable of undertaking combat missions in all weathers, by day or night. Tornado was developed in Europe as a multi-role combat aircraft to meet the operational needs of the air forces of the UK, West Germany and Italy and the West German Navy.

Tornado has been designed to serve in a wider range of operational roles, and carry a greater variety of external weapons and stores than any other modern combat aircraft. Despite these exacting demands, Tornado is a compact aircraft, smaller than other less-versatile in-service machines.

Tornado represents a considerable engineering achievement by Europe's aerospace industry. It is the largest and most important collaborative weapon programme ever undertaken in Europe. At its peak, more than 500 companies and 70,000 people were engaged in producing Tornado.

Three basic versions are built: Tornado IDS (interdictor strike); Tornado ADV (air defence variant); and Tornado ECR (electronic combat and reconnaissance). In addition, a special reconnaissance variant of the IDS is built for the Royal Air Force, and a combat-capable dual-control trainer is supplied.

Tornado was specified to fulfil several different combat roles. Missions for which it has been designed are: long-range interdiction; strike; naval strike; close air support; battlefield interdiction; air superiority; air defence; interception; electronic warfare; reconnaissance; and combat training.

---

* Text by British Aerospace.

Tornado IDS (Interdiction Strike)

The Tornado IDS is designed to fly at transonic speeds at low level, beneath the defensive radar screen, to reach its target. For such missions Tornado is capable of automatic terrain-following. A Tornado IDS can make a successful blind first-pass attack on any surface target on land or at sea. The Tornado IDS is equipped with a ground mapping radar, terrain following radar, doppler radar, laser ranger and marked target seeker, radar warning receiver and electronic countermeasures systems. A digital inertial navigation system provides data for the aircraft's nav/attack computer and autopilot/flight director. Ground speed is cross-checked by the doppler radar. The pilot also has a moving map display and a head-up display.

GR.1 is the designation given to its IDS aircraft by the Royal Air Force. The Royal Air Force has a dedicated reconnaissance version of the IDS, known as the GR.1A, equipped with sideways-looking infra-red imaging sytems and a downwards-looking Linescan, plus a video recording system.

Tornado ADV (Air Defence Variant)

The Tornado ADV was designed to meet the Royal Air Force requirement for a long-range all-weather interceptor. Although optimized for air defence, the ADV retains 80 per cent commonality with the IDS. The major differences between the ADV and the IDS are that the ADV has a front fuselage lengthened by 1.36m to accommodate the Foxhunter air-intercept radar and an extra fuel tank of approximately 500l capacity. Foxhunter is a track-while-scan pulse-doppler radar that detects both high- and low-flying targets beyond 100nm range. The Foxhunter radar keeps track of a large number of targets while continuing to search for additional targets. It can also receive target data from, or relay it to, other ADVs or ground stations, via a secure data link. Radar data may be displayed to the air crew in a variety of formats.

The Tornado ADV, the first of which were given the designation F.2 by the Royal Air Force, can speed in level flight to intercept a hostile target and launch a missile. It has an excellent range/loiter capability, remaining airborne for more than four hours. It can remain on station for over two hours during a combat air patrol some 550 to 740km (300–400nm) from its base. With flight refuelling, range and patrol period may be greatly extended. To increase its manoeuvrability in combat, the Tornado F2 was provided with fixed wing root extensions and the Kruger flaps were removed.

The F.3, the current production standard aircraft, is an improved version of the Tornado F.2 operated by the Royal Air Force. It was

The Tornado air defence fighter. Sky Flash missiles are recessed in the fuselage, while the Sidewinders are carried under the wing. The Tornado may change its wing-sweep angle in a dogfight, reducing sweep to increase turn radius but slowing acceleration. (British Aerospace)

introduced in 1986. It has more powerful RB199 Mk 104 engines with extended reheat, a twin inertial navigation system and provision for a JTIDS (Joint Tactical Information Distribution System) data link. The F.3 is also fitted with auto-sweep – a system that automatically adjusts the sweep angle of the interceptor's wings according to its flight speed and altitude.

Royal Air Force F.3s are armed with one 27mm cannon, four Sky Flash medium-range air-to-air missiles and, for close combat, four short-range AIM-9L Sidewinder air-to-air missiles.

In September 1987, a Tornado ADV made the first unrefuelled crossing of the Atlantic by a British fighter, flying some 2200nm (4077km) in 4 hours 45 minutes.

Tornado ECR (Electronic Combat and Reconnaissance)
Utilizing the IDS airframe, the Tornado ECR retains most of the capabilities of the German IDS but carries additional sensors and systems for its role of electronic intelligence gathering, reconnaissance, surveillance and defence suppression. It has forward and sideways infra-red imaging sensors, an automatic emitter locator system, a secure digital data link to ground and other forces and electronic countermeasures equipment and can carry a chaff and infra-red flare dispenser pod, plus anti-radar missiles and two Sidewinder air-to-air missiles for self defence. The twin cannon of

A photograph of the Tornado ADV. With wings swept back, empty missile racks and no extra fuel tankage, this aircraft is on a manufacturer's test flight.

the IDS are not fitted. The ECR can serve as a pathfinder and retains the capability for carrying out strike missions. The first ECR was handed over to the German Luftwaffe in April 1990.

Armament
The Tornado IDS has two Mauser 27mm cannon mounted internally in the lower front fuselage. Specially designed for the Tornado, the Mauser is a self-powered low-recoil revolver cannon with a high muzzle velocity firing electrically ignited ammunition. One of two rates of fire can be selected; high rate for air-to-air engagements, and low rate for air-to-ground attacks. On its seven external hard points (three fuselage, four underwing), Tornado can carry a mixed load selected from an extensive range of weapons and stores. These include air-to-air and air-to-surface missiles of different types, bombs, rockets, submunition dispensers, electronic warfare, decoy, sensor and reconnaissance pods, and fuel drop tanks. Two AIM-9L Sidewinder air-to-air missiles are carried by Tornado IDS for self defence. In addition to Sidewinder short range missiles, the ADV carries four Sky Flash medium-range air-to-air missiles in semi-buried positions beneath the fuselage.

Training
The air forces of the three nations agreed to the formation of a joint facility for the initial training of Tornado air crews. This was the Tri-National Tornado Training Establishment, situated in the UK at RAF Cottesmore. Here British, German and Italian air crews are trained to fly the Tornado IDS. Aircraft weapon training is a national responsibility. The Operational Conversion Unit for training Royal Air Force air crew to fly and fight the Tornado ADV was opened in July 1985 at RAF Coningsby.

THE HARRIER II

The Harrier II is an extensively redesigned version of the earlier Harrier GR.3/AV-8A Vertical/Short Take-off and Landing (V/STOL) Close Air Support aircraft, allowing even greater tactical employment. Developed jointly by British Aerospace and McDonnell Douglas of the USA, the Harrier II is able to carry double the payload of its predecessors over the same range or, conversely, the same payload over twice the range. Free from the constraints and increasing vulnerability of fixed-based operations, Harrier II's enhanced capability permits even greater advances in the art of dispersed operations from both concealed sites and forward operating locations (FOLs) and from a variety of maritime platforms. The AV-8B (United States Marine Corps), EAV-8B (Spanish Navy) and GR.5/GR.7 (Royal Air Force) are the four current variants of Harrier II. They benefit substantially from the use of carbon fibre composite materials in their construction, whilst a supercritical wing and other aerodynamic refinements greatly enhance air combat manoeuvrability. The new forward fuselage incorporates the Hughes Angle Rate Bombing System (ARBS) and a 'bubble' canopy for improved pilot vision. Pilot workload is also significantly reduced by the introduction of an advanced cockpit layout featuring a multi-function display (MFD), wide-angle head-up display (HUD) and up-front controller, a full-colour moving map display and hands-on-throttle-and-stick (HOTAS) controls.

Increased thrust from the well-proven Rolls-Royce Pegasus Mk 105 is complemented by underfuselage lift improvement devices (LIDs) and modified forward nozzles, to increase vertical lift performance. Incorporation of the newly developed Pegasus 11-61 engine, providing even greater thrust, will be yet another significant step forward in Harrier II's all-round agility. Entry of the Night

A Harrier II in the environment for which it was designed. Operating from rough airstrips, a piece of road or even just a clearing in a wood, the Harrier cannot be beaten for rapid-response firepower when and where the front line needs it. (McDonnell Douglas)

Left: This study of the Harrier GR.5 in the hover allows a good look at the aircraft's payload. Note the pair of AIM-9 Sidewinder missiles for self-defence nestling amongst the seven BL.755 cluster bomb units. With a capacity for this weight of ordnance and its unique operational flexibility, the Harrier is a potent aircraft. (British Aerospace)
Right: The greatest fighter of all time. Over 5,000 F-4s were built, and, thirty years after it began flying with the US Navy, the aircraft is still operational with several air forces. This is the E model, with the internal Gatling gun. (McDonnell Douglas)

Attack Harrier GR.7 into Royal Air Force service will ensure that enemy air defences and troop columns moving at night will no longer be able to exploit the relative safety provided by the cover of darkness. Utilizing the full potential of a forward-looking infra-red (FLIR) sensor and night vision goggles (NVGs), the Harrier GR.7 pilot will now be able to deliver a wide range of ordnance with pinpoint accuracy, by night as well as by day.

THE GREATEST FIGHTER ALL TIME

I was fortunate in flying all four models of the USAF F-4 in most of the different missions for which it was used in Vietnam and NATO. This unmatched versatility is the primary reason why I consider it to be the greatest fighter in history. Consider the different ways the same aircraft was used:

1. Long-range air-to-air interceptor   AIM-7 Sparrow
2. Intermediate-range dogfighter   AIM-9 Sidewinder
3. Short-range dogfighter   Gatling gun
4. Reconnaissance   Camera etc.
5. Carrier operations   USN, Royal Navy
6. Interdiction, close air support   Many weapons
7. Smart bomb delivery   Laser etc.
8. Long-range nuclear strike   Nuclear weapons
9. Wild Weasel anti-missile   Shrike, Harm etc.
10. Multi-national fighter   Israel, Japan etc.

That one single aircraft could do all these things, and for the most part do them better than the specialized aircraft designed for each role, is truly impressive. Consider my problem and great responsibility in training and operating a fighter squadron in NATO with 60 pilots and navigators and 24 aircraft worth 100 million dollars. One day they might sit on real, 5-minute nuclear alert for wartime targets in Warsaw Pact countries; the next day they might fly air-to-air, close-in, high-g dogfight training over the North Sea; the next day they might practise long-range interception of Soviet bombers; the next day they might fly to local ranges and practise the various nuclear weapons deliveries; and the next day they might fly to Italy or Spain and strafe or drop practice bombs on conventional target ranges, using a wide variety of simulated weapons and electronic delivery systems. For one crew to know how to do all these different things, at combat-ready standards, in the most complicated machine ever operated by man, was probably the most difficult flying job in the world. The F-4E, for example, contained 294 avionics black boxes. Not even an astronaut, although finely trained by necessity, faced such a diverse challenge.

On top of that, consider that the F-4 once held the following world performance records at the same time:

1. Time-to-climb to various altitudes:

	F-4	F-15
3,000m (9,843ft)	34.52sec	27.52sec
9,000m (29,528ft)	61.68sec	48.86sec
15,000m (49,212ft)	114.5sec	77.02sec
30,000m (98,425ft)	371.4sec	207.8sec

2. Maximum speed at low altitude: 753.6kt or Mach 1.18
3. Maximum speed at high altitude: 1395kt or Mach 2.42
4. Maximum altitude attained: 98,425ft
5. Maximum altitude sustained: 66,443ft

Most importantly, the F-4 has played a leading role in several major wars: Vietnam, the Middle East and, to a lesser extent, the Gulf. It has shot down more aircraft than any other jet except the F-86. Over 5000 F-4s were produced, more than any other modern fighter.

Now, 30 years after it went into production, it is still a front-line fighter for the United States, Japan, Britain, Germany, Israel, Greece, Spain, Korea and Turkey. It was used to great effect in the role of Wild Weasel, i.e. defence suppression, in the Gulf War. It cannot keep up with the advanced aircraft any more, but the F-4 is truly the greatest fighter ever produced. No other aircraft has been so important in aviation and air combat.

GREAT FIGHTERS OF HISTORY

Every new fighter pilot should have the opportunity to fly the Spad, the Spitfire, the F-86, the F-104, the Lightning, the Phantom, the F-15 and the MiG-29, just to know where he came from and to have a perspective on his profession. Individual fighters, because of the people who fly them and the wars in which they fight, take on a personality, a mixture of beauty, perversity, courage and determination. Can anyone in Britain look at a Spitfire flying at an air show without feeling emotions? Can any fighter pilot ever forget the fighter he once flew, which to him is more than just a machine?

WORLD WAR I: 1914–1918

Fokker DVII	Finest WWI fighter. Came too late in war.
Spad XIII	Flown by highest US French and Italian aces.
Albatros DIII	Richthofen's plane. Eventually outclassed.
Bristol F2B	Finest two-seater of WWI. Rear gunner protection.
Sopwith F1 Camel	Most successful killer of the war.
Royal Aircraft Factory SE5a	Favourite RAF fighter, flown by top ace Mannock (73 kills)
Fokker Triplane	Classic design. Later flown by Richthofen, who died in it.
Nieuport XVII	Popular French fighter, flown by Americans.

BETWEEN THE WARS

Armstrong Whitworth Siskin III	First all-metal RAF fighter. Served 1924–1932.
Boeing P-26	Big radial engine. Bridge between generations.
Fairey Swordfish ('Stringbag')	Brave old torpedo-bomber. Slow biplane in WWII!

WORLD WAR II: 1939–1945

Bell P-39 Aircobra	Early WWII fighter. Served well but became obsolete.
Curtiss P-40 Warhawk	The great 'Flying Tiger' of China.
Bristol Beaufighter	Two big engines made it a capable night and strike fighter.
De Havilland Mosquito	Fine twin-engined fighter-bomber which made memorable low-level attacks.

The Fokker DR. 1 triplane. Flown by Richthofen and other aces in the last year of World War I, it was capable of 122mph and 20,000ft. It had two Spandau machine guns mounted over the engine. (US National Archives)

Messerschmitt Bf 109	Greatest German aircraft of the war. 34,000 built.
Messerschmitt Bf 110	Major early night fighter. Gradually outclassed.
Hawker Hurricane	Immortal fighter which saved Britain. Served on 17 fronts.
Supermarine Spitfire	Most famous fighter of all. Supreme beauty and spirit.
Junkers Ju 87 ('Stuka')	The feared and potent dive-bomber.
Lockheed P-38 Lightning	Long-range escort. Highest Japanese killer. Flown by Bong.
Republic P-47 Thunderbolt	Universal fighter. Many aces. Known as the 'Jug'.
Focke-Wulf Fw 190	Versatile fighter-bomber. Had some advantages over the 109.
Mitsubishi A6M Zero	Japan's Spitfire. Couldn't compete in the end.
North American P-51 Mustang	Great escort dogfighter. Served with 55 nations.
Grumman F4F Wildcat	Main carrier fighter 1941–43. Rugged, with a 7-to-1 kill ratio.
Grumman F6F Hellcat	Superior to Japanese aircraft 1943–45, with a 19-to-1 kill ratio.
Messerschmitt Me 163	Innovative, hot rocket. Fast and dangerous.
Messerschmitt Me 262	First operational and combat jet fighter.
Junkers Ju 88G	Primary German night fighter. Took part in big night battles.
Vought F4U Corsair	Finest carrier fighter. Flew in Korea. Killed MiGs.
Yak-9	Modelled after Spitfire. Superior to Me 109 and Fw 190.

WWII TO KOREA: 1945–1953

Gloster Meteor	Only WWII Allied jet. World speed record 1945 – 606mph.
Lockheed F-80 Shooting Star	First US operational jet. Became T-33 trainer.
De Havilland Vampire	Diverse night fighter, interceptor and fighter-bomber.
Republic F-84 Thunderjet/ F-84 Thunderstreak	Even the swept-wing F model was not an F-86, but served well.
North American F-86 Sabre (D/L models with radar nose)	Great swept-wing, high-performance fighter of Korean War.
Northrop F-89D Scorpion	Initial bomber-interceptor with rockets in wing pods.
Lockheed F-94C Starfire	Improved F-80 with rockets for bomber-interceptor role.
MiG-15	F-86 won, but a fine early fighter.
Douglas A-1 Skyraider ('Spad')	Rugged WWII load carrier which became famous in Vietnam.

KOREA TO VIETNAM: 1953–1974

Hawker Hunter	Top RAF fighter of the 1950s. Aerobatic teams. Sold to 17 nations.
Hawker Siddeley Buccaneer	Nuclear strike, recce and low-level attack. Dependable and strong.

Lockheed F-104 Starfighter	First Mach 2 fighter. Held speed and altitude records simultaneously.
Hawker Siddeley (British Aerospace) Harrier	Revolutionary 'jump-jet' design. Hero of the Falklands.
Douglas A-4 Skyhawk	Popular little subsonic fighter. Still flying high.
McDonnell F-101 Voodoo	Tricky fighter. Became successful as recce bird.
Convair F-102 Delta Dagger	Major interceptor with improvements in radar and missiles.
Convair F-106 Delta Dart	Improved F-102. Mach 2. Semi-automatic control.
Republic F-105 Thunderchief ('Thud')	Largest single-seat, single-engined fighter. Heroic Vietnam bomber.
Cessna A-37 Dragonfly	Modified trainer. Small, nimble attack fighter.
Soviet fighters (by NATO designation):	
'Fencer' (Su-24)	Ground-attack fighter.
'Fishbed' (MiG-21)	'Fishbed-J' etc. means particular model.
'Flanker' (Sukhoi-27)	Great air superiority fighter.
'Flogger' (MiG-23)	Swing-wing fighter. MiG-27 is ground-attack variant.
'Foxbat' (MiG-25)	Mach 3 interceptor/recce
'Fulcrum' (MiG-29)	Popular air superiority fighter.
'Foxhound' (MiG-31)	Improved MiG-25.

Above: The Hawker Hunter served long and well with the RAF and many other air forces. It ended its career as an inexpensive two-seat training aircraft for Buccaneer crews. (Tim Laming)

Right: RAF Lightning interceptor – one of the greatest aircraft of all time. Its over-and-under engines gave it tremendous power for its time. (British Aerospace)

LTV F-8 Crusader	Early Navy bomber and MiG killer over North Vietnam.
LTV A-7 Corsair II	Baby brother of F-8 Crusader. Useful in Vietnam.
BAC Lightning	RAF's most exciting high-powered interceptor.
McDonnell Douglas F-4 Phantom	The greatest all-around fighter in history.
Northrop F-5 ('Freedom Fighter')	Developed from T-38 trainer as a low-cost, high-performance fighter.
General Dynamics F-111	Swing-wing fighter which finally earned its place in history.
Fairchild A-10 Thunderbolt II ('Warthog')	Slow but tough. A great tank killer.

SUPER-FIGHTERS

Dassault-Breguet Mirage F1	The French build them to fly them and sell them.
Saab Viggen	The Swedes build them to be independent.
SEPECAT Jaguar	Franco-British strike fighter.
Grumman F-14 Tomcat	Great strike/dogfight combination of the 1980s.
McDonnell Douglas F-15 Eagle	Great interceptor and dogfighter. Holds all time-to-climb records.
McDonnell Douglas F-15E Strike Eagle	Two-seater with advanced air-to-ground systems.
Panavia Tornado	Multi-national, multi-role. Impressive performance.
General Dynamics F-16 Falcon	The greatest all-around fighter of the 1980s.
Saab Gripen	Sweden's own super-fighter.
Mirage 2000	Successful French interceptor and strike fighter.
Rafale	France's own super-fighter.
F-22 Advanced Tactical Fighter	The major fighter of the next century.
European Fighter Aircraft	Joint fighter for NATO.

Sukhoi Su-27 Flanker. Very similar in design to the MiG-29, but much larger, the Flanker has also been modified for carrier operations. It is a superb air-to-air fighter despite its size. Its manoeuvring performance at Western air shows has impressed everyone. This aircraft was at Farnborough in 1990. (Author)

USAF FIGHTERS

During the First World War, the US Air Service, which became the US Army Air Corps in 1926 and then the US Air Force in 1947, flew a variety of aircraft with numbers in the manfaucturer's series rather than in sequence in the whole service. The Spad XIII was newer and better than the Spad XII, just as the F-15C is newer and better than the A model.

After the war, however, the service decided to identify aircraft by type rather than manufacturer, and in 1924 the first of the present series was designated: the Curtiss P-1 (P for Pursuit; after the Second World War this changed to F for Fighter).

Some fighters are developed but never reach full production. The United States, and other nations as well, often gave development contracts to two or more manufacturers because:

1. Competition encourages efficiency and technological imagination;

2. This helps maintain an industrial base of advanced manufacturers for the future; and

3. A test aircraft often served as a basis for the next generation of development.

It is fascinating to view the historical development of Air Force fighters, great stories of success and failure, the advance of technology, the urgent needs of wartime. It is one way to view the history of aviation, and the history of aerial warfare.

USAF FIGHTER AIRCRAFT 1924 TO THE PRESENT

Spad VII	French	1917	Big success. 6500 built.
Spad XIII	French	1917	Two guns, power, 8472 built.
Nieuport 28	French	1917	Important US machine.
Sopwith Camel	British	1917	Most famous Allied aircraft.
PS-1	Wright	1922	Single-wing. Prototype only.
PW-7	Fokker	1922	Only a few evaluated.
PW-8	Curtiss	1924	Produced in small numbers.
PW-9	Boeing	1925	Only a few made, but the best of the 1920s.

At this point, a new numerical system was started

P-1 Hawk	Curtiss	1926	Successful design and operation.
P-2 Hawk	Curtiss	1926	Variant not produced.
P-3 Hawk	Curtiss	1926	Successful test of radial engine.
XP-4	Boeing	1926	Modified PW-9 for supercharger.
P-5 Hawk	Curtiss	1928	Slightly improved Hawks. Only a few built.
P-6 Hawk	Curtiss	1928	With P-12, best between the wars.
XP-7	Boeing	1928	PW-9 with larger engine. Only one.
XP-8	Boeing	1928	Another engine test, but only one.
XP-9	Boeing	1930	First monoplane, but unsuccessful.
XP-10	Curtiss	1928	Good aircraft, but not produced.
XP-11 Hawk	Curtiss	1928	Never built.
P-12	Boeing	1929	Greatest biplane, built in large numbers.
XP-13	Thomas-Morse	1929	Only one. Engine problems.
P-14	Curtiss	1929	Never built.
XP-15	Boeing	1930	Testbed for P-12 improvements.

The Boeing P-26 Peashooter. The first all-metal monoplane fighter and a bold and popular aircraft of the 1930s, it could not cope in early fights against the Japanese in World War II. (US National Archives)

P-16	Berliner-Joyce	1929	First two-seat fighter. Not many built.
XP-17	Curtiss	1926	Testbed for various engines.
P-18	Curtiss	1930	Cancelled: lack of engine.
P-19	Curtiss	1930	Cancelled: lack of engine.
YP-20	Curtiss	1930	Service test. Not produced.
XP-21	Curtiss	1928	Yet another variation. Only two built.
XP-22	Curtiss	1929	Testbed for successful P-6.
XP-23	Curtiss	1932	Last biplane. Couldn't compete.
YP-24	Lockheed	1931	Sleek and promising, but company went broke.
P-25	Consolidated	1932	Promising but crashed.
P-26 'Peashooter'	Boeing	1931	Boeing's last. A great fighter.
P-27	Consolidated	1932	Two-seat testbed. Not built.
P-28	Consolidated	1932	Another two-seat testbed.
YP-29	Boeing	1934	Attempt to improve P-26.
P-30	Consolidated	1934	A few two-seat improvements.
XP-31 Shrike	Curtiss	1933	Couldn't compete with P-26.
P-32	Boeing	1933	YP-29 Variant. Never built.
P-33	Consolidated	1933	Cancelled. No breakthrough.
P-34	Wedell-Williams	1936	Racer design. Never built.
P-35	Seversky	1936	Good, but not good enough.
P-36 Mohawk	Curtiss	1937	Produced, but obsolete in war.
YP-37	Curtiss	1938	Failed attempt to improve P-36.
P-38 Lightning	Lockheed	1939	Great World War II fighter.
P-39 Airacobra	Bell	1938	No turbo: couldn't keep up.
P-40 Warhawk	Curtiss	1939	Okay, but inferior at high altitude.
XP-41	Seversky	1939	Immediately obsolete. Only one.
P-42	Curtiss	1939	Aero and engine testbed.
P-43 Lancer	Republic	1940	Produced, but forgettable.
P-44 Rocket	Republic	1940	Failed attempt to improve P-43.
P-45	Bell	1939	Variant of P-39.
XP-46	Curtiss	1941	Slightly improved P-40. Only two built.
Spitifre	Supermarine	1941	Many served with USAAF.
P-47 Thunderbolt	Republic	1941	Great World War II fighter.
XP-48	Douglas	1939	A designer's dream. Fast but impractical.
XP-49	Lockheed	1939	Replaced by better aircraft.

XP-50	Grumman	1939	Ugly and unsuccessful. Only one built.
P-51 Mustang	North American	1940	Greatest American fighter.
XP-52	Bell	1941	Pusher testbed. Never built.
XP-53	Curtiss	1940	An attempt to improve P-40. None built.
XP-54	Vultee	1941	Pusher with big guns. Not produced.
XP-55	Curtiss	1942	Pusher testbed. Not produced.
XP-56	Northrop	1943	Pusher testbed. Not produced.
XP-57	Tucker	1940	Experimental. Not produced.
XP-58	Lockheed	1943	Attempt at heavy, improved P-38.
XP-59	Bell	1942	First US jet. Not produced.
XP-60	Curtiss	1941	Another attempt to improve the P-40.
P-61 Black Widow	Northrop	1942	Good night fighter. Too late.
XP-62	Curtiss	1944	Dual-prop testbed. Overweight.
P-63 Kingcobra	Bell	1942	Not great. Many sent to USSR.
P-64	North American	1941	Only six built. Ordered by Siam.
P-65	Grumman	1942	Twin-engined. Cancelled.
P-66 Vanguard	Vultee	1940	Made for other nations. Weak.
XP-67	McDonnell	1944	Mac's first. Bypassed by others.
XP-68	Vultee	1941	Large testbed. Cancelled. None built.
XP-69	Republic	1941	Experimental. Never built.
XP-70	Douglas	1943	Pacific night fighter and trainer.
XP-71	Curtiss	1942	Long-range testbed. Cancelled.
XP-72	Republic	1944	Big P-47 for speed. Only two built.
P-73/P-74	–	–	Never assigned to USAAF.
XP-75 Eagle	Fisher	1943	Couldn't compete with P-51.
P-76	Bell	1942	P-39 Variant. Cancelled.
XP-77	Bell	1944	All-wood experimental. Cancelled.
P-78	North American	1944	P-51 upgrade. Redesignated.
XP-79	Northrop	1945	Flying wing, rocket-powered. Crashed.
F-80 Shooting Star	Lockheed	1945	First operational US jet.
XP-81	Convair	1945	Twin-jet pursuit plane. Cancelled.
F-82 Twin Mustang	North American	1945	Successful night fighter. Korea.
XP-83	Bell	1945	Advanced P-59. Not produced.
F-84 Thunderjet	Republic	1946	Successful, with many variants.

F-84 Thunderjet: this is the early, straight-wing version of the Republic jet. Even the swept-wing version, the F-84F Thunderstreak, could not match the F-86 in air combat. (Cradle of Aviation Museum)

XP-85	McDonnell	1948	Parasite on B-29/B-36 bomber.
F-86 Sabre	North American	1947	Great fighter. Korea.
XF-87	Curtiss	1948	Underpowered four-jet test fighter.
XF-88	McDonnell	1948	Forerunner to F-101.
F-89 Scorpion	Northrop	1948	Successful air defence fighter.
XF-90	Lockheed	1950	Supersonic fighter. Not produced.
XF-91	Republic	1949	Jet/rocket combo. Not produced.
XF-92	Convair	1948	Delta-winged research plane for F-102.
XF-93	North American	1950	F-86 variant. Not produced.
F-94 Starfire	Lockheed	1949	Successful interceptor. From F-80.
XF-95	North American	1949	Original F-86D radar interceptor.
XF-96	Republic	1950	Original F-84F swept-wing fighter.
F-97	Lockheed	1950	Original F-94C upgrade.
XF-98	Hughes	1950	Became AIM-4 Falcon radar missile.
F-99	Boeing	1952	Became Bomarc intercept missile.
F-100 Super Sabre	North American	1953	Great supersonic fighter.
F-101 Voodoo	McDonnell	1954	Successful interceptor.
F-102 Delta Dagger	Convair	1953	Successful interceptor.
XF-103	Republic	1955	Hypersonic interceptor. Cancelled.
F-104 Starfighter	Lockheed	1954	Great interceptor. Short legs.
F-105 Thunder-chief	Republic	1955	Great fighter-bomber. Vietnam.
F-106 Delta Dart	Convair	1956	Great interceptor.
XF-107	North American	1956	Variant of F-100. Cancelled.
XF-108	North American	1959	Delta Mach 3 fighter. Cancelled.
XF-109	–	–	Vertical/short take-off and landing. Never assigned.
F-110 Phantom II	McDonnell	1964	Original designation of USAF F-4.
F-111	General Dynamics	1964	Successful swing-wing bomber.

New designation system introduced in 1962, combining USN and USAF

F-1 Fury			USN F-86.
F-2			USN Banshee.
F-3			USN Demon.
F-4 Phantom II	McDonnell	1958	USAF. The greatest fighter of all time.
F-5	Northrop	1959	Light export fighter. From T-38.
F-6			USN F-4D Skyray.
F-7 Sea Dart	Convair		Experimental.
F-8 Crusader	Vought		USN. Successful in Vietnam.
F-9 Panther/ Cougar	Grumman		USN fighter.
F-10	Douglas		USN F-3. EF-10 in Vietnam.
F-11 Tiger	Grumman		USN. Blue Angels in 1960s.
F-12	Lockheed	1962	Secret interceptor. Led to SR-71.

F-13			Not assigned.
F-14 Tomcat	Grumman		USN. Great swing-wing carrier fighter.
F-15 Eagle	McDonnell Douglas	1972	USAF. Great air-to-air fighter.
F-16 Falcon	General Dynamics	1974	USAF. Great all-purpose fighter.
YF-17	Northrop		Lost competition with F-16.
F-18 Hornet	Northrop	1974	USN. Reworked F-17. Successful.
F-19			Never used except as disguise for F-117 Stealth.
F-112 to F-116.			Never used, but possibly for captured MiGs.
F-117 Stealth	Lockheed	1977	Secret for years. Big success.
F-20 Tigershark	Northrop	1982	F-5 follow-on. Never sold.
F-21 Kfir			Israeli fighter used for dissimilar combat training.
F-22	Lockheed	1990	Advanced Tactical Fighter winner.
F-23	Northrop	1990	ATF loser in fly-off.

FIRST FLIGHTS

It is instructive to view the development of modern jet fighters in different countries as they compete with one another to gain the upper hand in technology and weaponry. It is amazing that updated versions of many of those first aircraft of 35 years ago are still flying.

7 February 1954	XF-104	Lockheed	The great 'missile with a man in it'.
22 June 1954	A-4 Skyhawk	McDonnell Douglas	Great little fighter. Still going strong.
25 March 1955	F-8 Crusader	Vought	The Migmaster in Vietnam.
22 October 1955	F-105	Republic	Great fighter of Vietnam.
November 1955	MiG-21	USSR	Great fighter of Vietnam and many air forces.
17 November 1956	Mirage III	Dassault	Popular French fighter. Sold to 20 air forces.
30 April 1958	Buccaneer	British Aerospace	Multi-purpose fighter-bomber.
27 May 1958	F-4 Phantom	McDonnell Douglas	The last Phantom was produced in May 1981.

F-105 Thunderchief. The third of the great Republic fighters, the 'Thud' became immortal in reputation, if not in fact, in Vietnam. Originally designed to carry a nuclear weapon fast at low level. (Cradle of Aviation Museum)

East German MiG-21s. With reunification, the West German Luftwaffe suddenly inherited a lot of Soviet fighters. The MiG-21 was a formidable fighter in the hands of a good North Vietnamese pilot. (Tim Laming)

Date	Aircraft	Manufacturer	Description
30 July 1959	F-5	Northrop	Third World fighter version of T-38.
19 April 1960	A-6 Intruder	Grumman	Vietnam bomber with successful electronic upgrades.
21 December 1964	F-111	General Dynamics	Venerable swing-wing fighter, bomber and ECM aircraft.
27 September 1964	A-7 Corsair II	Vought	Sturdy strike fighter, developed from the Crusader.
23 December 1966	Mirage F1	Dassault-Breguet	Successful Mach 2 interceptor.
28 December 1967	Harrier	British Aerospace	Historic vertical take-off fighter.
About 1969	MiG-25 Foxbat	USSR	Powerful, record-setting, Mach 3 interceptor.
21 December 1970	F-14 Tomcat	Grumman	Primary USN carrier fighter.
10 May 1972	A-10	Fairchild Republic	The tank-buster and FAC aircraft.
27 July 1972	F-15 Eagle	McDonnell Douglas	Primary USAF air-to-air fighter.
20 January 1974	YF-16	General Dynamics	Multi-purpose, popular, 'Electric Jet'.
9 June 1974	YF-17 (F-18)	Northrop/ McDonnell Douglas	Multi-purpose USN fighter, originally to compete with F-16.
21 August 1974	Hawk	British Aerospace	Fundamental trainer, fighter and Red Arrow.
10 March 1978	Mirage 2000	Dassault-Breguet	Successful fly-by-wire interceptor.
27 April 1979	Tornado	Panavia	Primary RAF swept-wing strike fighter and interceptor.
June 1981	F-117 Stealth	Lockheed	High-tech fighter which avoids radar detection.
4 July 1986	Rafale	Dassault-Breguet	Advanced fighter as alternative to Eurofighter.
1990	F-22	Lockheed/ Boeing/ General Dynamics	Advanced Tactical Fighter for USAF next generation.

III

FIGHTER COCKPIT

THE COCKPIT of the modern fighter has become an electronic brain, connected to the pilot, the aircraft and various parts of the world. It ties them all together. The pilot is connected through his arms and legs, his fingers, his voice and ears, his eyes, his body sensations. He receives information, processes it in his own brain, and delivers responses. Various parts of the aircraft are controlled by the cockpit, and the condition of other parts of the aircraft are reflected there. Finally, the cockpit sees or hears the outside environment – weather, terrain, targets, friends, enemies, threats. The cockpit is just an extension of the fighter pilot's body, merely improving on the things God gave him. It enables him to move his body with great speed, to hear over great distances, to see in the dark, to thrust his fists, to defend himself – an extension of sword and shield.

The first cockpits were open to the air, and the only instruments were the sight of the ground, the noise of the wind in the wires, the feeling in the seat of the pants. Then in 1929 Jimmie Doolittle flew with an artificial horizon, without seeing the ground from take-off to landing, and instrument flight changed the air world. Nowadays the cockpit is an electronic game room. The pilot has so much information, so many things he can do in response, that there is often more than he can handle, and the little room becomes a jungle of impressions and tasks. After years in it, the fighter pilot loves it and feels totally at home, but he never loses his respect for its power and danger and the fighter he controls that is a terrible, awesome killing machine.

MODERN FLIGHT INSTRUMENTS

In the accompanying photos for this section you will see the cockpits of various aircraft. Let's make a quick trip around the Tucano cockpit. When the RAF arranged to build the Brazilian Tucano under licence, they redesigned the entire cockpit to provide a similarity and easy transition to the Hawk that the student would

69

fly next. (Note that even the advanced Phantom has a similar arrangement beneath the radar scope, but that the Tornado has centralized the radar and re-arranged the smaller instruments around it.)

1. At the top, where they intentionally interfere with forward vision, are the clock and magnetic compass, forcing the inexperienced student to be reminded of time (fuel consumption) and direction.

2. In the centre of the panel are the two main composite instruments of most jets prior to the new electronic displays. At the top is the ADI (Attitude Director Indicator), which, in varying degrees depending on the aircraft and systems it supports, is a more complex version of the old gyro attitude indicator. (Note that on the Hawk and Phantom there is a standby indicator just to the right.) On advanced aircraft, the ADI incorporates information from the navigation and weapons systems and other information for steering to targets, automatic bombing, etc.

3. Below the ADI is the HSI, or Horizontal Situation Indicator. It also uses various systems information to show the pilot his TACAN (Tactical Air Navigation) course and distance, heading to waypoints and targets, etc. Nowadays much of the information of the ADI and HSI is projected on to the HUD so that the pilot does not have to look down into the cockpit.

4. Left of the ADI is the Airspeed/Mach Indicator. The needle moves off the top in knots (170 at the six o'clock position) and then a smaller window begins to show the Mach number that is normally used during high-altitude cruise.

5. Below the Airspeed Indicator is an additional navigation indicator, with the needle pointing to the selected station.

6. To the left of these is a Multi-Function Display (MFD) which

Tucano cockpit (see the itemized discussion in the accompanying text). The cockpit of the trainer is designed to prepare the student for flying more advanced aircraft with similar cockpits. (Shorts)

can be selected to show various items like radio frequencies and cockpit procedures. This is much easier than reading the old paper checklist.

7. Below these is the gear handle and the navigation/communication selector.

8. To the right of the ADI is the altimeter. It covers 1000ft around the circle, and additional altitudes are shown in the numerical window. This is less confusing than the old-style indicator that showed higher altitudes with a smaller, less sensitive needle.

9. Below that is the Vertical Velocity Indicator, which shows the rate of climb or descent in feet per minute.

10. Below that is the ancient turn and slip indicator, which shows rate of turn on the needle and co-ordinated flight via the ball in the glass tube.

11. To the right of the altimeter is the G-meter. It moves from the nine o'clock position, up for positive g and down for negative, and other needles are carried along to remain at the maximum.

12. The remainder on the right are engine and fuel instruments.

13. Below those are warning lights that illuminate to show various problems or malfunctions.

The problem with older, crowded cockpits like that of the Phantom was that too many indicators and switches had to be placed in front of the stick, under the pilot's elbows or around the windscreen, often causing disorientation, poor flight control or accidents when the pilot moved his eyes from the proper place. The modern fighter cockpit is designed to place everything the pilot must look at or touch during most operations directly in front of him. In addition, many instruments or functions have been combined into improved electronic displays. The objective is to increase the amount of information received by the pilot, but in a more orderly, understandable way that can be analyzed and acted upon properly.

THE HEAD-UP-DISPLAY

The HUD, or HUDWAC (Head-Up Display Weapon Aiming Computer), presents a variety of flight parameters and continuously calculated weapon aiming solutions on a glass screen in front of the pilot. The pilot can look through the screen at the outside world, especially the target, while being provided with information required for flight and weapon delivery. The HUD shown on these diagrams is similar to the system provided by GEC Avionics for the F-16. The pilot selects the appropriate mode for landing, navigating, guns, bombs, air-to-air missile, lead-computing, snapshot

AV-8B Harrier cockpit. Modern cockpits are designed to enable the pilot to spend most of his time looking outside, with the most important switches directly in front of him, rather than under his arms where he would have to make sharp head movements to see. (McDonnell Douglas)

or dogfight. It requires a well-trained and nimble pilot to be able to switch around and handle all these different functions with the switches on the throttle and stick, known in the trade as 'varsity piccolo playing'. Technology is now in transition, with debate on the relative merits of helmet-mounted sights, night-vision goggles, HUDs and combinations with other systems like FLIR. There is a limit to the amount of information the eye can see, the brain can process and the body can act upon, especially during the physical demands of high-speed, high-g manoeuvring flight in a fight for life.

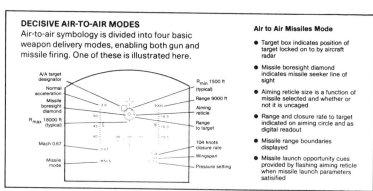

DECISIVE AIR-TO-AIR MODES
Air-to-air symbology is divided into four basic weapon delivery modes, enabling both gun and missile firing. One of these is illustrated here.

Air to Air Missiles Mode

- Target box indicates position of target locked on to by aircraft radar
- Missile boresight diamond indicates missile seeker line of sight
- Aiming reticle size is a function of missile selected and whether or not it is uncaged
- Range and closure rate to target indicated on aiming circle and as digital readout
- Missile range boundaries displayed
- Missile launch opportunity cues provided by flashing aiming reticle when missile launch parameters satisfied

COMMUNICATIONS AND IFF

The pilot's ears are now a much more important factor in the mission than even a few years ago. In effect, they can reduce the number of things the pilot has to look at. Of course, he has an intercom to talk to his navigator, and the standard UHF radio for talking to other flight members, ground control agencies, refuelling aircraft, etc. Some fighters, such as the A-10, also have additional radios for talking to FACs and Army personnel. The 'Have Quick' radio system uses frequency hopping by both transmitter and receiver to prevent listening or jamming. Other systems provide a secure voice capability. Various systems now transmit tones or warning signals to the pilot for operation of such things as terrain-following, navigation systems, missile systems and threat-warning systems.

Another innovation being developed is a computer which both transmits and recognizes human speech. A female voice can warn the pilot of a fire or other emergency. Similarly, the computer can understand the pilot say something like 'landing gear down' and perform the action without any physical movement by the pilot. More and more, the pilot becomes part of the aircraft.

IFF (Identification Friend or Foe), created during the Second World War, allows a radar set to interrogate a return and receive a verification code, if available. Thus it is possible for an AWACs or a fighter to identify all friendly aircraft on his scope by specific number.

The modern air battlefield is dominated by a sophisticated command, control, communications and intelligence capability. This is not as spectacular as 'smart' bombs, but it was the other major factor in the Gulf air war victory.

NAVIGATION SYSTEMS

Today's navigation system is designed not only to take the aircraft from one place on the Earth to another, but to be merged with the weapons delivery system so that the aircraft is precisely placed to put a bomb through a window.

Originally, the nav system was merely a needle showing the direction to a radio station or the route of an airway. Then radar enabled the pilot or navigator to see a rough picture of the ground which could be compared to a map. After that, more precise positioning was established for instrument landing systems, allowing the aircraft to find the end of the runway in bad weather. Later, terrain mapping displays and infra-red pictures of the ground enabled navigation to be undertaken without transmitting radar impulses that would betray a position over enemy territory.

In the cockpit, the pilot uses the Horizontal Situation Indicator (HSI) to give him a picture of his relationship to various nav aids or internal parameters for weapons delivery. Recently, the United States has been placing in orbit a series of navigation satellites for a Global Positioning System. By measuring the time for a signal to return from a triangle of satellites, it is possible instantly to locate the aircraft flying above the Earth to within a few feet.

Tornado GR.1 front cockpit. Radar scope centre, with flight instruments to left and engine instruments to right; weapons management controls below HUD. (British Aerospace)

Tornado GR.1 rear cockpit. Radar scope centre, flanked by TV monitors for various displays. Stick controls radar, not the aircraft. (British Aerospace)

The most incredible of all nav gear is the Inertial Navigation System. First developed for ships like nuclear submarines in their early days, the INS has now reached an amazing accuracy with the ringed laser gyro. In essence, the pilot dials in the co-ordinates of the base from which he takes off. The gyros of the system, much like those of the human inner ear, sense every motion of the aircraft in all three dimensions and adjust the reading of the geographical co-ordinates accordingly. In a similar way, the pilot may dial in an objective, and the HSI will point to it and show the distance. It will also give ground speed, drift angle, current winds and steering to a multitude of points worked out in pre-flight mission planning. It is accurate to within a few feet, despite all kinds of manoeuvring and accelerations along the way. Some new missiles, like the famous Tomahawk of the Gulf War or the AMRAAM radar missile, are guided by their own INS, which is updated by the aircraft INS. This takes them to their target area where a more accurate radar or imaging system provides the final precision. Because of the new accuracy in these navigation systems, it is now possible to position the aircraft in total darkness or bad weather so that the final TV, infra-red or radar weapons system can then deliver a bomb or missile literally through a window.

Much of this information is provided on the HUD. In normal, peacetime navigation, the pilot uses TACAN stations which provide distance and direction, and backs this up with INS, GCI/AWACS, visual map-reading and radar navigation. GCA (Ground-Controlled Approach) or ILS (Instrument Landing System) are used in bad weather for final landing.

ADVANCED FIGHTER SYSTEMS: JTIDS*

The Joint Tactical Information Display System is a jam-resistant, secure communications and navigation system that provides real-time data and voice information exchange between airborne, ground and sea tactical forces. It provides accurate position location, target acquisition and TACAN navigation capabilities. With it, the fighter pilot can see, on one of his coloured cockpit displays, a wide range of mission-oriented information taken from the JTIDS network that is fed by fighters, ground agencies, E-3 AWACS aircraft, J-STARS radar target identification aircraft and other sources.

---

* This information has been provided by the Collins Avionics Division of Rockwell International and Plessey Electronic Systems, who are designing and providing JTIDS terminals and data processors to US and NATO forces.

A JTIDS-equipped NATO fighter such as the upgraded F-16 will use on-board navigation, weapons and radar systems to feed status information automatically to the JTIDS network. This includes target data, own-aircraft position, altitude, ground speed, direction, fuel and weapon reserves and radar returns. In the cockpit, the pilot can select and display:

- Navigation situation, including waypoints and targets;
- Location of surface-to-air missile sites;
- Friendly air bases and alternative recovery bases;
- Location of friendly, hostile and unknown aircraft; and
- Location of friendly and hostile ground forces.

The pilot can select various display ranges from 5 to 320 nautical miles, to include information beyond the aircraft's sensor and radar vision. He can see a friendly aircraft's fuel and weapons, speed and track to determine if it could support him on a particular mission or target. He can also assign himself or be assigned a particular target, which all other JTIDS aircraft will see, in order to minimize battlefield confusion.

In another variation, the system can be tied in with the US Army Position Location and Reporting System (PLRS). This provides, to both air and ground units:

- Position and track of friendly ground forces;
- Position and track of hostile ground forces;
- Position and track of friendly and hostile aircraft for air defence operations;
- Fire and logistic support requests;
- Electronic warfare direction-finding; and
- Intelligence.

Thus fighter aircraft, ground forces and anti-aircraft batteries can all operate together in the same small battle area and reduce the problems of misidentification and control.

Thousands of users can participate on the same network. A fighter can tie-in to several different networks, perhaps using an air defence network for part of the mission and a ground support network at other times. This provides forces with a big improvement in joint force employment tactics, command and control and real-time battlefield pictures.

Of course, the success of this system depends on the reliability of the information fed into it and the ability of the command and control system and the fighter pilot to use the information easily and correctly. The primary airborne source will be the AWACS, with its huge radar and IFF systems sorting out everything over thousands of square miles. Similarly, the new E-8 (modified Boeing 707) J-STARS, which will be delivered to the US Air Force from 1995, has several different radar and sensor systems, such as

The array of dials and switches that faces the modern fighter pilot in his office. This is the driving seat of the Tornado ADV. (British Aerospace)

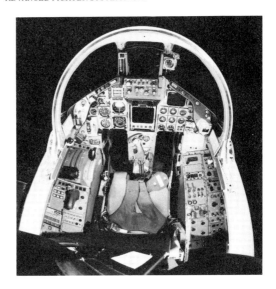

moving target indicators, that will identify targets in the ground environment. Both of these advanced systems were used successfully in the Gulf War. The J-STARS, although still under development, was brought in at the last moment; it was a great success in feeding target information, such as 'Scud' missile launchers moving at night, to A-10 and F-16 fighters.

ADVANCED FIGHTER SYSTEMS: GPS*

The Navstar Global Positioning System, now partially in use, provides the most accurate means yet of telling a pilot, a ship or aircraft navigator or a tank driver his exact location on the Earth. The system depends on a transmitter/computer that measures the time it takes for signals to return from three different Earth satellites. Because the system knows the relative positions of the satellites, accurately measuring the time permits a triangulation for position. Relying on an integrated circuit chip, the receiver has been condensed to a package as small as 100 cubic centimetres and weighing eight ounces. In addition to various kinds of manned sea, land and air vehicles, GPS is also used in Tomahawk cruise missiles and US Navy SLAM anti-ship missiles carried on fighters such as F/A-18s.

---

* This information has been provided by the Collins Avionics Division of Rockwell International, which provides GPS equipment to forces of several nations.

GLEAMING HORSES: THE COCKPIT*

Just before lunch, two hours before he was to fly against the enemy, 'Nails' Nicholson went out into the alert hangar and climbed up into the cockpit of the F-15. He turned on the battery switch and closed the canopy. He left the battery switch on because otherwise it was disconcerting to have the powerless Attitude Display tilted at some crazy pitch and bank angle, like a picture hanging crookedly on the wall, requiring adjustment before one could relax. Sometimes he felt his mind was like that, calling for the application of constant power to keep it on an even keel, lest it tumble, undisciplined, out of control.

The grinding wind-up of the gyros was also comforting: no pilot likes to sit in a lifeless airplane. After you live in the same cockpit for half your life, dominating the living machine, moving all the switches and controls, reacting to all the instruments and displays, feeling all the tiny vibrations and blinding pressures, seeing all the outside movements and shapes flashing by as you do your job – after all that, you cannot sit easily in the machine when it is dead, because that takes part of your own life away. When the airplane is alive, full of ominous energy and ambition and conceit that must always be controlled, you become part of it, and its joyful, deadly power mingles with your own.

Sometime, because you are trained to handle the most thrilling emergencies and utmost performance, the flying becomes mundane, although never boring, and even bold acts become routine. But you are never far from the edge and you are always part of the airplane, wired to all its nerve endings, as if a surgeon had spent hours connecting it to your brain, even when you sit in a silent hangar, even when you sleep, even when you are miles away in someone else's arms.

Nails moved his bare fingers over the protruding switches and controls, burned into his subconscious, that he normally touched with his Nomex, fire-proof gloves. He did not like the unfamiliar, cold sensations. He wasn't wearing his G-suit or survival vest. He wasn't fastened tightly to the seat and parachute and there was no security of other voices in his headset, no helmet blocking out a rush of air and the roar of the engines that seeped into the cockpit. He felt disturbingly naked.

He leaned back and closed his eyes and thought about the Russian pilot, sitting somewhere in Germany, eating lunch, knowing as he did that a conflict was coming. He tried to project himself into the air, tried to live the churning, wrenching manoeuvring and the control of his mind over the changing images and challenges. It would not come: there were too many possibilities. His training would give him the instant reactions and the brilliant imagination that were required by each surprising moment. No ground briefing today would give him advance notice of every part of the flight; the combat would not be planned in advance and simulated. For the first time in his three thousand hours of fighter time he would truly have to improvise, to tie together his intelligence and physical skill as never before.

He was anxious to go, wishing they would scramble him now. He thought of Liz. He wanted to go back home and take her to bed and hold her. But most of all he wanted to go. For fifteen years he had trained for this day. 'Now we'll see. Now we'll see, you son-of-a-bitch.' He raised the canopy and the cool air of Germany washed away the metallic, sweaty odours that filled the cockpit.

---

* Prologue to an unpublished novel by the author.

The accuracy is incredible: the system will consistently provide three-dimensional position within 16m, as compared to 180m for Loran and 400m for TACAN. Most fighters rely in combat on their INS for position, but these are accurate only to 1500m after one hour of flight and continue to degrade unless updated over known positions. The new ringed-laser gyro INS is a big improvement, but it is far less accurate than the GPS and it still degrades. Not all Navstar satellites are in position, nor do all fighters to receive the system yet have it installed, but GPS will become an important part of fighter navigation and weapons delivery accuracy in the years ahead. By knowing exactly where your aircraft is, you can more accurately tell a missile where to go relative to your position to destroy a target.

ADVANCED FIGHTER SYSTEMS: THE FUTURE COCKPIT

A major revolution in cockpit design and technology is in progress. The interim advanced fighters that will become operational a few years from now, such as the Eurofighter and the French Rafale, and to a much greater degree the F-22 Advanced Tactical Fighter a few years later, will have cockpits much different from those of relatively modern fighters like the Tornado and F-16. The new features include:

1. A shift from a multitude of cathode ray tube (CRT) displays, such as are now found on the latest fighters like the F-15E and the latest versions of the F-16, to a single, colourful liquid crystal display (LCD), a high-tech version of the self-illuminating screens found on the latest laptop computers. Because they are computer-generated, and do not lose resolution with an increase in size like a

High-resolution cockpit map displays can be colour-coded by the pilot to show high terrain, water etc. The moving map helps the pilot navigate and find targets in weather or at low altitude. When combined with other displays such as FLIR, terrain-following radar and the new JTIDS tactical displays, the pilot has a complete picture of his environment. (GEC Avionics)

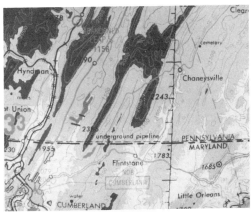

TV screen, and because they are flat and thin, the LCD can be expanded to fill the entire front panel of the cockpit, with various segments displayed or even moved around according to the phase of the mission.

2. Feeding this multi-purpose display with a variety of internal and external sources, including moving maps, forward-looking infra-red and radar, JTIDS battlefield networks, J-STARS radar target directions, pre-planned intelligence and flight data, instant reconnaissance information, navigation and other items. The goal is to provide the pilot with improved situational awareness through a complete picture of his environment, with as much as possible in pictorial rather than numerical form. This will assist understanding and help promote quick reaction, and simplify the basic problem of too much information in too little time. One picture is worth a thousand numbers.

3. Reduced use or elimination of the HUD, and reliance on the wider scope of helmet-mounted displays. The HMD has two big advantages over the present HUD and target lock-on systems: by viewing HUD information on the helmet visor, the pilot may receive this information while looking in any direction, instead of just through the HUD to the front; and the helmet system will enable the

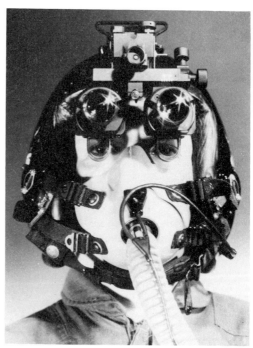

The revolutionary GEC Avionics 'Cats Eyes' night vision goggles represent an enormous step in improving night and foul-weather operating efficiency. They are the standard NVGs for all US Navy and Marine Corps tactical fixed-wing aircraft. (GEC Avionics)

pilot to identify targets in all parts of the sky and pass this data to the missile, which will then turn in the proper direction after launch to search for the target with its own seeker head.

4. Improved flow of information and commands to and from the pilot, using a wider variety of senses and controls. Under study are such systems as voice command, voice recognition, three-dimensional differentiation of sound inputs, touch command, 'smart' gloves, holographic imaging, night-vision and FLIR helmets, computer-copilots for some functions, eye position measurement and improved stick and throttle HOTAS controls. The goal is to provide a smoother, more sophisticated interface between the aircraft and the pilot's body and brain.

5. Improved surveillance of and response to the outside world. This calls for improved sensitivity, range and differentiation ability, plus cockpit displays and command input, in aircraft systems such as radar, infra-red, laser, voice and data communications, IFF, RHAW/ECM, TV, intelligence and navigation.

Not all of these advances will find their way to the F-22, for there is much to learn about pilot attitudes and abilities and the success of integrating all of these into a functional system that can be managed by one person. Nevertheless, the fictional account of the pilot whose brain and thought commands were wired directly to the aircraft controls and systems (published in 1977 in the best-selling novel *Firefox*, by Craig Thomas), is moving towards reality. The present rudimentary system of connecting the pilot to the aeroplane will soon be obsolete.

WEAPONS SYSTEMS

Thanks to the accuracy of the navigation systems, it is now possible to carry a weapon to the target in total darkness and the worst weather. It then becomes the problem of the weapons delivery system and the pilot to find the exact target and release the weapon so that its own system will guide it to the final pinpoint.

During most of the Vietnam War, bombs were dropped to free-fall on to the target as determined by the speed, altitude and dive angle created by the pilot as best he could in clear air, often while being shot at from the ground or air. As a result, many targets were never destroyed. With the introduction of the 'smart' bomb, a normal bomb with a laser sensor on the nose, it was possible to illuminate the target and guide the bomb directly on to the target. Within a few days, some bridges in North Vietnam were destroyed after years of trying. This same system was used effectively in the Gulf War.

Nowadays the pilot has in the cockpit an electronic display which gives him a TV, infra-red or radar picture of the target area. He finds his specific target and places cross-hairs, or cursors, on it. This information is then transmitted to the missile which has its own picture of the target. After release, the missile continues to guide itself on the shade or shape, previously identified by the pilot, until impact. At the same time, the pilot may leave the area in order to avoid groundfire. One can understand why the pilot or navigator is so busy and why the modern cockpit is dominated by glass screens.

ELECTRONIC COUNTERMEASURES

ECM became essential once radar-guided missiles became a threat to aircraft. Most fighters now carry an ECM pod or have a built-in capability. In the cockpit, the pilot (and the navigator if there is one) has a small scope and some indicator lights that warn of various threats. This is the Radar Homing and Warning indicator, known commonly as RHAW ('Raw') gear and sometimes known as the RWR (Radar Warning Receiver). If a specific radar frequency strikes the antenna, a line on the scope shows the direction and intensity of the signal. Different colours indicate different kinds of radar, and the indicator lights provide additional information. Since the system and the operator know about the frequencies of various threats, it is possible to judge what is looking at you, and what has been launched at you. Of course, the system detects only radar, not infra-red. There is, however, an infra-red detector built into the rear of some fighters that warns of an approaching missile. The pilot may then try to find it visually and perform a last-ditch, evasive manoeuvre or eject flares or chaff canisters to throw off the missile.

Under a specific threat, the operator may then turn on his

ECM pod on A-10. Electronic counter-measures pods jam enemy radars and missiles and are the primary means of defence in enemy territory. Most aircraft also have built-in or pod-carried flare and chaff dispensers to deter missile attack. If all else fails, look for the missile and pull hard when it seems too late! (Author)

'music', the ECM transmitter. He can select different kinds of jamming according to the frequency bands of the threats, and sometimes the jamming is done automatically. A large ECM capability is carried by specialized aircraft such as the EF-111 Raven. The enemy's problem is complicated by several aircraft jamming him and by the danger of the Wild Weasel missiles which can home in on his transmission. ECM, combined with flares, chaff and Wild Weasel, make it possible to operate successfully in a high-threat missile environment, as was successfully done over Iraq.

EJECTION SEATS

It may seem strange, but I am always more nervous about flying around in a little, single-engine light aircraft than I ever was in a Phantom. The reason is the ejection seat. If the engine quits in the Cessna, you have to find a place to put down very quickly and it may be hard to find. So, when you fly, you have constantly to be on the look-out for emergency landing areas as a prudent safety measure, even if the odds are slim that you will ever need one. If you get into trouble in a jet, you can eject safely in most situations, and this gives you confidence when flying in environments where you would not want to be in a small plane.

The ejection seat has saved many lives, although there have been many cases where it simply could not overcome a particular problem, like a high sink rate or high speed. The development of the seat over the years since the Second World War has been able to keep up with the increased performance of jet fighters, and better seats have saved lives that would have been lost in earlier years. Martin-Baker, the world's foremost manufacturer of ejection seats, tells me that nearly 1,000 US aircrew were saved by their seats during the Vietnam War.

There have been some unusual seats over the years. In the B-47, for example, the navigator below the pilot had a downward-firing ejection seat, and it took some time to iron out the problems of high-speed, high-altitude ejection. The F-104 also started life with a downward-firing seat, requiring the pilot to roll the aircraft at low altitude, but this was changed to an upward-firing seat later. In the A-1E Skyraider, a rocket pulled the seat up out of the aircraft. Some seats were designed to fire up through the canopy rather than wait for it too to be ejected. The F-111 has an entire cockpit capsule that is separated from the aircraft with both pilots enclosed.

The biggest problem in the early days was that seats did not have a 'zero–zero' capability, that is, you could not eject at a dead stop on the runway, but needed either airspeed or altitude to get the chute

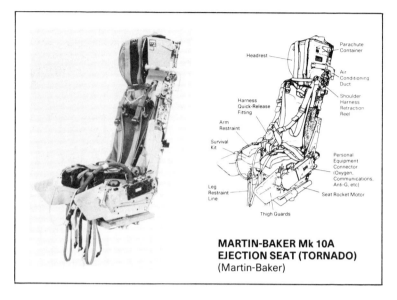

**MARTIN-BAKER Mk 10A
EJECTION SEAT (TORNADO)**
(Martin-Baker)

open before hitting the ground. Another problem, still with us, is that it is necessary to make the seat safe before and after flight so that inadvertent ejections do not take place on the ground: more than one pilot or ground crew member has found himself splattered on the ramp or the ceiling of the hangar when this has happened. The pilot therefore has some pins to remove and insert to prevent the handle from initiating the sequence. In some early seats, the designs had to measure the distance from kneecap to spine, since some long-legged pilots were losing their knees on the canopy rail during ejection. Nowadays, the parachute is built into the seat and the pilot wears only a harness that he connects after sitting in the cockpit.

Consider some other problems faced by the seat designers:

1. Get clear of the aircraft. The seat has to have enough power to push itself and the pilot clear of the aircraft, especially a high vertical tail, in a variety of attitudes and speeds. At first seats were simply blasted up by a cartridge shell, but this hit the pilot in the rear end with such a high g force that finally a rocket seat that provided a smoother and sustained force was developed.

2. Avoid wind blast, flailing arms and other damage to the body. The Phantom had a face curtain that came down over the helmet as the handles over the helmet were pulled, and this provided some protection. It had an alternate handle between the legs since g forces might make it difficult to reach the upper handles. The pilot is taught to sit up straight, pull the legs back off the rudders and

84

hold on tight to the handle until the seat separates. Many pilots who ejected received damage to the spine caused by ejecting in the wrong body position. There are also leg restraints that pull the legs back into the proper position. Seats now have drogue parachutes that stabilize them and prevent them from tumbling during high-speed ejection. Loose helmets and masks can cause head and face damage, so pilots are urged to keep them tight.

3. Get clear of the seat. Pilots with early ejection seats sometimes held on to the seat in panic and this prevented the parachute from functioning. Now there is a 'butt-snapper' which forces the pilot away from the seat as part of the sequence before chute deployment. This also helps to avoid the seat getting tangled in the chute.

4. Be able to get clear during ground emergencies. If you have to get out quickly when fully connected to the seat, there is now a handle available that severs all connections instantly.

5. Avoid parachute deployment at high altitude. You can freeze or suffer from lack of oxygen at 50,000ft, so there is a barometer built into the seat that causes it to open automatically at 10,000ft. However, the pilot can override this when ejecting over mountainous terrain. The seat also contains an emergency oxygen bottle that forces air into the lungs during the descent with only the stabilizing drogue chute in operation.

6. The seat won't fire. This problem can be fatal, but at least there is a way for the pilot to pull a handle and separate himself, and the parachute, from the seat and try a manual bail-out. I was taught to roll in heavy nose-down trim, blow the canopy and then release the stick, in the hope that I would then pop out of the cockpit.

7. Dual ejection. If the pilot in the front seat ejects, his rocket blast can roast the fellow in the back seat. So, in a normal sequence, the back-seater is fired first, no matter which crew member initiates the ejection. This mode can be de-selected by the back-seater so that he can eject without taking the pilot with him.

8. Survival equipment. Since the crew member may land in the water, he has a handle which allows him to deploy the life raft and survival kit that is stored in the seat. Once hitting the water, he releases the canopy and hopes it will blow clear so that he can crawl into his raft.

Seats are now very complicated mechanisms, designed to overcome these and many other problems encountered in the wide variety of situations that may occur. Martin-Baker designed the first British seats after a Meteor test pilot was killed during the war, and they have led the way in designing improvements over the years. Their equipment has been used in many US fighters, such as the Phantom, over the years, but McDonnell Douglas now makes its own seats.

PERSONAL EQUIPMENT

A fighter pilot no longer flies wearing a Class A uniform with tie, as some chaps did in the Battle of Britain. Under his flight suit, he may wear heavy underwear and/or a rubberized survival suit, like a diver's wetsuit sealed around the feet, wrists and neck, to protect him against exposure in cold water. At least this prolongs his survival time so that he can crawl into his raft and until a helicopter can arrive for pick-up. The suits are uncomfortable to fly in, but they save lives. Modern helmets made of new materials are much lighter than the older hard-hats.

Most fighters now have the parachute built into the ejection seat, and the pilot wears only a harness which is clipped to the seat once he is settled in the cockpit: plug in the radio cord and the G-suit air supply, and off you go.

The survival suit. On this rubberized suit, the boots are sealed and the wrist and neck openings fit tightly, preventing cold water from creating hypothermia. Otherwise, the pilot would die in a winter North Sea in a few minutes. (Author)

Another innovation is the Combat Edge system which increases the pilot's g capability. In addition to the usual G-suit which squeezes the stomach and thighs to prevent blood from draining from the eyes and brain, it consists of additional pressure applied by a vest to the upper body and a forced-breathing system which pushes air under pressure into the lungs when high g makes it difficult to inhale. This, combined with the F-16 seat reclined at 30 degrees, again slowing the drain of blood out of the head, gives the pilot several more gs before black-out. The F-16 and MiG-29 are stressed for 9g and the MiG can take several more safely, but the pilot is more limited. G-LOC, or g-induced loss of consciousness, has caused numerous accidents. Pilots are encouraged to stay fit, and many squadrons have exercise rooms for regular workouts.

A COMBAT MISSION IN THE COCKPIT

The pilot and navigator of an advanced fighter complete their pre-flight mission planning in the sealed and reinforced squadron building. All the information goes into a computer which produces a cassette, later to be inserted into the computer of the fighter. Moving-map pictures, waypoints, fuel computations, target data, threat locations, weapons load and other information can be called up on the cockpit displays during the mission. Later, the tape can be inserted into a TV machine to enable every moment of the flight to be analyzed, including voice records and a picture of the HUD during all manoeuvres.

The weather on this moonless night is zero-zero, both at home base and in the target area, but this is no problem. The fighters can take off down the runway using the infra-red system to keep them straight. Once airborne, the computer provides the course and the various turning points along the route; the autopilot and terrain-following radar carry the fighter towards the target at 200ft and 600kt while the crew monitor the action and look for problems or threats that have not been programmed in. The aircraft INS takes the fighter to each point, and the navigator cross-checks the system by watching offset points on the radar. If the INS drifts off, he can reset it to the actual position of the aircraft with the radar cursors. At the same time, the pilot observes his separate moving map and forward looking infra-red (FLIR) displays of the route on his cockpit TV screen. Tonight, he has selected the FLIR to be projected on the HUD, superimposed on the normal flight data, so that he can look ahead if visibility permits. Both crew members monitor their radar warning indicators for threats. Previously identified enemy missile sites appear on the moving map display.

Ready to go: all set in an F-15.

As they approach the target, an enemy aircraft locks on to the fighter and fires a missile. The pilot ejects chaff canisters, clicks off the autopilot and pulls the fighter around to attack, pushing a single button to switch the radar from the ground-mapping to the air-to-air mode. The radar automatically locks on to the enemy target once it comes into it view. The aircraft's INS tells the AMRAAM'S INS where the target is, and the missile is fired and heads for the point in space it has been given. As it approaches the enemy fighter, the radar of the missile sees it, takes over and accurately guides the missile in for the kill.

Having been delayed and thrown off course, our navigator switches to the target on the computer and flies a direct route in order to make the time on target. The RHAW gear signals a SAM site on the new route, one not considered in the pre-flight route planning. The navigator accepts the automatic ECM response his system provides. Then a SAM is fired, indicated by a red launch light on the RHAW. He selects a HARM missile from the fuselage station and tells it to lock on to the enemy SAM site. Although the site's signal drops off the scope, the pilot fires the missile, which homes in on the memorized co-ordinates of the target. As the HARM dives in at Mach 5, the proximity fuse detonates above the ground, spraying deadly missile fragments over a large area, including the enemy radar antenna. The enemy missile, accelerating toward our friendly fighter, is suddenly thrown off course when the navigator selects on ECM jamming mode that corresponds to the missile.

Coming up on the target, the navigator switches from radar to infra-red and picks out the specific corner of the building that the crew want to destroy with their missile. He places the cursors on a window and clicks a switch, telling the missile to watch that point and home in on it after launch. The missile is fired and the fighter turns towards home. The target is destroyed.

IV

FIGHTER MANOEUVRES

THE ESSENCE of good flying is to be able to put your aircraft where you want it, whether that is over the end of the runway in night weather, behind a MiG or in the groove for a dive-bomb pass. The problem is that you always have several things to do at once: you always have to be looking at the next thing and making decisions while your hands are attending to the current task. You always have a list of changing priorities – new, more important things always coming in and forcing the old things down the list. You live in three dimensions. You must talk and think while you act, you must watch and be decisive and you must manoeuvre your machine in a misty, fluctuating environment over which you have no control.

The fighter pilot has always had two basic functions: to attack the ground and to attack the enemy in the air. They are totally different, but they require similar skills. The goal is to be able to point the nose of the aeroplane at a target. It is very difficult, because your plane can have varying airspeeds, dive angles, banks and g-forces; it can be in varying winds and altitudes; and the target may be moving with its own varying airspeed, pitch attitude, bank and g-force. A change in any one of these factors will cause the bullet or the bomb to go somewhere else, and the pilot must watch and compensate.

Nowadays the pilot has a gunsight which adjusts for the ballistics of the weapon. He usually has a radar, lead-computing gunsight which adjusts for his own aircraft's conditions and those of the enemy aircraft. He has a weapons release system which compensates for changing conditions. The computers, the radar and the systems are making his job easier.

AIR-TO-AIR MANOEUVRES

This is not the place to try to teach the complexities of air combat, but it might at least be possible to convey the flavour, an idea of the problem, by describing a few basic manoeuvres. The difficulty most newcomers face is the geometric addition of the third dimension; instead of travelling on the surface of the Earth, you may now go up and down as well as forward and sideways. Consider the egg in Figure 1: this is the space in which two fighters can manoeuvre with maximum performance, and it is imprinted on or sensed in the mind of the air-to-air pilot. It is an egg, not a round ball, because at the top the aircraft turns a tighter circle with the one extra g caused by gravity. At the bottom, the circle is wider because the plane is losing a g by offsetting gravity. Moreover, airspeed is less at the top, increasing the turn rate. So a fighter may go to the vertical in order to improve turn performance.

A fighter in a level turn must pull the nose through 180 degrees of space in order to reverse direction from north to south. A fighter in a vertical climb has only to roll with ailerons, which can be done in an instant, to complete the same change of direction. Of course, at the same time, the level fighter can reverse direction with a quick roll while the vertical fighter will eventually have to pull the nose back down through 180 degrees of space to a vertical dive, which takes time. And, of course, these are just the very beginning of the endless alternatives. The point of all this is that the fighter pilot must see and take advantage of the best choices according to the dictates and opportunities of the fight. It's all obviously quite complicated, and you have to go up and do it before you even begin to understand.

Air-to-air students first practise individual BFM (Basic Flight Manoeuvres) before putting them together in a more complete sequence and in reaction to the opponent. In Figure 2 we see the classic High Yo-Yo. The White enemy is in a level turn. Our Black hero, instead of chasing White endlessly around the circle, pulls up instead into a vertical climb and uses a roll, and the egg advantage, to pull towards the other side of the circle. Thus he is able to close in on the enemy for a gun attack. As a counter to this (Figure 3),

The Lockheed F-22 Lightning II will be the best fighter in the world for many years to come. Note the engine exhausts, which may be vectored vertically (but not horizontally) to increase turn performance. (Lockheed)

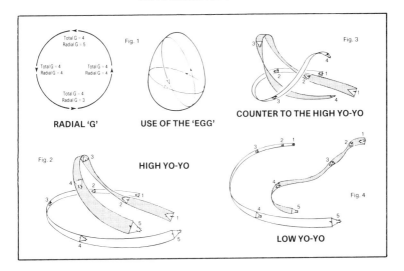

RADIAL 'G'   USE OF THE 'EGG'   COUNTER TO THE HIGH YO-YO

HIGH YO-YO

LOW YO-YO

White pulls up into the vertical also, killing off his forward velocity, and waits for the high-speed dive of Black to cause him to overshoot in front, where White can kill.

Another classic BFM is the Low Yo-Yo (Figure 4). Instead of chasing White around the circle and perhaps never catching him, Black pulls down inside the circle to cut him off. Instead of going around the edge of the bowl, he travels to the other side with greater speed in a dive and shorter distance down across the bottom of the bowl, gaining the closure he needs for an attack. Of course, White may then pull up and wait for Black to move out in front. Black must then decide what to do in return.

It soon becomes a three-dimensional chess game, different every time, with each fighter watching what the other does and trying to devise a manoeuvre that will improve his position. It becomes even more complicated if the aircraft are multiple or dissimilar, with different power, turn performance, weight, weapons or pilot ability. This is why only a few fighter pilots become aces: they seem able to grasp these concepts, string them together into complex permutations and convert them into victory.

AIR-TO-GROUND MANOEUVRES

Ignoring for the moment fancy technology and 'smart' weapons, let us consider the basics of delivering a bomb (or a bullet) on a ground target the old-fashioned way, i.e. manual bombing. The fighter pilot has a gunsight, a glass screen on which the round reticle and

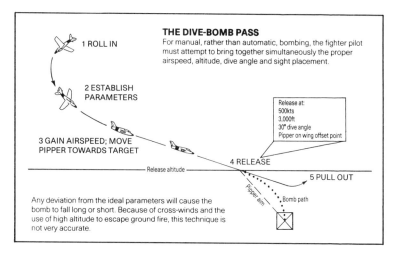

THE DIVE-BOMB PASS
For manual, rather than automatic, bombing, the fighter pilot must attempt to bring together simultaneously the proper airspeed, altitude, dive angle and sight placement.

1 ROLL IN

2 ESTABLISH PARAMETERS

3 GAIN AIRSPEED; MOVE PIPPER TOWARDS TARGET

Release at:
500kts
3,000ft
30° dive angle
Pipper on wing offset point

4 RELEASE

Release altitude

5 PULL OUT

Pipper aim

Bomb path

Any deviation from the ideal parameters will cause the bomb to fall long or short. Because of cross-winds and the use of high altitude to escape ground fire, this technique is not very accurate.

the dot inside it (called the pipper) are projected from inside the instrument panel. (The more informative HUD is merely an improvement on this concept.) The pilot dials in a certain number which rotates the reticle to the proper position on the screen for the weapons being delivered and according to such variables as release altitude, dive angle and airspeed. These are different for each weapon because, for example, a bullet will have a different trajectory from that of a bomb. The pilot then places the pipper on the target and pulls the trigger or punches the pickle button on the stick.

The next step is to hurl the weapon at the target from the proper distance and with the proper airspeed. By controlling the dive angle and releasing at a specific altitude, the pilot also controls the distance. The airspeed is controlled with the throttle and by rolling in on the target from a specific altitude and airspeed, so that the release airspeed is reached at release altitude.

Now the problems begin! Suppose the dive angle is correct but the airspeed is fast. The bomb will go 'long' because it won't follow the expected curve to impact as it slows in the air. Or, suppose the airspeed is right but the dive angle is too shallow, say 25 degrees instead of the desired 30. In this case the bomb will go 'short' because the pilot will pull the pipper up to the target but be farther out from it when the bomb is released. So the pilot corrects: if he sees that his airspeed or dive angle are wrong, he can compensate roughly by pickling early or late and offsetting one error with another.

But that's too easy. What if both his airspeed and dive angle are wrong. They may offset each other, or they may compound and

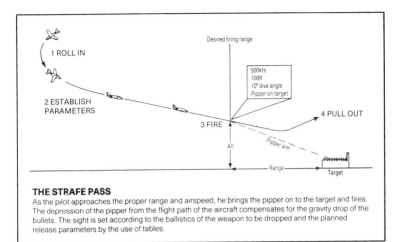

THE STRAFE PASS
As the pilot approaches the proper range and airspeed, he brings the pipper on to the target and fires. The depression of the pipper from the flight path of the aircraft compensates for the gravity drop of the bullets. The sight is set according to the ballistics of the weapon to be dropped and the planned release parameters by the use of tables.

throw the bomb extremely long or short. Now, it becomes more difficult to analyze in the few seconds of the dive pass and make a decent compensation. And then it becomes even more difficult, because the third factor, that of release altitude, also has a similar effect. Pickle high and the bomb will hit short because you have not driven up to the target yet. So now you have three variables to watch and compensate for, with many more combinations.

But what if, in your haste, you don't hold a level bank angle? This rotates your pipper up or down and causes a fourth possible error. And, what if there is a nose or a tail wind? This will throw the bomb long or short. And what if there is a cross wind? You have to know what it is, and aim left or right to compensate. And, what if the wind is a combination of cross and tail? How much do you adjust for each?

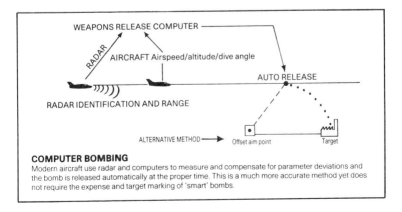

COMPUTER BOMBING
Modern aircraft use radar and computers to measure and compensate for parameter deviations and the bomb is released automatically at the proper time. This is a much more accurate method yet does not require the expense and target marking of 'smart' bombs.

The Lockheed F-117A 'stealth' fighter has been dedicated to the night bombing role. It flew 30 per cent of the strike missions on the first night of the Gulf War, with no losses and when Iraqi defences were at their peak. Its ability to escape detection depends on absorption and reflection of radar waves, engine heat dissipation and lack of emissions. New ground radars may learn to enhance and project limited returns, but the technology is being built into new fighters such as the F-22. (Lockheed)

And, what if you are getting shot at while all this is happening? Is it any wonder that a lot of bombs in combat don't hit the target? As fighter pilots say, 'Good bombing is magic.' What they really mean is that it takes a lot of experience and good co-ordination of mental and physical skill to sort all this out and make the bomb fall on the target consistently. First you try to eliminate as many variables as possible by trying to fly the perfect pass, and then you must decide how to compensate amid the variables and combinations that do arise. Bullets suffer basically the same problems, except that they are usually fired from a point much closer to the target, and they have a velocity imparted to them by the gun as well as by the plane.

Because of all this, 'smart' bombs were invented. The fighter has only to manoeuvre his aircraft into a general area and release the weapon into what is known as 'the basket'. If the bomb starts there, it has the glide distance or range to reach the target, and the guidance system will do the rest. In some cases, the target is illuminated with a laser from another aircraft and the bomber has only to dive in and release the weapon in the basket. In other cases, the laser is on the bomber itself, which is more complicated. Now the bomber releases the bomb, then pulls up and then back down again, giving the bomb time to fall towards the target. The fighter then illuminates the target in a dive, which the bomb sees until impact. In other cases, with powered weapons, the fighter may be able to continue to guide the weapon all the way to the target. Or the bomb may be given its own information about the target before release, so that the fighter can pull away as soon as the weapon is gone.

There are obviously lots of things for a fighter pilot to learn, since his aircraft may carry a wide variety of weapons and delivery systems.

THE SPORT OF KINGS*

Air Combat, the sport of kings. Detachment to Malta and intensive flying phase, twenty-eight sorties a day. 'Okay,' Boss says, 'take tanks off ships, let's go do ACM!' Here I get my first early taste of Phantom combat. Surely this is what being a fighter pilot is all about, me against him, one brain against another, one set of muscles against another, he who flies the smoothest, the meanest, the most cunning, most aggressive, most tactical fight within the legal limits wins, it is as simple as that. So all eyes brighten, secret pet theories germinate. We will start off with one versus one. We fire up the birds and all day long leap into a superb cloudless sky to trail thunder across the Mediterranean Sea.

'On east, outward split for combat . . . Go!' Fifteen miles and turn inwards. Inside my aircraft, two pairs of eyes scan carefully the piece of sky in which we expect him to appear. Today we are not using radar. Aerial lookout is a matter of practice and indeed my eyes sometimes take on the steely, faraway glint much beloved of fiction writers as I focus into the distance, and sometimes I amaze even myself with the acuity with which I detect distant minute objects.

In the crystal clear air I spot him, very low, very fast, curving up into a Sidewinder attack towards my blind quarter. The game is on. The stage is set, and like medieval combatants we set-up our opening moves as carefully as any Grand Master switching Pawn to Queen's Bishop Two. My left hand pushes the throttles through the gate into the far left-hand corner. As the surge of 'burner light-up cuts in, I crank on right rudder and roll down into him. My aim is to achieve a minimum displacement pass to prevent his gaining an immediate advantage as we commit into our hard turns. I am also going nose low to ensure a maximum build-up of energy. Thus we pass head on at a closing velocity of 1,000 knots and combat is joined.

He approaches me as a small, smoking speck to start with, the both of us pointed directly at each other on a collision course, his

---

* Extracted from *F-4 Phantom: A Pilot's Story* by Robert Prest (London: Cassell)

machine growing ever larger in my windscreen till it seems we must surely hit. But at the last moment, the instinct of self-preservation takes command and with a little twitch on the control column, I flash over the top of his canopy, clear by a thousand feet, a miss as good as a mile. I now have all the energy in the world stored in my metal body which is good, because in the F4 speed is energy, is performance, and thus a 6-G pull sends me racing skywards in a tremendous zooming arc. The F4 has not got the best turning performance of Western fighters, but using the right tactics, and in the right hands, even in a close turning fight it is a deadly machine. My plan is to remain in the vertical and use the phenomenon of radial G to give me the edge. Upside down and pitching over nose down, I can use my ailerons to change direction in an effortless instant, and so cut corners that would be impossible were I at the bottom of the circle.

However, even so there is a limited number of opening gambits available as options in Phantom combat. Hence we have both pitched up into similar enormous vertical 'yo-yos' and we pass inverted head on again at the top of the loop and start on down once again on opposite sides of the barrel. He disappears aft outside the limits of my vision, and I warn the navigator to screw himself round to look rearwards and report the 'enemy's' actions, a difficult task under 6 Gs. The aircraft is transitioning from Mach 1 plus at the bottom of the egg-shaped offset loop to under 200 knots at the top, from 10,000 feet up to 40,000, the physical laws of kinetic and potential energy are having a field day in this three-dimensional dance.

The game has moved into the development stage as we both try varying tactics and strategy to gain the advantage. My prime aim is to get him to lose sight of me, because we all know that in combat, he who loses sight, loses, period. That is why I try to direct my Saturn Five zooms towards the great white orb of the sun where I hang and poise momentarily before reversing my turn (if he is not threatening) to re-emerge from an unexpected angle. I go through the repertoire, trying reverse yo-yos, lag rolls, slice turns, rollaways, oblique loops and all the other curious manoeuvres peculiar to jet combat, yet it is all a game of chess because as I throw a move, so he counters, forcing me to counter his counter. I try more of the tricks taught to me at Phantom conversion school. Because he is a Phantom, I can afford to slow down and try to outfly him (a fatal move against low wing-loaded types) but anything goes in F4 v F4. Hence I can gamble on flying slowly yet as smoothly as possible, extracting every inch of performance without straying into the speed and energy sapping high drag regimes, aiming to force him out in front of me. I am conserving my performance by staying below nineteen units angle of attack, at every opportunity releasing to ten units to pick up those vital extra knots (when I have slowed down *too* much) that make all the difference between winning and losing (Air Combat gets so personal!).

The fight progresses. He tries to force me to fly through with a hard reversal, but this is an old trick and I pull up high, exchanging valuable speed for height, and yo-yo into the vertical plane. He follows, turning hard all the while and I am forced to turn with him, barrelling into one huge vertical 'scissors', as I look directly down on him through the top of my canopy. We are both operating the controls instinctively, one manoeuvre blending into another with an almost graceful precision.

The aerial ballet continues, for such it is because at times for a few seconds I become objective, calm, peaceful even, as I stare out at my adversary. His machine is like a fish, floating silently in the currents of the deep, gently quivering in slow-motion, twisting-and-turning elegance, puffy wisps of cumulus disintegrating round it gently like some marine foliage. And now it becomes gull-like, reversing and winging over, swooping in sudden plunges in the liquid atmosphere, seemingly delicate and frail as it glints in the sunlight. At one moment arching against the deep background blue of the sea and the next, arrowing straight up into the white heavens, scorched with sun, to hang and hover before slowly plummeting down again, wings shimmering with condensation. Condensation . . . that is the clue.

Dreamlike it may be looking down, but the reality in my own cockpit as I pull ever harder and commit back into the fight tells me the actual story of what is going on in that silver-grey toy wheeling before me. The engines at full afterburners are roaring in my ears, my eyes are foggy, senses reeling and blood pounding, all because the little clock marked 'G' on the instrument panel is steady at the figure 6. My arms ache, my neck muscles strain to hold up a head that is weighing six times its normal weight. My legs tense, assisted by the crushing, vice like grip of the G-suit to prevent the blood draining into those legs from my upper body and causing my eyes to go even foggier. As it is, I am still seeing stars, little flecks of black light that float across my vision. My breath in my own ears and my navigator's breathing over the intercom, both are harsh and heavy. We speak in grunts, forcing diaphragms to flex under the forces of gravity (hydraulic power is a wonderful thing). Right now this is war, and as I look out at that apparently serene object waltzing through the sky, I know the two bodies there are suffering the same torture, the same stresses, the same strain. They are sweating, groaning and cursing, necks twisting and eyes searching and their clock is probably reading 7 Gs. They are not at peace at all.

I sense that I am beginning to win because now, somehow, I have managed to work my way into his rear quarters. Now the ball is in my court for I must inevitably have an easier time when I am looking forward. He has to look back and fight as well, and every pilot knows he cannot fly his aircraft to the optimum under those conditions. My opponent is still turning hard, however, because I am still outside the ideal recommended cone for firing my Sidewinder, but I know it is only a matter of time. We have been fighting for three minutes – a long time in 1 v 1 combat – but I have the time and the fuel, as a quick glance at the gauge tells me, to continue playing my stalking game, because the cold certainty of victory has started washing over me in cooling waves and life is all of a sudden rosier.

He is beginning to lose sight of me for seconds at a time, perhaps tiring of the high G struggle as well. I can tell when that happens because I see his turn easing off for a moment, enabling me to bite off a few more degrees of angle off his tail. At last comes the major effort I have been waiting for. He loses sight of me under his tail and reverses his turn, attempting a barrel roll counter – fatal. I recheck Sidewinder selected, Master Arm still on, Coolant on, and pull into the uncomfortable twenty-three unit plus region with the aircraft buffeting and shuddering as I strive to control the heavy wing rock – symptomatic of approaching stall and disaster – with large inputs of rudder. I do not care, because I must kill, and kill quickly before the slot disappears and he recommences his hard pull into me, forcing me to disengage and reposition. Instead, with those extra units, I bring the pipper on the gunsight (check thirty-five mils set) to bear on his jetpipe, still glowing white-orange with 'burner, beautiful. Acquisition Sidewinder growls with delighted anticipation. I squeeze the trigger and . . . silence. The Winder is 'gone'. Five seconds later, had I fired the real thing, I would see a white puff as the explosive charge sent the metallic expanding rod slicing through his rear fuselage, severing hydraulic lines, control runs, electrical connections, and maybe then I would circle round the burning wreckage floating down, followed by two white parachutes of fallen foes.

But this is not war, this is peace. Instead I call 'Fox 2!' I win, you lose and combat is terminated. Then we either set up again, each determined to do better, sure, certain this time he will win, or else we call it a day and rush home short on fuel to smoke onto the strip, into the crewroom, coffee and argue over who did what, maybe look at films to confirm kills, and if you were vanquished, to secretly choke over it while sitting with a fixed grin – 'Waxed again!' Yes, Air Combat is the sport of kings.

V

FIGHTER MISSIONS

THE MOST FASCINATING thing about an aeroplane, aside from its speed and appearance, is what it can do. Some fighters, like the F-4, F-16, F-15 and Tornado, can perform a wide range of missions. In the first two instances, the basic aircraft is designed to do different things depending on what the pilot is capable of and what the mission calls for. The F-15 and the Tornado, on the other hand, have different versions: the F-15C is strictly air-to-air while the F-15E retains an air-to-air capability (although it does not have as much turning, acceleration and climb capability due to its extra weight) and adds sophisticated air-to-ground, all-weather systems and an extra crewman; and the Tornado IDS (interdiction strike) variant and the ADV (air defence) variant have different weapons systems and differently trained pilots.

Flying a multi-role fighter is a problem for the pilot and weapon systems operator, since they must be able to switch from one mission to another, perhaps at a moment's notice. The F-15C air-to-air pilot is more proficient at that mission than an F-16 or F-15E pilot who must train for other missions as well.

Nowadays, the classic fighter missions are a little mixed-up. With added range and payload, a modern fighter can now perform the roll of long-range bomber. A simple A-10 tank-buster carries Sidewinder missiles for air-to-air self-defence. Trainers have been modified into effective fighters. And day fighters, night fighters and

A-10 flight briefing: Captain Brian Maas briefs his flight for a four-ship training mission from 92 TFS, RAF Bentwaters, England. Briefings are thoroughly prepared, lengthy, professional and designed to ensure the maximum use of air time. 'Plan the flight and fly the plan' is the training motto. (Author)

Left: A-10 pilots of the 92nd TFS get their final briefing at the Ops Desk before going to the aircraft. (Author)
Below left: Final briefing at the duty desk. The Flight receives the latest information on aircraft, weather, gunnery ranges and safety notices. Always learn on the ground what you will be glad to know later in the air. Plan for all the contingencies, and be ready for anything.
Right: Fox Two: an F-18 fires an AIM-9 Sidewinder. The missile has been improved many times and has been the mainstay of the intermediate-range capability during most of the missile age. The new ASRAAM will replace it on advanced aircraft in the next decade. (McDonnell Douglas)

all-weather fighters are now all the same because of the improved systems they carry. Yet the basic missions of the fighter are still the same, and they are discussed in the following pages.

AIR SUPERIORITY

Douhet, the great, early air theorist, named his book *Command of the Air*. Since the beginning, every airman has known that control of the air, or air superiority, is the fundamental concept of air strategy. In order to use aircraft to accomplish national objectives, they must be able to fly relatively safely in the airspace over their own territory. Their airfields must be safe from destruction. If they are to be effective, they should be able to control the air over the enemy's territory. Each side must protect its factories and cities from attack. Each side must protect its armies and navies, so that they may control the more permanent ground and seas that may determine the victor of the war. Each side must try to carry the attack to the enemy and destroy his support for the battlefield. So

almost every use of the aeroplane in the scope of this book involves some aspect of control of the air. As a result, the technology of the air defence system often becomes at least as important as the technology of the aircraft that seeks to penetrate it.

Air superiority over your own territory involves an air defence system of fighters, surface-to-air missiles and guns, and a complex intelligence, radar and command and control system to operate these weapons. Air superiority over enemy territory involve neutralizing or attacking and destroying enemy airfields, missile sites and his command and control system, and engaging his fighters to prevent them from attacking the bombers. As in everything else, electronics and technology are becoming more and more important to the success of these missions.

CLOSE AIR SUPPORT

Control of the air over one's army is essential if the enemy has an air force. If, further, the army is engaged with an opponent's army, air power is important in supporting the army by attacking enemy troops and weapons. In addition, the same aircraft may be used further back from the battle area to attack enemy supply lines, depots, command and control centres, reserves, etc.

To illustrate the importance of this, the USAF recently decided to create a modified version of the F-16 for the close air support role. The regular F-16 can perform well in both ground attack and air superiority missions, but it can be improved. The F/A-16 will replace its 20mm gun with a 30mm cannon and it will improve its navigation and weapons systems by incorporating a day/night laser pod, forward looking infra-red and a terrain system. These aircraft will eventually constitute an entire quarter of the USAF fighter force.

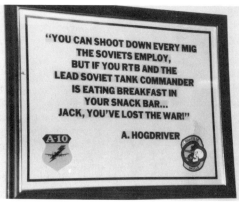

"YOU CAN SHOOT DOWN EVERY MIG
THE SOVIETS EMPLOY,
BUT IF YOU RTB AND THE
LEAD SOVIET TANK COMMANDER
IS EATING BREAKFAST IN
YOUR SNACK BAR...
JACK, YOU'VE LOST THE WAR!"

A. HOGDRIVER

Above: Quick check. The aircraft receive a final check by a maintenance team just before take-off. This system detects occasional problems that would be serious in the air, such as hydraulic leaks. A lot of work by a lot of people goes into each flying hour.

Left: Close air support. (Author)

Below left: The training missile. This Maverick inert missile remains on the aircraft and gives the pilot realistic in-the-cockpit displays for simulated attacks. Training missiles are less expensive and easier to maintain than the real thing, but the pilot cannot tell the difference. They also do not fire inadvertently, as has been known to happen with live weapons.

102

In addition, the multi-purpose F-16, which will comprise 40 per cent of the force, is now adding the LANTIRN system, auto terrain following and Navstar Global Positioning. Newer aircraft will have an improved engine, advanced threat warning, a digital terrain system and a flare/chaff dispenser. In other words, the USAF places great emphasis on close air support and battlefield air interdiction.

Close air support (CAS) involves intimate co-ordination with the army. This is accomplished by having Air Liaison Officers (ALOs), who have also been fighter pilots, located in army ground units and headquarters, and Forward Air Controllers (FACs) in flight who can communicate with ground commanders as the interface with the attack fighters.

The well-dressed A-10 pilot: Captain Maas wears full training kit, including survival suit and survival vest containing items of survival equipment. (Author)

Battlefield Air Interdiction (BAI) aims more at the non-strategic targets behind the battlefield that support the enemy ground forces. Here there is less need for army co-ordination by ALOs and FACs and a greater need for intelligence and finding targets of opportunity. Air defences are likely to be much stronger, and different weapons and attack methods may be required.

The US Army has always relied on the Air Force for CAS, although the larger and more sophisticated Army helicopter force of recent years has taken on some of this responsibility. An Apache helicopter can do much that an A-10 can do, so the distinction is becoming blurred.

After lengthy consideration, the Air Force has recently moved in the direction of planning the faster F/A-16 as the primary CAS fighter, preferring the speed and advanced systems of the little fighter to the two engines and rugged protection of the A-10. However, the current analysis of the Gulf War experience may show that the A-10 filled an important role in certain areas such as loiter time and observation capability, so the final answer to this question is yet to be determined.

THE FORWARD AIR CONTROLLER

The FAC is often, but not always, a fighter pilot, although he almost always acts and flies like one. His can be a difficult and dangerous mission, as it frequently was in Vietnam. The airborne FAC, as compared to an Air Liaison Officer attached to a ground unit, is the guy who puts the fighters on the targets in support of the army. Flying low and slow, in order to find and see his targets, he is vulnerable to ground fire. No fighter pilot who has seen a good one work in a dangerous situation can help but admire the motivation that seems to drive him. He reveals the fighter pilot background that is traditional to his breed, and he loves the 'grunts' he is protecting. This special combination of attitudes creates a unique individual flying a distinctive mission in a brave and commanding way. Just because you are flying behind a little propeller doesn't mean you can't fly like a fighter pilot.

FACs in Korea flew the O-1 Bird Dog, a small Cessna, just as they did in Vietnam. But it was too slow and took forever to climb back up from a target-marking pass. So the USAF bought some twin-engined Cessna O-2s and then, from the Marine design, the much faster turboprop OV-10. The Rockwell Bronco could carry many more rockets and it had its own miniguns built into the lower fuselage. The Marines used their updated version in the Gulf. The USAF are retiring theirs, and using the OA-10 to do the job. In

The Rockwell OV-10 Bronco, an outstanding FAC aircraft. This one is carrying extra fuel and rocket pods over South Vietnam. Miniguns were carried in the extensions above the rocket pods, but FACs were prohibited from using them much of the time. (US National Archives)

Vietnam, the Air Force was successful in Laos with the Fast FAC, an F-100, then an F-4, working with its own fighter Wing, finding and marking targets for the fighters in a high-threat environment that was too dangerous for the OV-10. This was tried again in the Gulf, and may be the way to the future.

INTERDICTION/STRIKE

Somewhere between the attacks on enemy troops in contact with your own on the front line, and long-range bombing attacks on the enemy heartland, lies interdiction: the attack on enemy supplies and support. The line between these roles is blurred as the fighter has developed longer range and payload and become more diversified in its mission capabilities. Now B-52s strike at tanks and troops, and long-range fighters like the Tornado or F-111 aim at long-range strategic targets.

You need an aircraft with some range and some ability to strike in the night and bad weather. This is what the Tornado, the F-111 and the F-15E were designed for; indeed, the Tornado version is known as the IDS for Interdiction/Strike. The F-16, with shorter range, no navigator and a weaker delivery system, is now moving

The Alpha Jet 2 is a joint venture between Dassault-Breguet and Dornier, designed as a tactical support aircraft and well able to carry a useful load of current weaponry, such as the gun pack and missile combination shown here.

105

F-16C with LANTIRN. Pods mounted on the forward fuselage provide terrain-following radar for navigation and infra-red for navigation and targeting at night in all weather. The pilot uses cursors to show the missile the location on an IR picture to home in on, then launches and leaves. (USAF)

further along the spectrum by adding the LANTIRN navigation and targeting system and other new technology for a more accurate all-weather capability.

Long-range strike is a complex affair, which may involve ECM, missile attack and suppression, enemy air attack, bad weather, heavily defended target areas and other problems. The top navigator in an F-15E is probably the best navigator who ever lived. The mission also includes nuclear strike, although this is more and more the responsibility of cruise missiles.

WILD WEASEL

In Vietnam, the USAF devised the Wild Weasel against the North's SA-2 ground-to-air missiles. The primary aircraft was the F-100 and then the F-105G, a two-seater modified with detection and jamming gear and anti-radar missiles. A navigator in the back seat, known as a 'bear' (because he was trailed around behind as though on a chain), helped to operate the systems. Teams of Wild Weasels accompanied strike forces and, when enemy radar was detected, the aircraft attacked with Shrike missiles which homed in on the radar. They also carried such things as CBUs to attack the SAM sites. It was a very dangerous business, a cat-and-mouse game with the radar operator trying to launch missiles against the Weasels who were in turn trying to launch missiles against the radar.

The latest Wild Weasel team comprises an F-4G, a Phantom with the nose gun removed and replaced by electronics, and an F-16 to carry additional HARM AGM-88 anti-radar missiles and provide a stronger air-to-air defensive capability. One interesting new development is a missile which hangs over enemy territory on a parachute, balloon or drone, waiting for enemy radar to betray its presence. The new missiles, such as the HARM, can remember the radar location, even though it is turned off after taking a quick look around. They are high-speed weapons, capable of around Mach 5 in order to destroy a site quickly when it transmits briefly.

The USAF, after considering a variety of replacements for the F-4G, is moving toward the development of an anti-radar capability for the overall fighter force. F-4G Weasels performed well in the Gulf, effectively preventing the Iraqi air defence system from denying entry to the Allied air forces.

IN-FLIGHT REFUELLING

Flying in formation is a lot easier than it appears to the non-pilot. Students placed near another aircraft bounce all over the place at first, but soon settle down. It is merely a matter of making tiny adjustments to power, pitch and roll in order to maintain position. Since you are both travelling at roughly the same speed, it makes no difference how fast you are going. When the leader makes rapid movements, it becomes more difficult for the wingman, but, as we all know, it is possible for the Red Arrows or Thunderbirds to appear as one through a wide variety of manoeuvres. The greater difficulty for the wingman comes when trying to hold position at night, when the visual cues are very limited – just a couple of lights in the murk. Depth perception becomes difficult, and spatial disorientation is common. Sometimes you could swear the leader is upside down and taking you into the ground, but you must trust your cues, just as you must trust your instruments in the weather when your body is trying to tell you something different.

In-flight refuelling from a tanker is always a little difficult, and sometimes very much so. The worst I have ever experienced was in turbulence on the edges of thunderstorms at night over Laos with a full load of bombs. The aircraft is very sluggish, you don't have the full power you want to move forward and you can't see – and the thought of a combat mission ahead doesn't make it any easier.

McDonnell Douglas KC-10 and F-4 Phantom. The merger of fighter and transport companies created one of America's most successful aerospace firms. A new concept in USAF organization, the Composite Wing combines tankers and fighters under one commander for flexibility and immediate response. (David Rothenanger)

In IFR the first job is to find the tanker, which is usually easy thanks to GCI assistance, your own radar and airborne TACAN. The harder task is to lead a flight of four fighters so that you end up just behind the turning tanker without either overshooting or having to drive up with power from a distant trail position, both of which are embarrassing for the leader. It is one of those many judgement skills where the rest of the troops can easily see how good you are.

Once in position, with your birds on each wing, you take turns dropping down into trail with the refuelling boom or basket. On KC-135 and KC-10 American tankers, the boom method is standard, whereas the British have always preferred the probe and drogue method. With the boom, the tanker has a fellow, the boomer, looking out of a rear window who controls the position of the boom with little elevons, flying it up, down and sideways with a control stick. The fighter moves into the proper position according to visual memory and the indicator lights on the bottom of the fuselage of the tanker. Once plugged in, he simply holds position by watching the lights. They tell him if he is too far forward or aft, or too high or low. At first, it is tricky getting the brain and muscles to respond to the lights; for example, it is sometimes easy to confuse an up signal with a forward signal.

If you get too far out of position, the boomer, or the boom automatically, will disconnect. He may tell you to break away for safety reasons. You may be a little nervous, especially on your first missions, because if you are all over the sky and can't take your fuel you may have to go home. And there were many instances in Vietnam where the fighter got to the tanker just in time before running out of gas.

With the drogue, which is being installed on some US tankers, the basket is bouncing around in the turbulence coming off the tanker, and you have to fight to stick your probe into it and hold the position visually. With both methods, there is always a danger that the boom or the basket will strike the aircraft and cause damage. I have known some back-seat navigators who could hold position and refuel without assistance from the pilot.

Refuelling is always an interesting experience, sometimes even a frightening one, and only pilots with self-confidence really enjoy it. There is always a feeling of pride when you pop right into position, get your gas without fuss and get out of the way.

VI

FIGHTER WEAPONS

WITHOUT WEAPONS, the fighter is useless. Since the first air-delivered weapons were created prior to the First World War, they have increased in size and accuracy. Now a pilot can deliver a 20mm round of M-61 high-explosive gun ammunition, or he can deliver a B-61 hydrogen bomb of 500 kilotons. Thanks to dramatic improvements in electronics, weapons can now be delivered more accurately, and in all kinds of weather. In the 20 years since the middle of the Vietnam War, technology has taken over many manual functions from the fighter pilot, giving him incredible accuracy in the delivery of his weapons.

The Gulf War was a showcase for the new weapons. Now, instead of raining bombs and bullets all over the area in hopes of hitting a target within it (although this was still the method on some targets), the weapons can be smaller and fewer because they are more accurate: if you can put the bomb through a window, you don't have to take six aircraft and drop 24 bombs in the general area of the building. Now, instead of having to place the aircraft in just the right place, in just the right conditions, for the bomb to fall on the target, the pilot has only to put it in the general area, and the bomb will guide itself to the target identified by the pilot or navigator with radar, IR or laser.

The 30mm gun on an A-10: Lt. Doug James, 92nd TFS, shows the size of the seven gun barrels on the GAU-8. The M-61 20mm cannon, carried on most other fighters, has only six barrels. (Author)

Yet there is still a role for such old-style birds as the A-10, which did magnificent work in the Gulf. With plenty of loiter time, a heavy load and its 30mm cannon, it was able to do a better job than the sophisticated F-16 in destroying tanks and other targets. On the other hand, stronger air defences move us more in the direction of using high technology, drones and stand-off weapons, relying less on basic weapon delivery skills.

These are just a sample of the huge range of weapons that can be carried by the F-4 Phantom. Each one must be tested and calibrated before operational use. The inventory is now considerably larger with the arrival of 'smart' bombs, not yet developed at the time of this 1965 photograph. (McDonnell Douglas)

Right: An RAF Tornado Mk. 1 of No. 27 Squadron, RAF Marham, with a mixed load of long-range fuel tanks and GP bombs slung under the fuselage. (British Aerospace)

BOMBS

The general-purpose bomb has always been the primary weapon of the aircraft: the gun and its extension, the air-to-air missile, often serve only to control the air so that bombs may be dropped.

The original high-explosive bomb has changed little in 50 years: it is still the most efficient way of destroying a typical target with shock and fragmentation. Nowadays, however, there are many kinds of bombs, some designed for a particular purpose and others using new technology to give the same basic effects – blast and fragmentation – in a more efficient way. In addition, the new technology has fostered wider applications, such as armour-penetration, large-area fragmentation or stand-off delivery.

In Vietnam, .50 calibre machine gun barrels were originally welded to the nose fuses of a 750lb bombs so that they would detonate above the ground and increase the distance of their effects on 'soft' targets. At the other end of a bomb might be a tail fuse with a short delay in it. Thus, depending on the target, the pilot could select the nose or tail fuse and determine whether the bomb would explode above the ground, for shock and fragmentation effect, or after penetrating it, for cratering and ground-shock effect. A bomb usually has a small propeller on the nose fuse, which has to spin a number of times before the fuse is armed, thus allowing the bomb to fall free from the aircraft before being dangerous.

The primary improvement to basic bombs has been the shaped-charge penetrator, which concentrates the blast directly ahead as the bomb strikes a hard target. Another improvement to the basic bomb has been the 'snakeye', folding fin or parachute, which would pop open after release and retard the bomb in flight, thus

Snakeye high-drag bombs are here shown being dropped from a Marine Corps AV-8B Harrier. The folding fins are clearly visible as they open to slow the bombs and allow lower, more accurate delivery with a reduced danger of fragmentation damage. (McDonnell Douglas)

allowing the delivery aircraft to fly lower for greater accuracy and have time to pull up and escape blast damage before the bomb hit the ground.

Some popular 'slick' bombs are the Mk 82 (500lb), the Mk 84 (2,000lb) and the Mk 117 (750lb). Bombs are usually mounted on a special rack which allows multiples to be carried on each wing or fuselage station, and which provides some ejection force to clear them from the aircraft's turbulence. There are also practice bombs, which are very small smoke bombs that simulate the ballistics of either slick or retarded bombs; they are carried in a dispenser, with doors for safe carriage, and are used on practice bombing ranges. Scorers in a tower will observe the smoke and tell the pilot where the bomb fell – for example, '100 [feet] at 3 [o'clock]' – so that he may learn from each delivery.

In the cockpit, the pilot can usually select individual bombs or pairs from each wing, or dump the whole load on one pass. One of the important skills that must be learned by new fighter pilots is getting the switches right. Mistakes are seen by the whole world. In the new cockpits, the pilot can call up a picture of his bomb and missile load, making it a lot easier to know what he has dropped and what he has remaining.

GUNS

At one time, with the invention of the air-to-air radar missile and a good radar set that would fit into the nose of a fighter, air theorists decided that guns were obsolete and air battles would take place at long range. A few fighter pilots tried to tell them otherwise, but they went ahead and designed the Navy Phantom without a gun inside.

Fortunately, gun technology did not stagnate, and a great leap forward was expressed in the M-61 Gatling gun which could fire 100 rounds of 20mm high-explosive shells per second. When you fire it – just a brief squeeze of the trigger – the gun goes *rrrrRRRRRRrrrrrr* and all that metal totally destroys whatever it penetrates. You only have about 1,000 rounds, so you have only about five decent trigger squeezes, but each one is deadly. The gun was first built into a pod that could be mounted under the aircraft, and the Phantom now had, by popular request from the users, a devastating gun in Vietnam. Then it was made a little smaller and fitted into the nose of the aircraft, which was now redesignated F-4E. Then, since bigger is often better, a 30mm version was made and installed in a tank-killer, the A-10 Warthog. When you fire it, the whole aeroplane shakes and you can't read the instruments. The very first time you do so, you think for an instant that the thing has come apart inside the aircraft. Depleted uranium is used in the shells, since it is heavier than lead and gives them greater mass, momentum and impact power.

The gun has been so successful that now we have a C-130 gunship that has 20mm Gatling guns, 40mm pom-poms and a 105mm howitzer. With infra-red sensing, it can see trucks and tanks in the dark and destroy them.

M-61 Vulcan 20mm Gatling gun

General Electric dominates the gun business. The company designed the original Gatling gun in the 1950s, based on the concept of rotating barrels to increase the rate of fire that had been introduced in the nineteenth century. With six barrels, each in a different stage of loading, firing and ejecting at any time, plus electric start-up and operation, the incredible rate of 6,000 rounds a minute, or 100 per second, is achieved. The M-61 is only the most popular gun in a wide family of weapons of varying sizes using the same concept. It was first used in the F-104 and it has been the primary gun in US fighters ever since. The number of rounds carried varies: the SUU-23 pod carries around 1,100, the re-

The bite of the Falcon: the rotary linkless feed system of the 20mm six-barrelled cannon. (General Electric)

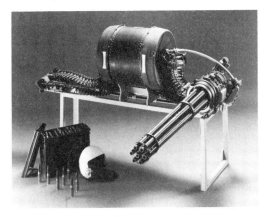

The 30mm cannon seen here is the GAU-8, carried as the main armament of the A-10 tank-buster. (Author)

designed gun carried internally in the F-4E holds only 638 and the F-15 holds 940. Newer versions allow the pilot to select 4,000 rounds a minute. Reliability is 15,000 rounds MTBF (Mean Time Between Failures). Other M-61 aircraft are the F-106, the F-111, the F-18, the A-7, the F-14 and the B-52H.

GAU-8 Avenger 30mm Gatling gun
Another important GE gun is the 30mm weapon carried in the A-10. Although larger, it has a 30 per cent improvement in velocity and its greater kinetic energy gives it a longer range. It has seven barrels and carries about 1,200 rounds. The recoil force is 9,000lb, equivalent to the power of one A-10 engine. The pilot can select either 2,100 or 4,200 rounds a minute, and the gun is designed to fire ten two-second bursts with a one-minute cooling period. This is the most powerful gun in the air, and it proved to be an all-important weapon against Iraqi guns, tanks and vehicles during the Gulf War. A 30mm gun, with modifications, will be installed internally in the new F/A-16 CAS fighter.

SMART BOMBS

The V-1 'Buzz Bomb' was, in a sense, a 'smart' bomb in that it had a self-contained guidance system that gave it an altitude, a direction and a certain amount of fuel so that it would run out over the target and then drop down. But, of course, it wasn't very accurate. After that, the US had cruise missiles like the Snark, Matador and modern AGMs, but mostly with nuclear warheads.

The real introduction for smart bombs was in Vietnam, when the USAF used Walleye, a TV-guided glide bomb, as early as 1966 and introduced the B-57G, which had a laser designator and guided bombs much like those we have today. The most successful use, however, came after bombing the North was resumed in 1972, and F-4s of the 8th Tactical Fighter Wing at Ubon were equipped with laser pods and 2,000 and 3,000lb bombs, ideal for the bridges up North that had resisted attack from a multitude of smaller 'hard' bombs in the earlier years: in just three months, the aircraft destroyed 106 bridges, including the famous Paul Doumer and Thanh Hoa bridges.

The greatest success for 'smart' bombs came, as we all know, in the Gulf War. The full range was used – TV, laser, IR and imaging. The effect on the war, and on the public, was remarkable. By being able to place a bomb, literally, down a ventilation shaft or through a door, it was possible to destroy a target completely with one large bomb instead of the multitude of 'hard' bombs previously used. This required fewer sorties and resulted in a more immediate destruction of key targets like command and control bunkers. The effect on enemy morale must have been devastating. It also greatly reduced the losses of Allied fighters, since they could stand off, away from heavy local gunfire.

Examples of the four major guidance systems are:

AGM-65 Maverick radar-guided, solid-propellant bomb

The Hughes Maverick, used on such aircraft as the A-10, has TV, laser and IR guidance models. The TV model, AGM-65A/B, weighs 463lb and has an 83lb shaped-charge warhead. The pilot has a small TV screen in the cockpit and the missile a small TV camera in the nose with a 2.5-degree field of view. The pilot identifies the target with cursors and the missile is told to see and remember the point based on black and white contrast. The CEP (Circular Error Probable) for 50 per cent of the missiles is only five feet. The problem, of course, is that the weapon is only useful in clear air, since both the pilot and the missile must see the target. The advantage is that the pilot does not have to continue to illuminate the target until impact, and in some situations TV sees better than IR.

Paveway laser-guided glide bomb

The Texas Instruments Paveway was the successful bomb used in Vietnam and it is still used as an attachment to the nose of ordinary 500, 750, 2,000 and 3,000lb 'iron' or cluster bombs. As compared to the Maverick, most of the weight is bomb, not rocket and guidance. The pilot, or that of a companion aircraft, illuminates the targets with a laser pod. The bomb is released into an area (the 'basket') from which it can glide to the target, homing in on the laser beam reflection. Paveway II is an improved version, with tailfins for additional manoeuvrability, and Paveway III has improved guidance controls, an autopilot and high-lift folding wings.

AGM-130 infra-red guided, solid-propellant bomb
An improvement on the Rockwell GBU-15 glide bomb, this system, still under test, has a strap-on rocket motor. It can be launched with or without target lock-on. Knowing the approximate location of the target, particularly if approaching at low altitude to avoid detection or missiles, the operator launches the weapon and then can guide it on his IR screen using the image transmitted from the missile. The operator may also control the altitude of the weapon as it approaches and searches for the target. The primary advantage of this weapon, in addition to its stand-off capability, is that it works in bad weather, as the IR head creates a TV-like picture of the different temperatures it sees. For example, a tank shows up at night in the desert, or an aircraft can be seen on a ramp. There is an airfield attack version, using kinetic-energy penetrators and area-denial weapons. A 15-mile range from a low-altitude launch, with a 2,000lb Mk 84 bomb, makes this a formidable weapon.

AGM-109 Tomahawk imaging cruise missile
The TV pictures of ship-launched Tomahawks racing down a Baghdad street, to impact without warning on a specific corner of a building, will be the lasting image of the Gulf War. The General Dynamics missile, driven by a normal jet engine after rocket launch, travels at 500mph, has a range of 1,500 miles and has a CEP of 65ft. It can be air-launched, typically from a B-52. It first flies to INS co-ordinates and then begins to look for pictures to match those placed in its memory before launch, gathered earlier by recce birds or satellites. Each picture in sequence brings it closer and more accurately to the target until it finds the door or aircraft it is looking for. Magnificent!

Pre-flight check: the pilot of a Phantom in Vietnam checks the TER (Triple Ejector Rack) mounted on the wing pylon, which here carries only two cluster bomb unit canisters. The rack contains safety pin mechanisms and ejection devices that push the weapons away from the aircraft on delivery. (US National Archives)

An F-16 with a heavy cluster bomb unit load. The CBU is a devastating weapon as each canister opens at a pre-set altitude, spreading a variety of submunitions over a large area. (USAF)

CLUSTER BOMB UNITS (CBU)

The CBU comes in many shapes and sizes, designed for a variety of targets that are vulnerable to a multitude of small weapons as compared to big bombs. Basically, the pilot drops a canister from the aircraft which opens in flight and sprays hundreds of small bomblets over a large area (alternatively, the canister remains attached to the aircraft and the weapons are ejected from it as the target is overflown). CBUs are primarily effective against 'soft' targets like personnel, vehicles or aircraft. Some of them are 'smart', set to go off only if disturbed later, or are activated by a timing device that sets them off over many hours. Examples are:

JP.233 airfield attack dispenser system
The Hunting JP.233 made its reputation in the Gulf War, serving to take out the major Iraqi airfields in some dangerous night, low-altitude attacks by RAF Tornados. The aircraft passes down the runway at low altitude and the dispenser drops 30 concrete-penetration bombs and 215 area-denial mines which make it difficult for crews to repair the damage.

CBU-87 combined effects munition
Popular with the USAF today, this dispenser has a proximity fuse that opens it at pre-set altitude. The dispenser rotates at up to 2,500rpm and the 202 bomblets each have an anti-personnel fragment casing over an incendiary device and a hollow-charge anti-tank warhead. Aircraft can be disabled by fragments at distances up to 250ft.

CBU-92 extended-range anti-armour munition
Due to equip the USAF in 1993, this dispenses a dozen anti-tank and area-denial weapons. Landing on legs by parachute, the

seismic/acoustic fuse finds a target, determines the range and bearing, and fires the warhead at it. IR fusing detonates it over the target.

AIR-TO-AIR MISSILES

The air-to-air missile revolutionized air warfare more than any other development since the gun was synchronized to fire through the propeller in the First World War. Suddenly, although it took a long time to develop the gun's reliability and accuracy, the fighter pilot could fire from long distance, in bad weather, from other directions than astern and without engaging in a dogfight in which either he or his aeroplane might be inferior.

The problem was that the other guy could do the same. And was that speck on the radar really the enemy, or was it a friend? The air-to-air (and the ground-to-air) missiles finally made the manned bomber a risky proposition (ECM and stealth technology notwithstanding), but they also greatly complicated the offensive and defensive problems of the fighter pilot and the designers of his aircraft.

The first air-to-air missiles were big and unreliable. Now, however, with chip electronics, super-cooled heat sensors, internal INS and the like, there has been a quiet revolution in capability and reliability. Examples are:

Sky Flash radar missile

An improved Sparrow for the RAF. The AIM-7, the major radar missile of the Vietnam War (and which is still on inventories today) had a habit of missing most of the time. The new ones have chips instead of vacuum tubes and are much better. The Sky Flash, four of which are carried under the fuselage by Phantoms and Tornado F.3s, has a range of up to 31 miles at high-altitude, at Mach 4.

AIM-9 Sidewinder heat-seeking missile

This has been much improved through many versions over the years and is still the primary air-to-air kill missile, but is to be replaced by the ASRAAM, which is still under development (and argument) by the Americans and Europeans. The new Sidewinders are true dogfight missiles because they are all-aspect: they are able to home on targets from all directions, not just the rear, because of their ability to detect minor heat differences with improved seeker heads. They have a better turning capability, with motorized foreplanes, more sensitive detonation devices and more powerful explosive warheads.

Above left: A Tornado with two JP.223 runway denial weapons. These are trials installations; in real operations in the Gulf, JP.233 missions were the most dangerous flown in the air war – at night, at low level and against heavy ground fire. (British Aerospace)
Right: The Soviets have a wider range of capable missiles than NATO, variation being aided by fitting different seeker/guidance systems on standard missile bodies. This MiG-29 carries two AA-10 Alamo radar missiles inboard and four AA-11 Archer IR dogfight missiles on the outboard stations. The red cones are to protect the highly sensitive missile heads from damage whilst on the ground. (Jon Lake)

The F-15, although nearly 20 years old, is the primary air-to-air fighter in the USAF. Future upgrades will include new radar and missiles, the latter replacing the Sparrows and Sidewinders carried by this example. (McDonnell Douglas)

AIM-120 AMRAAM

The Advanced Medium Range Air-to-Air Missile is now joining the inventory, eagerly awaited by today's fighter pilot. An F-15 has fired four of them simultaneously at separate targets, showing the ability of the fire control system to handle this complex problem and the ability of the missile to find its assigned target and kill it without further assistance from the mother fighter. It is not semi-active like the Sparrow, which needs projected energy from the mother ship to the target to be reflected back to its seeker while guiding; it is an active radar missile, a fire-and-forget weapon, meaning that it transmits its own radar, allowing the fighter to turn away and do something else after launch. It also has an internal INS, so that the fighter can tell it where to go by INS co-ordinates which can be updated after launch. The missile will go there, and then look for the target to home in on. Speed is Mach 4 to and range up 45 miles. The big deal is that you don't have to keep your aircraft pointed at the target while the missile is en route — and this can be a life-saver.

TRIPLE-A: THE FIGHTER PILOT'S ENEMY

It is ironic that in the most high-tech war in history, the Gulf War, most of the Allied aircraft to be lost were brought down not by enemy fighters or surface-to-air missiles but by 'triple-A', more properly known as AAA or Anti-Aircraft Artillery, and known since earlier wars as flak. Although there were some losses to SAMs, the Allies found sophisticated ways to neutralize or destroy most of the accurate, high-speed, radar-guided Soviet missiles that defended Iraq. At the same time, modern technology has not found a way to avoid the danger from masses of guns, from pistols to 100mm radar-guided artillery.

The North Vietnamese perfected the art: when an American aircraft flew over, everybody including grandmother pointed anything that would shoot into the air and blasted away in the general direction of the sight or sound of the enemy. I once had a tape made aboard a British ship in Haiphong harbour during an American air raid and there was a deafening rattle of thousands of small arms, automatic weapons and larger guns. With that much metal being thrown into the sky, some aircraft were inevitably hit even though most of the gunfire was grossly inaccurate. The Iraqis used the same technique and were successful. Countering this threat is a challenge. The only solution, and a partial one at best, seems to be to inundate the area with CBU munitions that will keep exploding and keep the enemy's heads down during the fighter passes across the heavily defended targets. However, this obviously does not work when you are talking about a whole city, or troops spread through the jungle. Gunners in South Vietnam knew that the FAC would drop the sky on them if they betrayed their presence with tracer, but that didn't stop them from scoring a lot of hits.

Few such small weapons are aimed accurately, as I once learned by looking down the four barrels of a ZSU-23 automatic weapon pulling off a target in Cambodia. He wasn't leading me at all and I was doing 600 miles an hour at a few hundred feet, or I would have been dead. I took a few small arms hits in South Vietnam, and never even knew it until I got back on the ground, but any one of them could just as well have penetrated my forehead. As you go higher, or as you go to areas more effectively controlled by the enemy, you face larger guns, some of which are radar-guided. Often the shells are pre-set to detonate at certain altitudes, such as 12,000ft – where we started our standard roll-in on target over Laos or North Vietnam.

One solution for the fighter pilot is to 'jink' – to rack the aircraft around in the sky, this way and that, pulling first right and then left, and perhaps back again, coming off the target at the lowest altitude, in the hope of throwing off the aim of the gunners (who are pointing at a piece of space through which they expect you to fly). Another method of reducing such casualties is to beef up the cockpit and the aircraft systems with armour plate, such as has been done on the A-10 and F/A-16.

The current solution is to develop stand-off weapons that can be guided to the target from the cockpit while the aircraft is miles away and going in a different direction. The TV camera or IR sensor in the nose of the missile passes the image of the target back to the cockpit and the pilot flies the missile on to the target. This is expensive technology, and not always as accurate as a low-altitude pass with cheap iron bombs, but in the long run it saves fighters if the environment is a high-threat one.

VII

FIGHTER ORGANIZATIONS

'THE PILOT IS of a race of men who since time immemorial have been inarticulate; who, through their daily contact with death, have realised, often enough unconsciously, certain fundamental things. It is only in the air that the pilot can grasp that feeling, that flash of knowledge, of insight, that matures him beyond his years; only in the air that he knows suddenly he is a man in a world of men. "Coming back to earth" has for him a double significance. He finds it difficult to orient himself in a world that is so worldly, amongst a people whose conversation seems to him brilliant, minds agile, and knowledge complete – yet a people somehow blind. It is very strange . . .

'He wants only to get back to the Mess, to be among his own kind, with men who act and don't talk, or if they do, talk only shop; of old So-and-so and his temper, of flights and crashes, of personal experiences; bragging with that understatement so dear to the Englishman. He wants to get back to that closed language that is Air Force slang.

'Though these men may seem to fit into the picture of everyday life, though they seem content enough in the company of other men and in the restfulness of their homes, yet they are really only happy when they are back with their Squadrons, with their associations and memories. They long to be back in their planes, so that isolated with the wind and the stars they may play their part in man's struggle against the elements'. *

In personal, daily terms, the young fighter pilot is part of different organizations, depending on the arrangement of his particular air force. In the USAF, he is part of a Flight, Squadron and Wing, usually all located on the same base. In the RAF, the chain of command is a little different, but it accomplishes the same thing. The central unit in all services is the fighter squadron, which flies and functions as a single unit. Above the organization on his base, the fighter pilot does not usually come in contact with (or care very much about) what goes on in some remote headquarters. As he

---

* From *The Last Enemy* by Richard Hillary (Macmillan, 1941).

rises in rank, however, he will gradually become more involved in the higher organizations because they inspect him and tell him what to do, he may have worked or expect to work there and, as life or wars become more complicated, they will help him do his job.

The modern US Air Force has Tactical Fighter Wings, usually with three Tactical Fighter Squadrons flying the same aircraft from the same base. There is a trend current in the USAF towards Composite Wings, with different aircraft mixed together, so that the wing can deploy and conduct operations without much outside support. For example, the Chief of Staff suggested in the Fall 1990 *Air Power Journal* a possible line-up for a Composite Wing:

Multi-role	24 x F-16C
Night/weather attack	12 x F-16C with LANTIRN
Long range/precision/all-weather	12 x F-15E
Air superiority	24 x F-15C
Air refuelling	6 x KC-135
Surveillance/control	3 x E-3 AWACS

This obviously would provide a more flexible combat unit under one commander for the smaller kinds of wars envisaged in the post-Cold War future. Various missions might also allow the attachment of different aircraft such as A-10 tank-busters, Wild Weasel anti-missile fighters or ECM/reconnaissance planes.

Regardless of how it is done, however, the essential unit will be the fighter squadron of similar aircraft. In the following pages, we will look more closely at this key organization.

THE FIGHTER SQUADRON

The heart of tactical fighter capability is the Fighter Squadron. Since the very beginning of air combat, the Squadron has been the home of the fighter pilot, without which he could not successfully function. The Squadron is divided into several Flights, but that is primarily for span-of-control, not because of any operational concept as it was in earlier days. The Squadron is one of several in the fighter Group (RAF) or Wing (USAF), but the Group/Wing is there primarily for good management rather than operational need. No, it is not the Flight or the Wing, but the *Squadron* which is essential to the flying mission.

A fighter pilot deals with his Flight Commander in many ways, but it is really the Squadron Operations Officer and Commander who decide how he will train and fly. His emotional attachment, his primary loyalty and his friends are spread throughout the Squad-

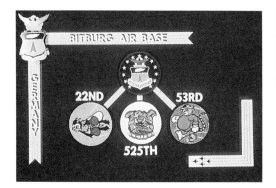

Squadron patches. Every fighter squadron in the world has a distinctive patch to be worn on the flight suit. The designs are occasionally found on aircraft too. (USAF: 36 TFW)

ron. Young pilots have very little contact with the senior officers above Squadron level, and tend to think of them as officers whose primary loyalty goes upward to the generals; the Operations Officer and Squadron Commander, on the other hand, are seen as loyal to and protective of the pilots in the Squadron, understanding their problems and sensing their attitudes and goals in ways that the Wing Leaders do not. This is not to denigrate the colonels, but simply to recognize that these officers hold stronger priorities – to larger missions and to higher headquarters which take less account of individual needs. Thus it is the Squadron which provides the emotional sustenance and outlet required by these highly talented, exuberant young men.

The Squadron is supposed to be able to function alone. In the US Air Force a Squadron can fly to a remote location or a site with pre-positioned equipment, and even personnel, and begin to conduct combat operations. In the first case, a flock of C-130s may join them, bringing the men and equipment. Much of the support is provided by the same people, the Aircraft Generation Squadron which supports them at home and shares the Squadron number. These are the crew chiefs and maintenance personnel who keep the aircraft flying. More complicated maintenance is provided by a central shop, such as engines or electronics, and elements of these units may also be deployed. But the point is that it is the *Squadron* which is the unit that can go to war.

The Squadron Commander is one of the most carefully selected officers in the Air Force. He must have the respect of both the people below him and those above. With his loyalties torn in two directions, he must walk the fence and get the job done. Sometimes the troops are unhappy, and he must try to sympathize, even though he must also try to explain the reasons for the unpopular policies which have hurt morale. The fighter bureaucracy, like any other, has its inefficiencies and stupidities. The Commander bridges the gap and motivates the force. Rarely does he do so by being a hard and unfriendly disciplinarian.

The 'Boss', and his second-in-command (who often stands in his place), must be the friend and hero of the fighter pilot, yet enforce the rules and hand out the punishment for those who fail to comply. There is a genius to this role which many men simply do not have. The fighter pilot, on the one hand, is a spirited, single-minded individualist who by nature does not take well to discipline and orders. But he flies a twenty- or thirty-million-dollar aeroplane and defends the nation, and the system requires that he perform his heavy responsibility to exacting standards and constraining rules and regulations. The Squadron Commander is the man who successfully resolves this incompatibility.

Above all, the Squadron gives the fighter pilot the greatest friends he will ever have. They share the same job and feelings and ambitions; they are mates and comrades; they love each other. As a result, they tend to be snobs, not unfriendly, but certainly aloof, to outsiders who do not understand their unique passion and skill. They gather around each other, supporting and joking and pushing, and they become superior as a result. The Squadron, like so many of life's training experiences, breaks a man down and then rebuilds him in the desired image. His inexperience and wrong thinking are illuminated, and then he is shown the way to gaining the respect of his compatriots, by conforming and performing. In the end, the Squadron becomes a perfect team that thinks and acts as one. The corporate mentality, the family, the interchangeability of the members, the self-love, the cohesive unit – these win wars.

THE 92ND TACTICAL FIGHTER SQUADRON

A USAF fighter squadron is led by a Commander, an Operations Officer, several Flight Commanders, one or more Weapons Officers who are graduates of the USAF Fighter Weapons School, and assorted other people with various duties.

The 92nd Squadron, at RAF Bentwaters, has flown the A-10 since 1980. The aircraft it has flown in its 50 years since being established in the Second World War, as shown elsewhere in this book, amount to a veritable history of fighter aviation. In the Second World War, especially, the Squadron had a distinguished combat record; since then it has been a mainstay of NATO.

During my four years in the Squadron, flying the F-4 and trying to provide some decent leadership for 60 sharp guys 10 or 15 years younger than me, it was, like all fighter squadrons, a very special place – a home, a place where all my friends were, a place where I

THE FIGHTER SQUADRON

There is a film clip from the Vietnam War. An F-105 fighter pilot is standing in front of the Squadron. It is his going-home party: he has survived his 100 missions over North Vietnam. He is holding a gift, a framed picture of the Squadron that his comrades have given him. He is trying to speak, but he cannot because he is crying. Then he smashes the picture repeatedly, with frustration, on the table, shattering the glass in the collapsed frame and cutting his hand. He chokes out the words: 'I don't need this to remember you guys.'

---

felt happy again when I went back 16 years later. So much happened to me there. Such trials and disappointments and joys, such fun and laughs and friends, the utter happiness of flying at the most demanding level – no other period of my life is so embedded in my memory. When I left, I went into the civilian world and never really found close friends again. They don't understand out there.

NO. 74 SQUADRON RAF

British fighter pilots, God bless 'em, are a cheerful and spirited lot, made that way by their culture and their special history. After the Battle of Britain, and then the Falklands and the Gulf, fighter pilots are something very special in Britain, much more than in the United States. I spent a day with No. 74. They were great guys, friendly and open, and I felt as though I were 20 years younger.

January 31, 1991. Wing Commander Graham Clarke nods his head forward as a signal to his wingman, and releases the brakes of his old but airworthy F-4J Phantom. He pushes the throttles into afterburner and glances to see that his wingman is rolling with him for their formation take-off down Runway 23 at RAF Wattisham in Suffolk. Behind them, the second element has completed its engine run-up; twenty seconds later it follows Clarke on radar into the low ceiling of wet clouds. Thus begins the final flight of the former US Navy Phantoms; they have served the RAF reliably since they were reconditioned from desert storage in 1984 as a result of the need for Phantoms in the Falklands. Even today, one crew from the Squadron rotates to temporary duty in the South Atlantic. Now, with the reduction of NATO forces, these older F-4s are no longer needed and have been replaced by newer Phantom FGR.2s returning from Germany. The USAF has retired all its Phantoms, many to the Air National Guard, except the special F-4G Wild Weasel anti-radar birds. Other nations, such as Germany, Japan

No. 74 Squadron RAF: the key personnel of one of the RAF's most distinguished squadrons, now flying Phantoms. (Author)

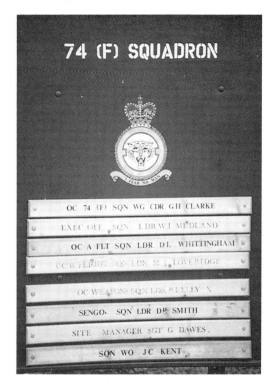

74 (F) SQUADRON

OC 74 (F) SQN WG CDR G H CLARKE

EXEC OFF SQN LDR W J MEDLAND

OC A FLT SQN LDR D L WHITTINGHAM

OC B FLIGHT SQN LDR M J LOVERIDGE

OC WEAPONS SQN LDR N KELLY

SENGO SQN LDR D P SMITH

SITE MANAGER SGT G DAWES

SQN WO J C KENT

and Israel, continue to fly the aircraft. In the RAF, only a few squadrons in the UK will continue to fly the F-4.

Breaking out on top, the four Phantoms of Tiger Flight join up into tactical formation and begin to look ahead for the C-130 tanker from RAF Lyneham. After joining on the slower tanker, each aircraft tops off its fuel from the single basket trailing from the centre of the Hercules. This method of refuelling is difficult because the tanker's trailing turbulence throws the basket around, making it a challenge to insert the probe extended from the fuselage just outside the front cockpit. USAF Phantoms, in contrast, are refuelled with a boom into the receptable behind the rear cockpit while the pilot flies in formation beneath the tail of the KC-135 or KC-10.

Tiger Flight then proceeds north-east, going 'feet-wet' over the Norfolk coast, into the circular air-to-air practice range over the North Sea. Splitting into autonomous elements, the back pair of Phantoms set themselves up for simulated combat against two 'MiG-29 Fulcrums', the world's top dogfighters. In Clarke's back seat, Squadron Leader Ned Kelly, the squadron's Senior Weapons

Instructor and Officer Commanding/Navigators, directs the mission through the sequence of individual training situations that he had briefed on the ground beforehand. RAF 'fightergators' are given more responsibility in flight and on the ground than their USAF counterparts. Although the front pilot may sign for the aircraft, the navigator may often be the flight leader, with full responsibility for the direction of the mission. RAF navigators may also serve as Squadron Commanders.

Head-on, 2-v-2, the opposing flights lock on to each other at long range with radar. Tiger 3 calls Fox One on the radio, indicating that he has established the parameters to fire his Sky Flash radar missile, an improved variant of the US AIM-7 Sparrow. This completes the first exercise. Then, as the flights close, the Phantoms manoeuvre for position to attain a heat lock-on with the seeker head of their captive AIM-9 practice missiles. On active patrols or real combat, each Phantom would carry four radar and four heat missiles.

As the Phantoms achieve a head-on, heat lock-on, Clarke's simulated Fulcrums split sharply in different directions in an attempt to confuse their attackers. Tiger 3 engages reheat and instructs his wingman to take on one of the enemy fighters while he attacks the other. With their inferior Phantoms, they must not get into a turning dogfight with the more powerful, superior MiGs. With the lock-on growl of the heat missile in their headsets, the two F-4s call Fox Two, radar missiles fired, almost simultaneously and then lower their noses to 'blow through' the MiGs at high speed. As they pass by their targets and expose their tail, they eject missile-distraction flares from the canisters built into the rear of the fuselage. Exercise Two complete.

Having served as a high-speed target for the radar and heat lock-on attacks, Clarke and his wingman, Tigers 1 and 2, haul their Phantom-MiGs around to engage in the third pre-briefed situation, a close-in dogfight. Heat attacks are now extremely difficult, as the target rarely stays long enough within the seeker-head limits of the missile to allow completion of the firing sequence. Often, even if the missile is fired, the target will pass out of limits and the missile will go ballistic without a target to guide on. So the gun often becomes the weapon of last resort, with 'snap shots' the only opportunity. Before the internal nose gun was installed in the F-4E, earlier models of the F-4, including the Navy's J model, carried only the SUU-23 Gatling gun in a pod mounted on the centreline station. More than one embarrassed pilot in Vietnam managed to pickle off a gun instead of a wing-station bomb due to a simple switch error. The result: a short, but expensive, dud. But the 6,000-round-a-minute gun is effective. The USAF learned in Vietnam that many situations degraded into gun attacks – hence the reversion to internal guns and the correction of the erroneous long-range-missile thinking that developed in Britain and the US in the 1960s.

The Phantom attackers of Tiger Flight break off their high-speed escape and reverse to take on their leader and his wingman. Each opposing element in a 2-v-2 flight performs co-ordinated man-oeuvres as a team: each aircraft tries to provide support for its partner against the opponents, who may have split vertically and/or horizontally. The innumerable permutations of this swirling battle, with each member of the two teams trying to gain a firing position on the enemy while still protecting himself and his partner, make for a new training situation on every flight, with new lessons and three-dimensional experiences to be analyzed and remembered. Even more situations are possible when the squadron practises other combinations such as 1-v-2, 2-v-4 and 4-v-4. Before they retired last year, the USAF 527th Aggressor Squadron, flying F-16C Falcons from RAF Bentwaters, often conducted Dissimilar Air Combat Tactics training against RAF fighter units. Now USAF and RAF flights meet frequently on pre-briefed DACT flights. In addition, different flights may 'bounce' each other during un-expected encounters over Britain, although only in certain areas under controlled safety conditions. This teaches crews to stay alert and be prepared to fight different aircraft at any time. Crews also fly often at very low altitude, maintaining the difficult mental and physical skills necessary to fly as low as 100ft in order to avoid radar and missile detection.

Eventually the heavy manoeuvring at high g kills off energy and carries the planes down to the safety floor of their airspace and Kelly calls, 'Knock it off'. This is the standard call when anyone in the flight approaches safety parameters, has a problem with himself or

No. 74 Squadron RAF operations. Phantom aircraft and crews are managed by Ops, the central communications and management facility in the Squadron building. Elsewhere, efficient flying and training schedules are prepared on similar wall-boards. (Author)

his aircraft or loses situational awareness. The danger of mid-air collision is high in these aggressive training situations, and strict rules are observed. The two elements climb back up, separating, and join battle again, until Tiger 4 calls 'Bingo fuel' – time to go home. Sweating heavily from the physical exertion of trying to breath rapidly under the pressure of 5–6 gs in their rubbery, sea survival suits, the crews relax. Back-seaters tune in the home TACAN and check the airspace ahead on radar for bogeys.

Clarke talks to Eastern Radar and brings the Flight of four down the chute for a GCA and high-speed pass down the Wattisham runway. The weather is terrible, but this is the last flight, so they manage. Members of the Squadron are gathered outside to watch the final pass, laughing at the problems of the wingmen in hanging to their positions in the turbulence and limited visibility. There seems to be a little sadness, even though new Phantoms will replace these old warriors, some of which flew from US Navy carriers against North Vietnam. The crew know that in about two years all the Phantoms will be gone, and No. 74 Squadron will be retired. It is also an eventful day for Squadron Leader Dai Whittingham: this is his last flight with the Squadron before he moves on to take command of the RAF Phantom Training Flight at Wattisham. When he arrives at his Hardened Aircraft Shelter, he'll be met by squadron mates, champagne and the fire truck for the traditional last-flight hose-down.

The Tigers are one of the most famous of all RAF squadrons, with a proud combat history in both World Wars. Formed at Northolt in July 1917, the Squadron moved to France, its motto 'I fear no man'. One of its Flight Commanders was Mick Mannock, perhaps the greatest British ace of the First World War and holder of the Victoria Cross. In the Battle of Britain, the Squadron was led from Biggin Hill and other fields by the great 'Sailor' Malan. After the war, it became the first Lightning squadron. After some years in the Far East, it was disbanded, to be re-formed again with the F-4J. As one of the famous 'Tiger Squadrons' in air forces around the world, No. 74 meets often with 14 other sister 'Tiger' units to exchange ideas, fly and enjoy the companionship of pilots from other nations. Bitburg 53rd Squadron F-15s, Upper Heyford 79th Squadron F-111s and Canadian F-18s from Bad Sollingen are some of the great units in this unique international organization.

The Navy Phantom has the improved, General Electric J79 engine, which gives it more power at high altitude than the British-built Phantoms with the Rolls-Royce Spey bypass engine. So the squadron's newer FGR.2 (F-4M) Phantoms will give greater performance in the thicker air at low altitude. No. 74 Squadron pilots flew FGR.2s when they attended the Red Flag combat exercise at

Nellis AFB, Nevada, so the aircraft is not new to them. Now the J aircraft, and later all the Phantoms, will retire to hangars to await new owners, or perhaps an honoured place in museums or mounted in concrete, where future generations will admire the strange, formidable lines of the world's greatest fighter aircraft.

At the same time, the crew will move on, perhaps to the Tornado, while the pilots dream of the European Fighter Aircraft, where once again they may practise the unique skills of the dogfighter, the ace, the Real Fighter Pilot. For a time, between the retirement of the last Phantom and the introduction of the EFA, the RAF will not have a dogfight aircraft. Only the less-manoeuvrable Tornado F.3 Air Defence Variant, backed up by the lower-performing Hawk and Jaguar, will guard these islands. RAF thinking is that either it will go to war supported if necessary by the USAF's F-15/F-16 dogfight capability as in the Gulf, or its tactics will avoid dogfight situations against more capable aircraft like the MiG-29 or Su-27 Flanker and try to keep the fight on its terms. This gap in tactical capability does not leave leaders like Wing Commander Graham Clarke happy, but he understands the budget imperatives, and looks forward to the day when the RAF will once again have a complete air-superiority force.

THE FIGHTER WING

The US Air Force is organized a little differently from the RAF, with the Fighter Wing playing a more direct role in the operations of the Fighter Squadron. In the RAF, the Squadron is a little more independent, without so much Wing staff assistance and supervision directly at hand.

The USAF Wing usually consists of three Squadrons, with one of them in a state more akin to a training (i.e. less combat-ready) squadron than the other two. In the Wing, there are a variety of offices designed to assist the Squadrons, even though the latter are able to go off to another location and function for a period of time all by themselves. The Wing has weapons, plans, standardization/ evaluation, intelligence and other functions centralized so that all Squadrons may call on them.

All of these functions, in addition to the Squadrons themselves, fall under the responsibility of the Deputy Commander for Operations, a full colonel like the Wing Commander and the Vice Wing Commander. In addition, the Deputy Commander for Maintenance provides all the necessary support to keep the aircraft flying. Each Fighter Squadron is mirrored by an Aircraft Generation Unit that provides the crew chiefs and other immediate support for the aircraft. Each plane has a crew chief, with an assistant or two, who take pride in their machine, ensuring that it is ready to fly and kept in top condition.

If necessary, the Fighter Squadron, with its maintenance unit, can deploy to another location and fly combat missions without the Wing staff. In the long run, however, the Wing provides centralized support and control.

UNITED STATES AIR FORCES EUROPE

USAFE is the finest air combat force in the world; that means I think that it is better than the Navy, the Marines, the Pacific Air Forces, Tactical Air Command, the RAF, the Soviet Air Force and anyone else who can go to war on a mass basis. Of course, the reasons stem primarily from the fact that for over 40 years it has been the leading edge of the West's stand against the Soviet threat, and all the others I mentioned do not have the same mission or money to create such a powerful force. So no one in the other services should take offence at what I have just said. Man for man, the pilots of the others compare favourably.

USAFE, as the primary arm of NATO air forces, maintains a string of fighter bases, with combat-ready Wings of F-15s, F-16s and F-111s, primarily in Germany and England. Although the Soviet threat is now much reduced, it still maintains powerful air forces, with superb fighter aircraft like the MiG-29 and Su-27 that are as good as or better than anything USAFE flies.

With better relations with the Soviet Union and the resulting budget cuts, USAFE will be reduced. The F-111s and A-10s will go home, but F-15Es will come to RAF Lakenheath to maintain a strike capability. LANTIRN-equipped F-16s will increase USAFE's all-weather performance. USAFE and the RAF will become more flexible and mobile, designed to move to other trouble spots and operate independently and, if necessary, with hard and precise impact. Bases will remain in caretaker status, with pre-positioned

Many USAFE F-16s are being modified to carry the Low Altitude Navigation and Targeting Infra-Red system for Night, or LANTIRN. The navigation pod permits automatic terrain-following by radar and the IR pod provides navigation vision and target identification. (General Dynamics)

support, ready to accept squadrons deployed from America and conduct deterrent or combat operations quickly. As US Army forces withdraw from Europe, much of USAFE will remain as the extension of American and NATO power.

THE RED RIVER RATS

The Red River of North Vietnam flows out of China, through Hanoi to the sea. If, during the Vietnam War, you flew a fighter north of that line, to the targets of Hanoi and Haiphong, you flew into one of the most heavily defended areas the world of war has ever known. There is no greater hero to me, in all of history, than a United States Air Force F-105 pilot who flew 100 missions up North or, worse, flew less than 100 and spent years in a North Vietnamese prison under torture and miserable loneliness. A story that every person, not just fighter pilots, should read is Jack Broughton's *Thud Ridge*: it will tell you about the soaring, searing achievement of these brave men.

After the war, with the pride of their accomplishment, and with so many comrades killed or missing, some of these pilots formed the Red River Valley Fighter Pilots Association, more commonly known as the 'River Rats'. Aside from the satisfaction of staying in touch through the newsletter and having frequent reunions, which continue to this day, the members of the association have made a great effort to raise scholarship money to send to college the children of those who never came home.

After some years, the association's charter, or qualified, members decided to let other Vietnam veterans become associates if they are invited by a charter member. As the scholarship motive and the membership slowly decline, let us hope that the Rats will find new ways to foster the ideals of the Fighter Pilot among the new members of the breed. They can be contacted at the Red River Valley Fighter Pilots Association, 6237 S. Greenwich Road, Derby, Kansas 67037.

AERIAL DEMONSTRATION TEAMS

Over the years there have been many jet demonstration teams. Some have proved to be temporary – just the best pilots in an operational squadron somewhere. A lot of countries see the value of having a team to 'show the flag', however, and show the public what their tax money creates. Even Jordan had a small team of Pitts Specials flying around a few years ago.

The 1974 Red Arrows: the author stands with Squadron Leader Ray Hannah and the Red Arrows after flying with them in a show at RAF Cranwell. The Gnat was a nimble little aircraft. (Author)

Today's Red Arrows. The nine Hawks of this famous display team replaced the Gnats in 1980. (British Aerospace)

Because they have the money to support a large team of nine F-16 first-line fighters, and they have been in the business since the early days, the USAF Thunderbirds are said by many to be the best of all the teams, providing a slick, professional show every time. But, national preference aside, other fighter pilots say that the RAF's Red Arrows have a special flexibility and verve that make them the best. Some years ago I travelled with a close friend who flew with the Thunderbirds and saw a lot of shows, but I have also had the opportunity to fly with the leader of the Red Arrows in a show at Cranwell, and I must say that they did things in a way that the Americans did not. Perhaps it was just the difference between

134

AERIAL DEMONSTRATION TEAMS

US Air Force	Thunderbirds	General Dynamics F-16A
US Navy	Blue Angels	McDonnell Douglas F-18B
United Kingdom	Red Arrows	British Aerospace Hawk
Canada	Snowbirds	Canadair CT-114
Italy	Frecce Tricolori	Aermacchi MB-339
France	La Patrouille de France	Dassault Alpha Jet
Portugal	Asas de Portugal	Cessna T-37C
Switzerland	La Patrouille Suisse	Hawker Hunter
Sweden	Team 60	Saab SK.60
Spain	Team Aquilla	Casa C-101 Aviojet
Yugoslavia	Flying Stars	Soko G-4 Super Galeb
Morocco	Green Marches	CAP 230
Ireland	Silver Swallows	Fouga Magister
Chile	Halcones	Extra 300
Japan	Blue Impulse	Mitsubushi T-2
India	Thunderbolts	Hawker Hunter
Singapore	Black Knights	McDonnell Douglas A-4
Australia	Roulettes	Pilatus PC-9
Brazil	Smoke Squadron	Embraer Tucano
New Zealand	Kiwi Red	McDonnell Douglas A-4
South Africa	Silver Falcons	Atlas Impala

the highly supervised, impressive Americans and the smaller, aggressive British, who had a little more freedom to be daring.

Others love the Italian Frecce Tricolori because of the romantic enthusiasm that shows up in their flying, or the Patrouille de France because of a certain panache. The Canadian Snowbirds fill the sky with aeroplanes and are fun to watch, and the Asas de Portugal are good too. But all these teams fly trainers, because they are cheaper to fly and easier to maintain. So I must give my vote to the Thunderbirds, although, for me, they have never had the same impact since they stopped flying the huge, noisy and powerful Phantom. Watch for the Soviet Su-27s!

The US Navy's Blue Angels – the only other team apart from the Thunderbirds to fly an operational fighter, the F/A-18 Hornet. The 'Blues', stationed at Pensacola, Florida, rival the Thunderbirds and the Red Arrows. (McDonnell Douglas)

THE USAF THUNDERBIRDS*

The Thunderbirds were activated at Luke Air Force Base in Arizona on 1 June 1953. In the ensuing years, they have displayed their aerial artistry for millions of spectators worldwide. Although the faces, names, aircraft and number of team members have changed over the years, the team's reason for being remains the same: to plan and present precision aerial manoeuvres demonstrating the capabilities of Air Force jet aircraft. Its men and women exhibit the exacting professional skills the Air Force develops in its people to fly and maintain a readiness capability to rapidly reconfigure and integrate their jets and people into a combat role if needed. The Thunderbirds history reflects the development of American air power in the jet age:

1953	F-84G Thunderjet
1956	F-100C Super Sabre
1964	F-105B Thunderchief
1969	F-4E Phantom II
1974	T-38A Talon
1983	F-16A Fighting Falcon

Training for the entire team takes place from mid-November to mid-March, in preparation for the show season. It is both concentrated and rigorous. The months of intensive training and careful planning come down to this: with hundreds of thousands of people watching, six Thunderbirds pilots and aircraft will weave their magic in the blue sky.

The pilots hone their skills to a fine edge through a highly structured training programme. Starting with basic two-ship formations, they progress through the complete air demonstration sequence until flying their aircraft with exquisite precision becomes second nature. The new Thunderbirds pilots learn the fundamentals of flying tight, precise formations; they work to perfect their timing; and, most importantly, they develop a high degree of confidence and trust in each other and their leader. Maximum-performance take-offs, 'lazy eights', rolls, loops and whifferdills are all flown with minimum wing-tip clearance in formations of four, five or six aircraft.

Highly trained technicians, expert in more than 32 Air Force career fields, fine-tune the aircraft prior to their departure from Nellis Air Force Base. A selected group of these exceptional technicians and support specialists travels to each show site to ensure that these aircraft remain in top condition, ready for a

---

* This extract is quoted from *USAF Thunderbirds: 1990*, a product of the USAF Air Demonstration Squadron, Box 9733, Nellis AFB, Nevada 89191.

Right: Thunderbird Four's view from the cockpit. Flying the slot, Four must watch three aircraft at once during a variety of manoeuvres. (USAF Thunderbirds)
Below: Thunderbirds take-off. The F-16, with all its power, puts on an impressive display. (USAF Thunderbirds)

flawless performance. The Thunderbirds' air demonstration is more than an aerial ballet, choreographed purely for spectator entertainment. It also represents a practical demonstration of the skills and techniques each US Air Force tactical fighter pilot holds. Each flight manoeuvre represents a carefully selected blend of aerobatics and combat tactical manoeuvres, performed with Thunderbirds flair within the constraints of a live-audience air demonstration.

In 37 years, only 185 officers have worn the Thunderbirds emblem. While the reasons for joining the élite team have been expressed in many different words, pride is one word that seems to explain it best – pride in being a key part of what the Thunderbirds represent.

VIII

FIGHTER HISTORY

I T IS THE look back at history that motivates us to the future. We study the great events and people in fighter aviation, challenged by both war and peace, and we see what we must do to keep going, to survive all the impediments to progress that lie ahead. We learn that we must continue to grow, to develop technology, to train better, to fight bureaucracy, to stay ahead of our enemies, to be strong in peace and war. We know that democracy is stronger than the other forms of government, that in recent years the people have had enough wisdom to maintain a strong military establishment in a dangerous world. But it has not always been so, and we must always guard against those who want us to be weak and give the world to the tyrants.

History is full of wonderful things, and, without exaggerating their importance, we can say that fighter pilots have a brave and spontaneous little history of their own – one that illuminates some of the best characteristics to be found in mankind.

THE FIGHTER IN WAR

The fighter aircraft was not a major factor in the First World War – it was too new, too weak, too uncertain about what it was supposed to do. Yet the war laid the foundation for the major missions that air power would perform in all future wars. Between the wars, the air power theorists and leaders, like Douhet, Mitchell, Trenchard and others, sorted out the ways to use the new weapon, overcome

The Albatros DV was an attempt by the German Air Force to improve on a successful WWI design and to maintain the superiority over the Western Front first gained by the Albatros DIII.

P-47 Thunderbolt. Republic's versatile World War II fighter performed well in long-range escort fighter and ground-attack operations. (Cradle of Aviation Museum)

the resistance of the armies and the bureaucrats, and prepared the nuclei of the huge air forces that would quickly grow to fill the needs of the Second World War.

In the First World War the fighters began to take 'pot shots' at each other with pistols and rifles to try to prevent reconnaissance, but nothing much else happened. Then, in a revolutionary technological breakthrough. Anthony Fokker, a Dutchman working for the Germans, created a system that would enable a machine gun to fire through a propeller arc without hitting the blades. Air-to-air combat was born. Fighters were also used to drop grenades and small bombs on enemy troops, and some strategic bombing with larger aircraft was developed. But the armies were too huge, too well dug into the mud, like great elephants, to be influenced much by these aerial insects buzzing over them.

In the Second World War it was different. The bombers developed enough range and carrying power to fulfil Douhet's vision of strategic attack on the enemy heartland. Cities and war industries were totally destroyed. Fighters ranged over the battle area and its hinterland, destroying rail and road traffic, supplies, troops, tanks, guns, headquarters, airfields. Fighters also developed the range and speed to intercept or escort bombers, and to fight against each other for the freedom to do these things. In contrast to the First World War, the ground war could not have been won without maintenance of control of the air over Europe. Japan, of course,

The Messerschmitt 109 was the mainstay of the German Fighter Arm throughout WWII and in its earlier variants was an exceptional fighter. Up to the late summer of 1942 it was still superior to anything else flying.

139

F-105 'Thuds' from Korat bomb North Vietnam. The Vietnam War demonstrated the vulnerability of the fast jet to determined anti-aircraft fire. (US National Archives)

was different, because it was the bombers, and 'The Bomb', that achieved victory without an invasion.

In the smaller wars that followed – in Korea, Vietnam, the Middle East and elsewhere – the limitations of air power became more apparent, as other factors on the ground and in the halls of diplomacy prevented control of the air from achieving total victory – until, finally, in a unique little war that was perfectly designed for the aeroplane, high technology and overwhelming firepower destroyed the enemy before the ground war even began.

Moving a decade into the era of jets and nuclear bombers, air force planners began to envisage huge, long-range, unmanoeuvrable, Mach 3 interceptors with missiles to match. They put in computers, took out the guns, and thought about taking out the man, until suddenly, in Vietnam, the supersonic fighters found themselves trying to out-turn each other at 300kt in old-fashioned dogfights. So, today, the prototypes of the fighters of the next century once again turn like 1914–18 fighters and carry powerful guns and dogfight missiles as well as the longer-range radar kind. Fighters started to fly alone, then gathered into groups and then

The bottom of a well-armed Phantom. Air-to-air missiles are carried recessed in wells under the fuselage, air-to-ground rockets are carried on the wing racks, conventional bombs are carried on the centerline and fuel tanks are carried on the outboard stations. (US National Archives)

Bitburg F-15Cs in flight over Germany. The F-15 at Bitburg has been the primary interceptor of USAFE for 15 years, joined by others at Soesterberg in the Netherlands. (USAF 36th TFW)

into armadas, but now, with power and manoeuvrability, they once again fly alone or in pairs to perform their mission of intercept or strike. But one thing never changes: the fighter pilot is still in control, and he is the one factor around which everything else is designed.

CHUCK YEAGER BREAKS THE SOUND BARRIER
14 OCTOBER 1947*

Bob Cardenas, the B-29 driver, asked if I was ready.

'Hell, yes,' I said. 'Let's get it over with.'

He dropped the X-1 at 2,000 feet, but his dive speed was once again too slow and the X-1 started to stall. I fought it with the control wheel for about five hundred feet, and finally got her nose down. The moment we picked up speed I fired all four rocket chambers in rapid sequence. We climbed at .99 Mach and began to buffet, so I flipped the stabilizer switch and changed the setting two degrees. We smoothed right out, and at 36,000 feet, I turned off two rocket chambers. At 40,000 feet, we were still climbing at a speed of .92 Mach. Leveling off at 42,000 feet, I had thirty percent of my fuel, so I turned on rocket chamber three and immediately reached .96 Mach. I noticed that the faster I got, the smoother the ride.

Suddenly the Mach needle began to fluctuate. It went up to .965 Mach – then tipped right off the scale. I thought I was seeing things! We were flying supersonic! And it was as smooth as a baby's bottom: Grandma could be sitting up there sipping lemonade. I kept the speed off the scale for about twenty seconds, then raised the nose to slow down.

---

* From *Yeager: An Autobiography* by Chuck Yeager and Leo Janos (US: Bantam Books, division of Bantam, Doubleday, Dell Publishing Group; Commonwealth: Hutchinson), pp. 129–130.

I was thunderstruck. After all the anxiety, breaking the sound barrier turned out to be a perfectly paved speedway. I radioed Jack in the B-29. 'Hey, Ridley, that Machmeter is acting screwy. It just went off the scale on me.'

'Fluctuated off?'

'Yeah, at point nine-six-five.'

'Son, you is imagining things.'

'Must be. I'm still wearing my ears and nothing else fell off, neither.'

The guys in the NACA tracking van interrupted to report that they heard what sounded like a distant rumble of thunder: my sonic boom! The first one by an airplane ever heard on earth. The X-1 was supposedly capable of reaching nearly twice the speed of sound but the Machmeter aboard only registered to 1.0 Mach, which showed how much confidence they had; I estimated I had reached 1.05 Mach. (Later data showed it was 1.07 Mach — 700 mph).

And that was it. I sat up there feeling kind of numb, but elated. After all the anticipation to achieve this moment, it really was a let-down. It took a damned instrument meter to tell me what I'd done.

FIGHTER PILOT BOOKS

THEORY AND PRACTICE

The Ace Factor: Air Combat and the Role of Situational Awareness, by Mike Spick (England: Airlife, 1988). A good historical analysis of what it takes to be one.

Air Power: Aircraft, Weapons Systems and Technology Series (London: Brassey's, late 1980s). Nine-volume series by senior RAF leaders, especially the volumes on air superiority, air defence, ECM and air-to-ground and the Vol. 1 survey of roles.

Combat Missions: From the Cockpit, by Ken Delve (London: Arms and Armour Press, 1990). Insider's realistic view of RAF fighter and support missions, emphasizing crew duties.

Fighter Combat: The Art and Science of Air-to-Air Combat, by Robert L. Shaw (England: Patrick Stephens, 1985). The 'Bible' of air combat – the complete, expert textbook by a fighter pilot.

Fighter Missions, by Bill Gunston and Lindsay Peacock (London: Guild Publishing/Salamander Books, 1989). Best-yet survey of seven different fighter missions, with simulated combat scenario for each.

Fighter Pilot Tactics: The Techniques of Daylight Air Combat, by Mike Spick (Wellingborough, England: Patrick Stephens, 1983). Well-researched history and analysis of the major conflicts.

Flying Modern Jet Fighters, by Robert Jackson (Wellingborough, England: Patrick Stephens, 1986). Harrier, Tornado, Hawk, F-14, F-111, F-4 and a good chapter on air superiority fighters.

Hungry Tigers: The Fighter Pilot's Role in Modern Warfare, by Frank J. O'Brien (Blue Ridge Summit, Tenn: 1986). All the missions, with an F-4 accent, by a Vietnam veteran.

In the Cockpit: Flying the World's Greatest Aircraft, edited by Anthony Robinson (London: Orbis Publications, 1979). Pilots' descriptions of flying Harrier, F-4, A-4, F-86, F9F, A-1, Me 109, Me 262 etc., plus bombers, transports.

Jet Fighter Performance: Korea to Vietnam, by Mike Spick (London: Ian Allan Ltd, 1986). Well-illustrated and readable analysis of technology.

The Story of Air Fighting (revised edition of *First Circle*), by J. E. 'Johnnie' Johnson (England: Hutchinson, 1985). Historical analysis of fighter combat by the WWII ace who became an air marshal. Excellent!

HISTORY

Air War Hanoi, by Robert F. Dorr (London: Blandford Press, 1988). Fine illustrated history.

Air War South Vietnam, by Robert F. Dorr (London: Arms and Armour Press, 1990). Companion volume to previous book.

Famous Fighter Aces, by Bryan Philpott (Wellingborough, England: Patrick Stephens, 1989). Readable summaries, each of a few pages.

Fight for the Sky, by Douglas Bader (New York: Doubleday, 1973). The great fighter pilot's own story of the Hurricane and the Spitfire.

Fighter Pilot: Aerial Combat Aces from 1914 to the Present Day, edited by Stanley M. Ulanoff (New York: Prentice Hall, 1986). Anthology of writings by aces.

Fighter: The Story of the Battle of Britain, by Len Deighton (London: Jonathan Cape, 1977; also a UK Collins/Grafton paperback, 1990). The ability of the novelist shines through in this well-researched and readable history.

The Right Stuff, by Tom Wolfe (New York: Farrar, Straus, Giroux, 1979). The astronauts and Yeager, written with panache.

They Fought for the Sky, by Quentin Reynolds (London: Cassell, 1958). Favourite summary of WWI air combat.

The United States Air Force in Korea: 1950–1953, by Robert F. Futrell (Washington DC: Office of Air Force History, USAF, 1983). The definitive history in 700 pages.

Wolfpack: Hunting MiGs over Vietnam, by Jerry Scutts (Shrewsbury, England: Airlife, 1987). Story of Robin Olds and the 8th Tactical Fighter Wing during the war.

PERSONAL STORIES

Baa Baa Black Sheep, by Gregory 'Pappy' Boyington (New York: Putnam). Book by the Flying Tiger and Pacific ace (the TV series was fun but lost the flavour).

F-4 Phantom: A Pilot's Story, by Robert Prest (London: Cassell, 1979). Superbly written description of life in the great fighter in the RAF.

The First and the Last, by Adolf Galland (London: Methuen, 1955; Germany 1953). The Luftwaffe leader tells of his battles with the Allied air forces and of Nazi incompetence.

Going Downtown: The War against Hanoi and Washington, by Jack Broughton (New York: Orion Books, 1988). F-105 commander's Air Force career and his battle against political restrictions in Vietnam. See also his earlier book, *Thud Ridge*.

Reach for the Sky, by Paul Brickhill (Glasgow: Collins, 1957). Story of Douglas Bader.

Stranger to the Ground, by Richard Bach (New York: Harper & Row, 1963). The first book by the author of *Jonathan Livingston Seagull*, a realistic description of an F-84 flight across Europe. A testament to flying.

Wing Leader, by J. E. 'Johnnie' Johnson (London: Goodall Publications, 1990; originally 1956). The great RAF WWII ace and leader.

Yeager, by Chuck Yeager and Leo Janos (New York: Bantam Books, 1985). The life story of the man who broke the sound barrier.

FICTION

Flight of the Intruder, by Stephen Coonts (Annapolis: Naval Institute Press, 1986). Authentic and well-written story of A-6 pilot attacking North Vietnam. Made into a movie.

Steel Tiger, by Mark Berent (New York: Putnam, 1990). Authentic story of Vietnam air combat by a three-tour veteran.

SOME GREAT FIGHTER PILOT FILMS

The plot and the acting may not always be great, but the flying scenes make up for this. Best of all – *The Right Stuff.* On the ground or in space, the astronauts were fighter pilots.

Wings (1927; Silent; Gary Cooper, Buddy Rogers). First Academy Award.

Flying Tigers (1942; John Wayne, Paul Kelly). Yanks in China.

Spitfire (1942; Leslie Howard, David Niven). Story of the designer.

Flying Leathernecks (1951; John Wayne, Robert Ryan). Marines in WWII.

The Bridges at Toko-Ri (1954; William Holden, Grace Kelly). Korean War Navy pilots.

Reach for the Sky (1956; Kenneth More, Nigel Green). Story of Douglas Bader.

The Blue Max (1966; George Peppard, Ursula Andress). Lone German in WWI.

The Battle of Britain (1969; Laurence Olivier, Michael Caine, many others). WWII Epic.

Tora! Tora! Tora! (1970; Many US and Japanese actors). Up to Pearl Harbor.

The Right Stuff (1983; Sam Shepard and the Seven). Yeager and the astronauts.

Top Gun (1986; Tom Cruise, Kelly McGillis). Brash Navy pilot.

The Flight of the Intruder (1991). Navy A-6 over Vietnam.

T-38 Thunderbirds, here over the Hoover Dam near their home at Nellis Air Force Base outside Las Vegas. It was a great satisfaction for student pilots in the 1960s and 1970s to fly the same aircraft as the Thunderbirds, as astronauts (for proficiency and cross-country flying) and as combat pilots (F-5 single-seat version). (USAF Thunderbirds)

144

POEMS

The troubles of our proud and angry dust
    are from eternity, and they shall not fail.
Shoulder the sky, my lad
    and drink your ale.

A. E. Housman,
Last Poems, 1922

A steed, a steed of matchless speed!
    A sword of metal keen!
All else to noble hearts is dross,
    All else on earth is mean.

Robert Cunningham-Graham,
'Cavalier's Song', c.1920

FLIGHT OF THE SABRE JET

Then, suddenly, the band of tempered steel was gone;
I screamed defiance at the Universe . . . Mach One!
I caught Time's wings and fettered them,
With bolder searching hand I touched the hem
Of Dawn's empurpled robe of grace
And flesh-free, soul-borne rose to conquer space.
Then in my car of silvered fire-motion
Pursued the sparking tail of Comet through the Ocean
Of Cloud. Looked down the passage on a world to be,
Fed at the breast of Knowledge, stained her white knee
With thwarted-angel tears. And from the macrocosmic view
Saw souls ascending . . . glowing . . . new.

Then whirling, soaring, arching looked at Noon
And turned in ceaseless circles round the Moon.
I bludgeoned Earth's eternal pull, assailed a Star,
Beat off foul Flux and Change, and turning from afar
Swooped down. Headlong on that great arc of speed,
I saw where Thunderheads are born and feed.
Drew quarrels of Force at the quiver of God.
And launched them down to scorch the sod
Where earth-bound mortals met for the comedy of Day.
From my bold vantage point I laughed and turned away.
Laughed loud for Man how harnessed Might,
But never shared the passion of my Flight.

Ronald R. Jeffels,
Air University Quarterly Review, 1954

P-51

It fills the sky like wind made visible
And given voice like drums through amplifiers,
Too great a terror to be lost on death
Remembering that all our dreams are fliers.

This terror, cannoned as the hawk is billed,
Taloned with lusty boys who love their toy,
Mounts on the living energy of grace
Whose passing cracks on burning lathes of joy.

Piston by piston they made fumes of flight
Frenzy the startled air her passing sears.
Fast as a head can turn from East to West
She summons distances and disappears.

That moment only – glancing up and gone –
And see, her boy outburns the burning year.
And we are clod and pasture fixed upon
Her birth above the hills like a crowd's cheer.

John Ciardi,
Poetry, May 1945

A PILOT'S POEM

If you are able,
save for them a place inside of you
and save one backward glance
when you are leaving
for the places they can no longer go.
Be not ashamed to say you loved them
though you may or may not have always.
Take what they have left
and what they have taught you
with their dying
and keep it with your own.
And in that time
when men decide and feel safe
to call the War insane,
take one moment to embrace
those gentle heroes you left behind.

*Written on 1 January 1970 by Major
Michael O'Donnell, who was killed in
action on 24 March 1970 while flying a
rescue helicopter in Cambodia, and
quoted in MiG Sweep, the newsletter of
the Red River Valley Fighter Pilots
Association, Fall 1985.*

146

FIGHTER PILOT SONGS

These songs are taken from the extensive collection in *The Wild Blue Yonder: Songs of the Air Force* (The Redwood Press, PO Box 3323, San Mateo, Ca 94403, or by purchase through the Red River Valley Fighter Pilots Association). There is a Volume II, 'Stag Bar Edition', but caution is urged if it is used in the presence of children. Look also for the recordings of Dick Jonas, an F-4 pilot in Vietnam, and Oscar Brand, who made several fighter pilot records in the 1950s.

THE AIR FORCE SONG

Off we go into the wild blue yonder,
Climbing high into the sun;
Here they come zooming to meet our thunder,
At 'em boys, give 'er the gun!
Down we dive spouting our flame from under
Off on one helluva row!
We live in fame or go down in flame,
Nothing'll stop the Air Corps now.

Minds of men fashioned a crate of thunder,
Sent it high into the blue;
Hands of men blasted the world asunder,
How they lived God only knew!
Souls of men dreaming of skies to conquer
Gave us wings, ever to soar.
With scouts before and bombs galore,
Nothing'll stop the Army Air Corps!

Off we go into the wild blue yonder,
Keep the wings level and true.
If you'd live to be a grey haired wonder,
Keep the nose out of the blue!
Flying men guarding the nation's border,
We'll be there followed by more.
In echelon, we'll carry on! Boy!
Nothing'll stop the Army Air Corps!

Major Robert M. Crawford
Carl Fischer Inc. Copyright, 1939

Set to music, this became the official song of the United States Air Force, changing the last three words to 'US Air Force!'.

World War I

STAND TO YOUR GLASSES

We stand 'neath resounding rafters,
The walls around us are bare,
They echo back our laughter,
It seems that the dead are all there.

CHORUS
Stand to your glasses steady,
This world is a world full of lies.
Here's a health to the dead already,
Hurrah for the next man to die.

Denied by the land that bore us,
Betrayed by the ones we hold dear,
The good have all gone before us,
And only the dull are still here.

We loop in the purple twilight,
We spin in the silvery dawn,
With a trail of smoke behind us,
To show where our comrades have gone.

In flaming Spad and Camel,
With wings of wood and steel,
For mortal stakes we gamble,
With cards that are stacked for the deal.

World War II

GIVE ME OPERATIONS

Just give me operations,
Back home on some lonely atoll,
For I am too young to die,
I just want to go home.

Don't give me a P-38,
The props they counter-rotate;
They're scattered and smitten,
From Burma to Britain,
Don't give me a P-38.

Don't give me an old Thunderbolt,
It gave many pilot a jolt,
It looks like jug,
And it flies like a tug,
Don't give me an old Thunderbolt.

Don't give me a P-51,
It was all right for fighting the Hun,
But with coolant tank dry,
You'll run out of sky,
Don't give me a P-51.

*The poem continues in similar
vein, commenting on various
aircraft up to the present day.*

Korea

HALLELUJAH!

CHORUS
*Sing hallelujah! Sing hallelujah!
Throw a nickel on the grass,
Save a fighter pilot's ass.
Sing hallelujah! Sing hallelujah!
Throw a nickel on the grass,
And you'll be saved.*

Cruising down the Yalu,
Doing three-twenty per,
I called to my Flight Leader,
'Oh, won't you save me, Sir?
Got two big flak holes in my wing,
My tanks ain't got no gas.
Mayday, Mayday, Mayday,
I've got six MiGs on my ass.

The boys up from Misawa,
Think they are so hot.
They brag about the 'Bluetails'
That they have often shot.
One thing they don't remember,
Whenever they holler and hoot,
Is to look into their mirror.
Just before they shoot.

I flew my traffic pattern,
To me it looked all right.
My airspeed read one-thirty,
My God, I racked it tight!
I turned onto the final,
My engine gave a wheeze.
Mayday, Mayday, Mayday,
Spin instructions, please.

Vietnam

SONG OF THE WOLF PACK

Oh, pilots of the Wolf Pack,
Go to the briefing room.
This mission is a good one,
To the MiGs it will mean doom.
We're going up to Hanoi,
To Kep and Phuc Yen, too,
To write our bloody record,
In the annals of the blue.

We take off in our Phantoms,
To play our deadly cards.
The engines make our thunder,
And our eyes are steely hard.
We're on the way to battle,
The forces of the foe.
We're certain to destroy them,
We'll seek them high and low.

We battle today, and make our kills.
The Wolf Pack in the sky.

We cycle through the tanker,
The tension starts to rise.
We go to meet our destiny,
Awaiting in the skies.
We tune and arm our missiles,
As we streak across the black.
Our boss is in the forefront,
Leading the Wolf Pack.

We're showing on their radar.
Their hearts are full of hate.
They rise to meet our challenge,
To meet their bloody fate.
They're headed for disaster,
As any fool can tell.
They dare to face the Wolf Pack,
We'll shoot them clear to hell!

We battle today, and make our kills.
The Wolf Pack in the sky.

Wolf Pack lead says, 'Contact'.
They're MiGs, a flight of two.
I'm too close for the Sparrow,
The Sidewinder will do.
I'll roll into the six o'clock,
Behind the trailing MiG,
And let him have a missile,
Just like a fiery Gig.

Oh, other flights engaged more MiGs,
Hot action filled the air.
The Wolf Pack's lust was sated,
Before heading for their lair.
The enemy won't soon forget
The awesome deadly toll,
As the 8th Wing troops return to base,
And make their victory roll.

We battle today, and make our kills.
The Wolf Pack in the sky.

This song, of the 8th Tactical Fighter Wing at Ubon, Thailand, may not be great music now, but at the time, sitting around the bar after a combat mission, it gave the men something to do and was good for a laugh. I once recorded four hours of songs I collected from all the Wings in South-East Asia for General George Brown, our commander, and we gave copies to a lot of people. Together they told a whole, interesting history of the air war – planes and people and events – in ways that never got into the history books. I lost mine. Anyone have one?

IX

FIGHTER WARS

O VER TIME we have learned that it is imperative to maintain control of the air over a land or sea battle. Most forces engaged in war will have some kind of air power that poses a serious threat to the opposing side. Thus almost all war depends on tactical air power, on the fighter pilot, for its outcome. A fighter pilot can't stop an ICBM or a Viet Cong guerrilla, but in most cases he can make a big difference in the ability of the enemy's army, or his own, to fight, either by attacking the enemy ground forces or by preventing the enemy air force from attacking his own.

In the four decisive air battles outlined below, the fighter pilot was the decisive factor. Contrast these to the Vietnam War, where his efforts, however valiant, were restricted and the war was lost partially as a result. In another contrast, largely because of the lessons of Vietnam, the Gulf War was won with a textbook application of modern air power. For once, instead of fighting the last war, we learned what we did wrong and did not repeat the mistakes. Even more important, we advanced to new strategy and technology without error.

War is a great stimulus to technological development, and to the budgets that support it. The message of the Gulf War, and of this whole book, is that fighter pilots are important, that their new technology – new cockpits, new weapons, new delivery systems –

The Fleet Air Arm fighter pilot was crucial to the outcome of the 1982 Falklands War. His mount was the BAe Sea Harrier, which achieved results out of all proportion to its numbers. Two FRS.1s are seen here. (British Aerospace)

and their superior training, skill and aggressiveness can be decisive factors in warfare. The nation that allows its fighter force to stagnate, to lose the technological edge, to weaken the key elements of motivation, spirit and leadership, may some day pay a terrible price.

DECISIVE AIR BATTLES

Although the First World War did provide some major air engagements, none of them played a decisive role in the outcome on the ground. It took more than the limited firepower of these early aeroplanes to upset the grand armies embedded in the muddy line across the centre of Europe.

In the Second World War things were immediately different. In Europe, Hitler's initial *Blitzkrieg* against Russia and the West took place in the air as well as on the ground. The shock of massive air attacks accompanied and reinforced the mobile devastation inflicted by the tank divisions. Lacking a front on the ground, the Japanese used carrier air power to shock the United States and destroy a large part of the Pacific Fleet. The war then produced two monumental air battles, each of which saved the West, turned the tide, showed the new importance of air power and depended on fighter pilots to win great victories. After that, except for the long but inconclusive bombing campaigns against Germany and Japan, air power never achieved the same dramatic decisiveness in the war.

Thirty years later, the fighter pilots of Israel, along with their brothers in the tanks, proved to be the deciding factor in saving the country from being overwhelmed by superior Arab forces. And then, a decade after that, the fighter pilots of Great Britain fought off those of Argentina to win the Falklands War.

Looking back now at these four engagements, it is clear that air power, and fighter pilots, were the overwhelming factor in great victories. In the first three, at least, the winners were in grave danger of losing their ability to defend themselves against being overrun and totally defeated. In the last, the outcome caused the fall of the Argentine military government (and had Britain lost, the Thatcher government would have been brought down). There have been other occasions in history when the use of air power has been important, but in none of these has the outcome been so dependent on air power and so vital to the very survival of the combatants.

The Battle of Midway
After Pearl Harbor, and the destruction of a major portion of the US Pacific Fleet, the Japanese moved a superior force to capture

Midway Island as a preface to an invasion of the Hawaiian Islands. This could have led to the blockade of the US West Coast, possibly worse, and turned the Pacific into a Japanese lake, making it impossible ever to mount an attack on Japan. The fighter pilots of the US Navy, after four unsuccessful attacks with heavy losses, suddenly turned the tide, destroying all four of the Japanese aircraft carriers with dive-bomb attacks. The Japanese Fleet withdrew, and thereafter was never able to stop the inexorable advance of American forces that brought the B-29s within range of Japanese cities and the end of the war.

The Battle of Britain

Everyone knows that story: Hitler needed to conquer Britain so that he could turn to his great enemy, Russia, with his rear protected from a future US invasion. Only 'The Few', the outnumbered Hurricane and Spitfire pilots of several nations, prevented him from taking control of the air over Britain and enabling a sea invasion to be mounted against a weakened British Army. With better German leadership and strategy, and less resolve by Fighter Command, the battle probably would have turned the other way. It was a very near thing, but the fighter pilots chopped away at the German air fleets until Hitler saw no use in further attack and losses. As a result, the islands remained free, and served as the launching pad for the massive Allied attack which destroyed the German Army and won the war.

The Yom Kippur War

In 1973 Egypt and Syria attacked Israel with a massive tank force, supported by large air forces and a superior air defence network of advanced Soviet missiles. On the eighth day of the 19-day war, the

Despite its low quality, this photograph demonstrates well the advantages of effective camouflage. At first glance only the upper F-4E is apparent: had the photo been taken from a higher altitude or from a more oblique angle then these Phantoms would be virtually impossible to spot over the Israeli landscape. The F-4 was an important aircraft for the Israelis in their war against the Arab forces. (McDonnell Douglas)

154

Israeli Air Force flew 1,000 missions over the largest tank battle since the Second World War. The nation was in danger of being overrun by the surprise attack, but the Air Force, with new ECM pods and tactics, managed to carry the attack to the enemy while the ground forces tenaciously held on, recovered and mounted a successful counter-attack. Eventually the politicians put an end to it, but in the early stages it was the fighter pilots who made the difference and saved the Army, and thus the nation.

The Falklands War

The Falklands War may seem in retrospect a 'teapot' war, not so important in military or world history, yet on its outcome depended the fate of the two governments involved (although not, of course, the nations themselves). By losing, the Argentine generals were toppled from power and democracy began an unsteady return. By winning, the Conservative Government remained in power in Britain for the remainder of the decade, conducting a major revolution in the way Britain functioned. All this hinged on a tiny force of ships and men, protected by a handful of just twenty Harriers, without an early warning system, against the brave, long-range air attacks of the numerically superior Argentine Air Force and their deadly Exocet missiles. Thanks to superior training and a driving confidence and will to win, the British pilots fought off the heavy air attacks and just saved the invasion fleet. Eventually, despite serious British ship losses, the air attacks died off and the ground forces were able to capture the islands. Once again, against great odds, the British fighter pilot demonstrated the value of courage, skill and determination as decisive factors in air combat.

COMBAT MISSIONS: VIETNAM

Very few fighter pilots saw as much of the air war in Vietnam as I did. I never saw a SAM or a MiG, and I was never called upon to enter 'Route Pack Six', the heavily-defended area around Hanoi, none of which I regret. I did, however, have the unusual experience of flying all four USAF models of the F-4 in combat, flying missions in South Vietnam, North Vietnam, Laos and Cambodia. In addition to the C and D in the South, I flew the E model up north; I also flew a dozen RF-4C reconnaissance missions out of Saigon and several F-4 strike missions from other bases while serving nearly a year as the Aide and Executive Officer to the Vice Commander of the US Air Forces in Vietnam. This kept me current in the aeroplane between combat tours. Thus, I had the unique opportunity to fly a wide range of missions throughout the battle area, and to witness at

Phantom gunsight over Vietnam. This is the simple, pre-computer gunsight in the F-4C, looking at beautiful Cam Ranh Bay, South Vietnam. The mils dialled in on the left tilt the glass so that the pipper, projected from below, moves to the proper position for the weapon being used. (Author)

close hand the briefings, planning and highest-level command operations of the air war in the headquarters as well. In addition, I flew frequently as an observer on combat missions in the O-1, O-2 and OV-10 FAC (Forward Air Controller) aircraft, the A-1E Skyraider, the AC-47 gunship and army UH-1 helicopter. I visited every USAF base in Vietnam and Thailand, and spent many hours talking with the General about the air war. It was always most interesting to go out and fly an F-4 strike mission and then come back to Saigon and hear about the operation in the command briefings. Sometimes the loss in translation was quite remarkable.

After Vietnam, I flew the airplane for four years in NATO, with a different variety of air-to-air, conventional and nuclear missions. It all shows what a truly versatile and great weapon system the F-4 was, for nearly 30 years. Today, the F-16, with one pilot and improved avionics, has a similar diversified capability. Here are the missions I flew in 1969–70:

Close air support
When the Army on the ground had a TIC (Troops in Contact) with the enemy, they often called for air support through the Direct Air Support Centre or the FAC who was working with them. We would fly in flights of two or four Phantoms to specific coordinates and then look for the FAC orbiting the target area. The weather was often bad, making it difficult to find him, keep everyone in sight, look out for the constant air traffic, and get the weapons on the target, especially at night. The ground commander liked 'snake and nape', where we carried cans of napalm on the wing stations and high-drag Snake-eye bombs on the centre-line. These could be delivered down to a few hundred feet on low-angle passes over the

more typical, but less accurate, 30 degree dive bomb attack with slick bombs. We were more likely to take small-arms hits on these low level passes, despite a delivery speed of 500 plus knots. When I flew low-angle bomb missions in the slow, World War II-vintage A-1E Skyraider, I was not at all comfortable with how long it took a particular tree to go by, wondering why some VC (Viet Cong, Victor Charlie) didn't step out and shoot me in the forehead with a pistol. That extra 300 knots makes a world of difference. But in either case, there is a wealth of satisfaction in putting your weapons on the bad guys when your own troops are up against it. Flying around at low level in an OV-10 and watching those poor grunts walking around in the hot jungle, when you can go back home to your air-conditioned bed and bar, makes you highly motivated to help them all you can.

The only VC I ever saw the whole time I was there was on my very first combat mission: wearing the standard black pyjamas, he ran out and took off just before I put a can of napalm through the front door. We didn't concern ourselves much about killing the enemy; we had heard enough stories about what they did to innocent civilians or what they would do to us if they captured us, and we were highly motivated to help the Army. Many a trooper bought me a beer in Saigon on learning what I did for a living.

Ground alert

We had half-a-dozen fighter wings strung the length of South Vietnam, and one of our missions at Cam Ranh Bay, in the middle of the country, was to keep three two-ship flights on five minute alert 24 hours a day. With two wing tanks, we could reach both the Southern Mekong Delta and the DMZ on the North Vietnamese border. Sitting around in the alert shack, sleeping at night in our *g*-suits and boots, a few feet from our aircraft, we would launch instantly on TIC or other immediate requests from the Army. We sometimes flew three two-hour missions in an eight-hour tour, jumping from one aircraft to another loaded one when the action was heavy. There is nothing quite like being dead asleep, to be awakened by an awful, ear-shattering Klaxon horn and a loud-speaker shouting: *"Three and Four, out the door"*, scrambling into the cockpit 15 seconds later, starting engines while strapping-in and trying both to wake up and relax, then launching into the murk at 3am. You don't stay sleepy very long when you are suddenly rolling down the runway at 150 knots with a max-loaded 50,000 pounds of bombs and fuel, off to get shot-at and to save some guys out in the middle of the jungle. Dropping bombs at low altitude at night is Really Exciting. They fire some flares into the soggy atmosphere, and it feels like you are flying around in a bowl, the dangerous milk-bowl effect, wondering which way is up, one eye in the cockpit and the other trying to see everything and everyone else out there in the darkness. But, maybe you are saving some kid's life, and after getting all pumped-up, you are disappointed if you get there and nothing happens. Killing the enemy is your reason for being, and your strongest motivation.

Sky Spot

This was the mission we hated: a boring, wasteful 'milk-run' at high altitude. When weather was bad, they directed us with the old SAC bomb scoring radar and gave us a kind of high-altitude GCA and a countdown to pickle (bomb release). It was the same system they used to guide the B-52s, which typically came across in flights of three from Guam or Thailand to drop 108 500-pounders apiece. After dumping the whole load from two or four F-4s into the clouds at 20,000 feet, we went home thoroughly dissatisfied. Almost all fighter pilots in Vietnam were eager for action, the tougher the better, especially when the FAC or later the Army gave you some specific and meaningful results of the effort. Spraying bombs on the jungle with wishful thinking was usually unproductive, although there were occasional solid targets, or surprising secondary explosions. I once flew over the jungle in a helicopter a minute after a B-52 strike and the deep plowing of the earth for thousands of yards was devastating, but only to the trees. The same weapon against an Iraqi Maginot line would be more appropriate.

LZ prep

We would prepare a landing zone for Army helicopters by dropping a couple of 2000-pound bombs in the middle of the jungle. The blast would knock down all the trees for a few hundred feet and also alert any VC in the area that something was about to happen. It seemed like a waste of a valuable mission but I guess the Army needed the space.

Interdiction (easy)

There were lots of places where we just went and dropped bombs in the jungle, trying to blow up supplies that someone thought might be there, along the supply trails that laced southern Laos and North Vietnam. There wasn't much gunfire, and there wasn't much in the way of results, either. Once, in Cambodia, I looked down from 500 feet directly at the orange muzzle flashes from a four-barrel 23mm gun, and I was glad I was doing 600 knots at the time. The guy had obviously never shot ducks. It was very frustrating to have to go after supplies strung out in the jungle in little piles because the political leaders were afraid of antagonising the Russians or the Chinese by hitting the same supplies when they were concentrated on ships or trucks in Haiphong harbour, or on the main rail and road arteries coming out of China.

Interdiction (hard)

It was more dangerous to try to cut the roads in northern Laos, and the passes into North Vietnam along which the larger trucks travelled at night. Here the guns were much bigger, 37mm, 57mm, 85, even 100mm shells, often radar guided, which could knock a Phantom out of the sky. We would roll in steeply from 12,000 feet, pickle off the bombs around 8,000 feet and jink hard back and forth while pulling out of the dive. It was unusual not to see some orange streaks or golf balls or triple-A shells flashing over the canopy in the dive. Once I got too interested in the target and the gunfire and I forgot to pull the power back when I rolled in; I went supersonic in the dive, which was not healthy because the bombs might do crazy things in the shock wave. My back seater laughed all the way home, and I'll bet the North Vietnamese did too, considering where the bombs probably went. At night, they would bring their bulldozers out of the trees and fill in the holes and we would go back the next day and do it again. When the monsoons turned the roads to mud, they quit and went somewhere else.

MiG Cap

We weren't allowed to go up north and hit strategic targets or look for MiGs during my tours in 1969 and 1970, something about 'encouraging the enemy to come to the bargaining table'. But we did fly combat air patrols, armed with four AIM-9 Sidewinder and four AIM-7 Sparrow missiles and the internal gun. Our mission was to protect U-2 reconnaissance flights from MiG intercept. We never saw any, and just as well, because we had not been properly trained, 'Top-Gun' style, in air-to-air tactics at that point. Earlier, Robin Olds, with carefully selected people, and later similar specialists like Steve Ritchie from the USAF Fighter Weapons School, did great work against the MiGs.

When we weren't flying, life was pretty relaxed. At the bases, in South Vietnam there wasn't much to do outside the gate, and it wasn't the safest place to be anyway. So, we built our own bars in the Sqaudrons, and were free to drink or hang around as long as we got good rest before flying. At Cam Ranh, there was a secure beach, and we spent a lot of time there swimming and sunning. Cam Ranh also had a big Army hospital, and the nurses to go with it. Once a mortar shell hit the hospital in the middle of the night and more fighter pilots than patients came stumbling out into the street while the fire fighters put out the blaze. But the vast majority of pilots led a quiet life: writing letters, working out, reading, borrowing and building a library of tapes on the new stereos bought in Japan or Hong Kong on R & R. In general, life on the ground was so boring, and life in the air so exciting, that we were usually anxious to fly and do something.

In Saigon, there was a lot more to do, and it was reasonably safe, although we didn't wander around much at night. When I rode around town with the General, he sat up front with the driver and I, being a more expendable captain, sat in the back, where the hand grenades were more likely to be dropped from a motor scooter; we lost a few that way, but it was too hot to roll up the windows. Who worries about that after you've been up north? I started smoking again, for the same reason.

In Thailand, we could go into the Thai towns and enjoy the restaurants and shopping. The real treat, which we could manage about once a month, would be to hop a ride on the 'Klong' (C-130) which made a regular round-robin of the bases from Bangkok. The large tourist hotels were as civilised as could be, and the lucky, good-looking bachelor might even make a date with a Pan Am stewardess while sitting around the pool. It was a long way from the war. A few guys even had their wives in Bankok, illegal but unenforced; one guy got killed rat-racing while coming home from his last mission of his second tour, and his wife was waiting for him in his room. Tragic. Much as we loved our work, Rest and Recreation was what we lived for – you had a choice of a week in Hong Kong, Sydney. Taipei, Tokyo or Singapore. For some it was a lot of sex and/or drinking, but for most it was just a chance to do some sight-seeing, sleeping and forgetting about the war. I did Tokyo, and went to the World's Fair. My other week was spent in Honolulu with my wife, probably the happiest, shortest week I ever had in my life.

I'm sorry we lost the war, because we could have won it. It wasn't a total loss, because it set the North Vietnamese back when they had the virility to take over all of South-east Asia. Now, as we have seen, they don't have the strength, and they look like they might decide to join the real world. I look back on it as just one of the battles of the Cold War, a long process of wearing down the communist world until it finally collapsed under the pressure. A lot of what we did was pretty senseless, but all wars are like that.

My experience added some fibre and toughness and made me a much better fighter pilot, but the other side of that coin is that no one came away without being changed forever into something less admirable; a post-combat syndrome of impatience, drive, ego, a short attention span and personal hardness that sometimes conflict with the normal world. Above all, in my mind, are those brave and bold fighter pilots who went 'Downtown', to Hanoi and Haiphong, who fought the SAM missiles and the MiGs, and the guards in the POW camps who tortured them for six or eight years. No sky warrior in history showed as much guts and courage and determination and professionalism as the Fighter Pilots of Pack Six. God bless 'em all.

THE MIG KILLERS

After his first Vietnam tour, Steve Ritchie went to the USAF Fighter Weapons School at Nellis and made a thorough study of air-to-air combat. The Navy had just started Top Gun, when experience in the first MiG battles proved that their pilots had a lot to learn. Ritchie was ambitious. He saw what needed to be done and he hoped that he would be able to get back to South-East Asia and apply what he had learned. The handsome, young Air Force Academy graduate had applied for the Thunderbirds, but they had not accepted him. The team was more relaxed, individualistic, hell-raising in those days. Ritchie, said one, still had a little too much 'Zoomie tightness' in him. His intensity was to pay off in a different way.

The Air Force saw the possibility of renewed action over North Vietnam as peace efforts dragged on under Lyndon Johnson's failed effort to bribe the enemy to the bargaining table with a bombing halt. Richard Nixon would be different: he and Henry Kissinger knew how to apply power. The MiG killers were assembled primarily in the famous 'Triple Nickel', the 555th Squadron in the 432nd Tactical Reconnaissance Wing at Udorn, in northern Thailand, near the Laotian border. Randy Cunningham and Willy Driscoll had just knocked down their first MiG with a Sidewinder, flying an F-4J from the *Constellation* on 19 January 1972. It was the 122nd kill of the war and the first in almost two years. In April, North Vietnam

USAF Vietnam aces Steve Ritchie and Chuck Debellevue. Most of their victories were achieved as a team. Crew co-ordination – knowing what the other man is thinking and going to do, reducing conversation and uncertainty, exploiting the advantages of two minds, two sets of eyeballs and two pair of hands – gives the well-trained team an edge in air combat. (US National Archives)

invaded Quang Tri, the capital of a South Vietnam province. Nixon resumed bombing strikes on the North, and the air war began again in earnest. On 16 April Jeff Feinstein got his first MiG. On 8 May Cunningham and Driscoll got their second and two days later they got 3, 4 and 5. Cunningham, now a US Congressman from California, had been to Top Gun at Miramar. In drama like fiction, Cunningham's fifth MiG was flown by Colonel Toon, the famous leader of the North Vietnamese fighters. In a lengthy, hard-turning air battle, in which Toon and Cunningham used every trick they had learned, the Navy lieutenant finally outwitted Toon by pulling his throttles to idle in a vertical climb. Extending his speed brakes and then his flaps, pulling 8g, he slipped behind the MiG-17. Toon, losing sight of his enemy and knowing he was up against the best, decided to dive away, but Cunningham, rolling at slow speed, fell in behind him and killed him in the dive with a Sidewinder. On the way home, low on fuel, Cunningham was hit by a SAM, but managed to get feet-wet, where he and his back-seater were picked up and returned to an exciting celebration aboard the carrier. They were the first American aces of the war, having killed the top ace of the enemy in the process. He was 'the best pilot I ever encountered, American or otherwise', said Cunningham. The same day, Bob Lodge and Roger Locher, with three kills to their credit, were shot down and Locher was picked up after spending 23 days in North Vietnam. Also on the eventful day of 10 May, Steve Ritchie got his first kill, a MiG-21.

Cunningham and Driscoll were not just lucky, they were really a great team, well-versed in all the manoeuvres and tactics of air-to-air combat. Their fifth victory and third kill of the day over North Vietnamese Colonel Tomb was the greatest single one-on-one air battle in history. Cunningham is now a US Congressman for California. (US National Archives)

Jeff Feinstein was the third USAF ace. Here Jeff congratulates Terry Murphy, who was shot down while covering Madden and DeBellevue during their two MiG kills on 9 September. Murphy and his pilot, Bill Dalecky, were picked up quickly and returned to Udorn and a joyful welcome. (Terry Murphy)

Ritchie killed his second MiG-21 on 31 May. Then on 8 July, flying with Chuck DeBellevue, he killed two more MiG-21s with Sparrows from his F-4D. He had matched Robin Olds with four, but was one behind the Navy. The same day, Jeff Feinstein got two more, bringing him to three, matching DeBellevue. The 432nd at Udorn, commanded by Chuck Gabriel (later to be Chief of Staff of the Air Force), was doing good work. Led by Wayne Frye, himself a MiG-killer, the 'Nickel' was killing MiGs thanks to the expertise of Lodge, Locher, Ritchie, DeBellevue and others. They were passing their knowledge on to new members of the squadron. They were determined to control the air over North Vietnam so that the bombers could do their job.

Finally, on 28 August 1972, Steve Ritchie got his fifth MiG, another MiG-21, and became the first USAF ace since the Korean War. DeBellevue was with him for his fourth, and later got two more to become the highest scorer of the war, with six. Feinstein ended up with five. The two navigators, as Driscoll before them, had shown that the Phantom was a two-man aircraft, and that a team of experts, knowing how to fly and communicate and use the systems of the Phantom to the best advantage, could go into heavily defended North Vietnam 'and kill MiGs'. That is the title of the book that describes their victories.

The last big action took place on 9 September. Ritchie had gone home, and DeBellevue was flying with John Madden. In a furious, low-altitude fight, they killed two MiG-19s, raising DeBellevue to six, while Bryan Tibbett and Bud Hargrove knocked down another with the gun. But then a third Phantom in the flight, flown by Bill Dalecky and Terry Murphy, took a hit and began to lose fuel. Murphy transmitted its co-ordinates and the crew ejected. Within half an hour, they were picked up by the Jolly Greens and returned home. Later, Murphy showed up in my F-4 squadron at Bent-

163

waters, where he enjoyed telling the new guys about the day Murph and the MiGs got shot down. It was congenial pros like him that made a fighter squadron a great place to be. A couple of years ago, we took my boat from Tampa to Miami and drank a little beer along the way – two old Phantom drivers reminiscing about the war and tasting a little of the comradeship that can never be found again.

THE PHANTOM IN EUROPE

From 1966 until the present day the F-4 Phantom has played a major role in the NATO mission. With the acquisition of the Phantom – by the USA. Britain, Germany, Greece, Turkey and Spain – NATO made a vast leap in defensive and offensive capability. The primary aircraft of the early 1960s were designed for specific purposes and lacked the electronics, range and payload to perform many missions; among the primary NATO aircraft, the USAF F-100 had no radar and the Luftwaffe F-104 lacked range, a bomb load and all-weather bombing systems. NATO mission performance thus suffered large deficiences in its overall capability. The Phantom changed all that. Suddenly, with one aircraft, the West could perform all the major roles across the fighter mission spectrum:

1. Nuclear strike to Eastern Europe
2. Nuclear support of ground war
3. Conventional strike to Eastern Europe
4. Conventional interdiction and close air support
5. Long-range interception
6. Close-in dogfight
7. Long-range deployment

In my job as the Squadron Operations Officer of the 92nd Tactical Fighter Squadron at RAF Bentwaters in the early 1970s, I was responsible for training and operating a squadron of 60 pilots and navigators and 24 F-4D aircraft. Except for hard combat, it was the greatest challenge a fighter pilot can face, because we had to be able to perform each of the missions above at any time. The first F-4s in Europe were introduced in 1966 by the 36th Tactical Fighter Wing at Bitburg, Germany, which has often been the first to re-equip with new fighters – such as the F-80 in 1948, the F-84 in 1952, the F-86 in 1953, the F-100 in 1956, the F-105 in 1961 and the F-15C in 1977. My Wing, the 81st Tactical Fighter Wing, converted from F-101 Voodoo fighters (Robin Olds commanded in 1963–65 and then recruited some of his best pilots for the MiG-chasing mission of the Wolfpack) to the F-4C in 1966, along with Bitburg. In 1973 the

Wing upgraded to the F-4D with advanced bombing systems and radar and flew these aircraft until the arrival of the first A-10s in Europe in the 92nd Squadron in 1979. Eventually all fighter Wings in USAFE flew the F-4 except the F-111 Wing at Upper Heyford.

The 81st Wing has a long and proud history and celebrates its 50th anniversary in 1992. The Wing's aircraft history is literally a history of the development of US fighter aviation:

1942:	P-39 Airacobra
1943:	P-38 Lightning
1944:	P-40 Warhawk
1945:	P-47 Thunderbolt
1946:	P-51 Mustang
1949:	F-80 Shooting Star, F-86A Sabre
1953:	F-86F Sabre
1954:	F-84F Thunderstreak
1958:	F-101A Voodoo
1966:	F-4C Phantom II
1973:	F-4D Phantom II
1979:	A-10 Thunderbolt II
1988:	F-16C Fighting Falcon (Aggressors, retired)

Other services still flying the Phantom are the Luftwaffe, which still flies the F-4F and the RF-4, and the RAF, which flies the Phantom FGR.2 (F-4M) in the air defence role. RAF Phantom squadrons in Germany are being withdrawn and only Leuchars and Wattisham in the UK, plus the alert force in the Falklands, will fly the aircraft until it is finally retired in about two years' time. In addition, Greece and Turkey fly the F-4E and RF-4, while Spain and the Royal Navy have retired their aircraft.

Let us go back to the early 1970s:

Nuclear Strike to Eastern Europe
Victor Alert. Two- to three-day tours sitting and sleeping in a separate, secure area within feet of the aircraft, ready to jump out of bed and go to nuclear war, was a very important, very boring job. Our targets were primarily the Warsaw Pact fighter and naval bases within the range of the Phantom. Our Wing also maintained alert birds in Northern Italy and the Madrid Wing did the same in Turkey. Last summer I drove into East Germany and through a small town near a Soviet command centre which had once been my nuclear target. It was a strange feeling to think that I could have been sent to destroy this drab, old village and its people, who are now our allies, 20 years ago.

The alert aircraft carried one B-61 thermonuclear weapon on the centreline, two fuel tanks and an ECM pod on the wings and the usual four Sparrow AIM-7 radar missiles in the recessed fuselage wells. This bomb was only 13–14in in diameter and just under 12ft long, with a parachute-retard capability and selectable yields for various targets. The pilot had to receive a special PAL (Permissive Action Link) code in order to arm the bomb. The handling and delivery of nuclear weapons required heavy standardization and supervision. Each year a crew was required to give a professional certification, briefing a senior officer of the Wing on an entire nuclear mission, including the memorized recitation of the checkpoints on the target run-in. I once got carried away and gave a two-hour presentation while the Wing Commander tried not to fall asleep. No-notice certifications were also conducted on alert. About once a year, the Wing was subject to a no-notice Operational Readiness Inspection (ORI) by the ORI Team from Headquarters, United States Air Forces Europe. A complete war scenario was enacted with all possible realism over a period of several days, ranging from early conventional attacks escalating to an all-out simulated launch of the fleet on a nuclear strike. Everything from individual crew performance to weapons loading and maintenance to command and control procedures was thoroughly evaluated. Failure in any area might cause the entire Wing to fail: heads would roll, and a heavy training schedule was undertaken to prepare for the re-test in a few months' time. It was no fun, but it ensured that the mission was performed properly. The ORI system continues today and NATO also continues to conduct Tactical Evaluations of all NATO flying units.

With the introduction of the cruise missile, the Phantom alert mission was discontinued and the missions themselves are now being phased out along with the missiles as a result of the nuclear disarmament treaty. It was the introduction of those missiles by NATO (not the peace protesters who objected and now claim victory) that forced the Soviets to negotiate and allowed the missiles to be withdrawn. But there was a time, opposing massive conventional forces, when the nuclear strike capability of NATO served well to deter Soviet aggression.

Nuclear support of ground war
A key element of NATO doctrine in the 1970s was the strategy of limited nuclear counterforce – a willingness to escalate a conventional war to a single or extremely limited nuclear strike to convince the enemy that the West was willing to take the risk of a larger nuclear war in defence of its interests. So we practised and were constantly prepared for surprise nuclear tasking. A crew would be given a target and be expected to prepare maps, navigation information and target attack tactics for a briefing to Standard-

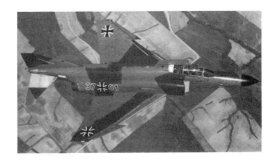

Luftwaffe F-4F. Among the more recent Phantoms produced, these F models are still operational for NATO. (McDonnell Douglas)

ization/Evaluation or ORI teams. The crew would then fly an actual mission against a target somewhere in Europe and be expected to arrive over the target within seconds of the designated time. Practice missions were also frequently flown on scored bombing ranges, such as those in the Wash area of England, delivering small smoke bombs with high-speed, low-altitude lay-down or toss bomb techniques using the F-4D's WRCS (Weapons Release Computer System).

Conventional strike to Eastern Europe
The first objective of any European war was to avoid going nuclear. Training was therefore also concentrated on the use of the Phantom to deliver the full range of conventional weapons. We frequently practised briefing mass conventional bomb attacks on enemy airfields, then conducting low-level attacks with co-ordinated pop-up tactics on simulated targets. These missions are still flown, with airfields coming under noisy attack by other NATO fighter units. With new all-weather weapons and delivery systems, these dangerous, daylight mass attacks are now unlikely against defended targets.

Conventional interdiction and close air support
The F-4D on gunnery range missions carried a dispenser with six practice bombs (four slicks and two which simulated parachute retard) and a Gatling gun mounted centreline. After a low-level training mission, a range attack began with two radar nuclear lay-downs, followed by four dive-bomb deliveries and about four strafe passes which used up the half-hour range time. Squadrons deployed to ranges in Sardinia, Aviano in Italy and Zaragoza in Spain or flew locally to English ranges when weather permitted. We spent several months a year in Spain or Italy, where better weather allowed concentrated practice on gunnery and air-to-air ranges.

Long-range interception
The original purpose of the Phantom in the United States Navy was

167

to defend the carrier against long-range air attack, so it has always had a superior air-to-air radar for the firing of the Sparrow missiles which are built into the design of the underside of the fuselage. On a typical intercept mission, one Phantom would act as target while the other set up for various kinds of attacks – head-on, stern conversion, snap-up – with the Sparrow and then the Sidewinder and gun as the attacker closed.

Close-in dogfight

Air Combat Tactics ability in those days was not up to current Top Gun/Fighter Weapons School standards. We learned the basic manoeuvres and tried to put them together into some meaningful engagements. As an ACT instructor pilot, I would typically take two clean Phantoms out over the North Sea and there would be time for three or four good engagements before reaching minimum fuel. Occasionally we would encounter an RAF Lightning or Buccaneer over the water and do some limited, illegal turning. Nowadays, dissimilar ACT is authorized and practised according to safe, prebriefed procedures. In addition to ACT manoeuvring, we also flew hot-gun firing missions against a target known as the Dart, towed behind another Phantom in a racetrack pattern over the Mediterranean.

Long-range deployment

NATO extends all the way to the Turkey/Iraq border. We once deployed half our squadron to Turkey and operated for two weeks out of a bare site with support from Britain. In addition, each year we would conduct a six-aircraft exchange with a squadron from another nation. We would also occasionally land at stations in other countries to give them experience in turning-around foreign aircraft.

It was a good life, flying around Europe, enjoying other countries, using the aircraft to its fullest extent. Everyone had just come from Vietnam, so we were all a little crazy by today's sober standards. The nuke standardization and unattainable training requirements were a pain, but the mission was accomplished and we all look back with strong feelings about this important time in our lives.

The primary fighter in NATO today is the F-16, which is flown by many nations. This aircraft is similar to the F-4 in that it can also perform all the diverse missions once performed by the Phantom. Most squadrons, however, concentrate on some missions, such as air-to-air, and maintain lower proficiency in others, such as nuclear strike. Whether flying combat or sitting nuclear alert, it was all part of the same war – now won, but never forgotten.

GLEAMING HORSES: HOSTILE INTENT*

Lt. Colonel Donny 'Nails' Nicholson and Major Joe 'Jabber' Jarnigan over Berlin, 1 May 199X.

'Texas, Magic. Be advised your targets have departed orbit and turned head-on. They're 5000 feet low and climbing. In addition, there are two bogeys, apparently hostile, just took off from Oranienburg, headed west on the deck. Be prepared for missiles or a pop-up to your six o'clock; we'll keep you posted. They're also Flankers, over.'

'Texas, Roger.' Nicholson already knew this, and he was growing concerned. He had seen the target flight change direction and altitude on his radar and the sudden signal from his RHAW gear told him that the Flankers had locked on to him with their radar. Then his Doppler search radar had picked out the new targets moving against the ground clutter and his RHAW had recognized the Flanker radar band when they had looked at him on their radar. His flight was now in grave danger, threatened by the two separate flights of enemy fighters, not to mention the other aircraft 70 miles to the north.

The Flankers carried three AA-10 Alamo radar missiles with a range of nearly 30 miles, two of them mounted on pylons under the engines and the other mounted on the fuselage between the engines. In addition, they carried four AA-11 Archer heat-seeking missiles, two of them mounted on outer wing pylons and two on the wing tips. As with the Eagles, they had not carried wing tanks on the other wing pylons. There was one major difference, however. The Eagle could identify, lock onto and track numerous targets at one time. It was possible even to fire at several maneuvering targets while the radar continued to track others. That way you could handle more than one enemy at a time. The Flanker's radar, on the other hand, could handle only one target at a time. Locked onto Texas Flight, they might not spot Jersey Flight behind at low altitude, even though their radar was also capable of finding targets against the terrain background and they had AWACS assistance.

'Magic, Texas. Put Jersey Flight on those bandits on the deck and we'll continue with the high flight; and I think it's time to put the Linebackers on the bandits north, over.'

'Roger, Texas, that's already being done and should work out. We've already told Jersey and Linebacker to push it up and they should be able to intercept both flights before they reach you.'

'Good thing,' Nicholson spoke to himself. 'I don't need six of you bastards just yet.' He transmitted: 'Texas, afterburner.'

Donny moved the throttles forward into burner and the Eagle quickly slipped into supersonic flight, with only a slight ripple on a couple of the gages to indicate the passage through the Mach. He wanted max energy, and the ability to climb vertically, when they engaged. The two different fighters were comparable in a turn, but the Flanker had an electronic, fly-by-wire flight control system, which might give it some advantage compared to the normal mechanical/hydraulic controls of the US fighter. The difference would be in the pilot if they got into a turning fight.

The Rules of Engagement said that Nicholson and Jarnigan could not just plow on in there and fire. They had to wait and see what the Flankers did,

---

* From Chapter 10 of an unpublished novel by the author.

whether they fired or threatened or ran or evaded or did something in between that was hard to evaluate in a few seconds. They could defend themselves, but could not initiate the first shooting. It wasn't long before the decision was taken out of their hands: the enemy fired.

The two flights of fighters, each line abreast, raced toward each other at nearly 2000 miles per hour. Each flight knew from its RHAW gear that the other had a radar lock-on. What each did not know were the Rules of Engagement under which the other was operating.

The Russians took the advantage; each of them locked onto one of the American fighters and they simultaneously fired two Alamos each on the leader's command at six miles. They could have fired at more than 30, given the great closure rate, and that had lulled the Americans into some doubt as to their intentions. More importantly, it had reduced their reaction time.

The missiles began life supersonic and moved immediately to Mach 3. It took less than seven seconds for them to reach their targets. The Americans had split as briefed at 25 miles, but the Russians had split also, each maintaining an F-15 head-on. Jarnigan had his eyes in the cockpit, trying to figure out what the radar was telling him, scanning for other bogeys, deciding on an ECM response; then he saw the launch light and was jarred by the fearful audio sound which confirmed it. He decided to fire back. That was what killed him. 'Nails' was looking through the HUD watching the Flanker blips; suddenly there was a missile launch-light on his RHAW gear. There was no time to notch 90 degrees left to try to break the lock of the Doppler radar and cause the missiles to go stupid. In a second he could see the expanding missile trails emerging out of the cloudy background; he pulled in maximum Gs and yelled at Jarnigan. 'Jabber, pull up! Pull up! Now!'

The radar missiles passed a few hundred feet below Nicholson's F-15, unable to correct enough for the sudden upward change in the fighter's vector. Jarnigan fired a missile and then reacted to the launch-light and Nicholson's shout, but was one second too slow. The first missile, closing at 4000 feet per second, struck the bottom of the aircraft just aft of the cockpit, in the middle of the internal fuel cells, and the aircraft exploded. Suddenly, the sleek, fifteen-million-dollar aircraft was no longer a single supersonic projectile; it was thousands of pieces going sideways, tumbling in all directions, unable to pierce the air. The momentum of the two huge Pratt & Whitney turbofan engines still trying to rotate at 10,000rpm, the explosion of the missile warhead and 1500 gallons of JP-8 jet fuel, and the sudden immense deceleration totally destroyed, really totally, the aircraft and the body of Major Joseph A. 'Jabber' Jarnigan, United States Air Force, 22nd Tactical Fighter Squadron, Bitburg Air Base, Germany. Husband of Karen. Father of Jamie and Joanie. Deceased.

X

FIGHTER CONCEPTS

W E HAVE looked at the fighter pilot – what he is, how he is created, the equipment he uses – but we still do not quite understand him. There are some aspects to his make-up, some attitudes and concepts that are part of his profession, that we need to understand. Every fighter pilot concentrates on these, and they become building blocks for his character. There are, of course, more than I describe here, but these will tell us something about the way the fighter pilot thinks and acts, give us an insight into the requirements of the job and show us why he must learn to be different from the rest of the world.

SITUATIONAL AWARENESS

Every person can recall an incident in life, perhaps driving a car or dealing with some minor emergency, when there seemed to be too much information arriving in too short a time, too much to do in the seconds available before the freedom to act disappeared forever. The fighter pilot faces this experience every time he flies. He can remember his days as a student, his first whirling launch in a high-speed jet aircraft after the slow-motion flight of the little prop plane in which he started. He was, as the instructor said later, 'ten miles behind the airplane'. His untrained mind was unable to keep up with the rapid, unfamiliar change of the multi-dimensional world through which he was thrown. But, as time went by, he learned to think and act at the same time, to pick out the bits of information he needed from all those available and put them together to form a decision; then he acted with his hands, even while his mind was sorting through all the new information and re-arranging priorities and preparing new decisions. Slowly, he built a picture of his condition, a knowledge of his situation, that of his airplane and that of the world around it, and he was able to use this information to make correct decisions to stay alive and get the job done.

The modern jet fighter has, on the one hand, increased the flow of information to the pilot to the point where there is simply too much available, too much to handle; but, on the other hand, the new fighters have systems which help the pilot to sort out the information and select what is needed, in effect reducing the amount of information which actually goes into his computer-brain to make decisions. The modern cockpit is simply a machine for doing this, and then, as efficiently as possible, translating his decisions into action. Yet the danger of overload, of piling too much information on the pilot when stress and lack of time prevent him from using it, is always there. Consider a pilot in a typical overload situation:

1. He is flying at low altitude, trying to watch the ground and the flight instruments simply in order to avoid flying into the ground 100ft below him while travelling at 1100ft a second.

2. He is talking on the radio to his wingman and to a combat controller, accepting and giving information. He must think ahead and make decisions about what the flight will do, where it will go. He must protect his wingman and he must think about the objectives of the battle in which he is engaged.

3. He has weapons on board and must be thinking of how to deliver them, which ones are best and what switches must be remembered and selected.

4. He must navigate, find his way to the target and avoid enemy defences and operate various systems which compete to do this. The closer he gets, the more this rises to the top of his priority list.

5. Enemy missiles are fired, causing flashing lights in his cockpit; enemy aircraft are seen on his radar scope which must be interpreted. He is in danger of dying.

A Marine Corps AV-8B demonstrates its famous short take-off capability during forward site operations at Camp Lejeune, North Carolina. (McDonnell Douglas)

6. Something goes wrong with his complex machine: warning lights tell him what, he must remember correct procedures and actions must be taken. Which is more important, the target, the enemy or the aircraft? What must be done first, what can wait ten seconds, what is he forgetting and what must be anticipated that he cannot yet see?

7. The weather may be bad, even terrible. It may be night. This is unnerving, making everything more difficult.

8. The battle plan, as always, deteriorates and things start to happen that he has not anticipated. The enemy surprises him.

9. Things start to go wrong. Little things combine with other little things and become important. The tanker is late, his wingman is out of position, the AWACS warns him of bogeys, the radio isn't working correctly, sweat is running into his eyes . . . and on and on.

10. The problems start to overlap. There isn't time to handle all of them so some must be postponed. His mind is having trouble thinking of everything and doing what is necessary. At the extreme, the mind simply stops functioning when the overload becomes too great. He has to force himself to relax and try to get things done as best he can in the best possible order. It may be too much: he may simply fly into the ground or fail to see the missile coming because he is engaged in something else. He may die because he has lost his total awareness of the situation around him.

Situational awareness comes from training, training, training. That is what gives the pilot the coolness which slows up his mind. As he practises, he discovers that he can do more and more without panic or overload. The new cockpit helps him: he can do things with one switch that used to require several; he can see what his aircraft is doing in the HUD without having to look inside, so he can look for MiGs and fly at the same time; the voice warning system tells him in words that something is wrong – much better than seeing a warning light and deciding what it means; he says a word, recognized by the computer, and the matter is corrected – faster than finding a switch under his elbow; he sees a MiG and turns his head to look directly at it, which tells the missile seeker head to do the same – easier than trying to find it on the radar scope. He is learning to pat his head and rub his stomach and whistle a tune and dance a jig simultaneously. He is Bach, with part of one hand playing one kind of music, part of the other hand playing another kind of music, the middle fingers of each playing a third. His eyes look at a dozen things, his left hand moves throttles while fingers control radar, his right hand moves the aircraft while fingers control weapons. The aircraft is wired into his brain. He is Clint Eastwood, in *Firefox*: his brain flies the aeroplane without bothering to go through the muscles of his body. It is all just a trend in that direction.

TEAMWORK

The fighter pilot is something of an individualist, a loner, someone capable of acting without support. Yet almost all of his flying is done in concert with other fighter pilots. Modern combat requires that they support and defend each other. They fly in formations and they join together to maximize their impact and confuse the enemy.

Despite the vast changes in the speed and technology of aerial combat, one thing has not changed: the wingman is crucial to the safety, and therefore the success, of the fighter pilot. In essence, the flight leader concentrates on the kill and the wingman protects him so that he can do so. The more the battle degenerates from long-range radar into a dogfight, the more important is the information provided by the wingman to the leader. But now, far more than a second set of eyes, the wingman shares complicated tasks of weapon systems management with the flight leader, operating radios, radar warning gear and radar search and identification and undertaking separate target tracking and attack.

A thing of beauty to a fighter pilot is a well-trained team – a leader and a wingman, able to function to the fullest without needless conversation and to anticipate each other's movements – gold-medal figure skaters moving together perfectly on the slippery ice of combat. We call it flight discipline: the aircraft operate as a team. They go by the rules: there are standards, things which must be done, so that each pilot can count on the other to be at the right place and do the right thing. There is no time in high-speed jet combat for discussion and instruction, and no room for mistakes.

The flight may be four ships, even eight or sixteen, depending on the mission. The flight leader must not only control his flight but co-ordinate with support aircraft as well. But in most situations the two-ship element leader and his wingman are the fundamental unit.

Although the words have changed since the first aerial combat of the First World War, the concepts are the same. Captain Kurt Geerer, once an F-16 pilot in the ace 526th Tactical Fighter Squadron in Germany, said, 'The wingman has three big jobs when I go into a threat area: check six, sanitize the area and know the exit. In other words, the leader may pursue his objective, knowing that there will not be a surprise attack from the rear, that he will be told about any other aircraft entering the area and that the most appropriate, safest exit from the battle will always be updated as the

The Tornado crew. Crew co-ordination and efficient communication are essential for each man to understand important things that the other knows. Sometimes a simple expletive gets the message across. (Author)

situation changes. While doing all this, the wingman must also be prepared to shoot, evade or even take the lead. It is hard to imagine any human activity which calls for more quick thinking, reaction ability and simultaneous management of multiple complex tasks.'

It's not easy being a wingman: sometimes you don't get to shoot unless the big guy gives you permission because he missed, blew the switches or has fired all his weapons; you have to have lots of eyes and a fast neck; you have to stay with the leader while he gyrates all over the sky, but you must look everywhere else for the bad guys; and if somehow the leader gets shot down and you don't, you have a real self-image problem.

The tactical situation may change and it may be better for the wingman to direct the fight. Before a fighter pilot can be a flight leader, he must demonstrate that he can be a good wingman, to follow orders before giving them. He must learn to trust his leader and to give instant and disciplined response to orders. He must be a professional and do his homework on the ground so that there will be no failure in the air. At the same time, the leader must take care of his wingman: give him a good briefing so that he knows exactly what to expect and do; protect him from the enemy, since he may be less experienced; and not exceed the wingman's ability to stay with the leader during heavy manoeuvring.

General Robert Dixon, whom I served as Aide in Vietnam, was later the Commander of USAF Tactical Air Command. In Korea, as a lieutenant-colonel, he flew the wing of Ralph Parr, only a captain, who became a jet ace in the F-86. Parr got all the glory, but General Dixon was extremely proud of the fact that he had been part of the team, putting aside rank to support and protect the best shooter. In aerial combat, the wingman is just as important to the success of the mission as the leader.

In the RAF, there is a different philosophy. The student pilot in the Hawk begins to practise leading missions. By the time he arrives at, say, the Tactical Weapons Conversion Course in

Thunderbirds in the F-4. Most USAF fighter pilots would love to spend a tour with the Thunderbirds, who symbolize their professionalism and spirit. (McDonnell Douglas)

Tornados, he will be expected to lead flights in combat situations. His final phase consists of five flights in which he must lead to several targets while being bounced by another Tornado as an air-to-air threat. This is very difficult for a new pilot to handle, and some of them are eliminated from the programme at this late stage because they cannot handle the complex thinking required.

The other type of teamwork is that between the crew of a two-seat fighter. The pilot in the front and the navigator in the back perform different but co-ordinated tasks. They must think alike and communicate perfectly. Often the back-seater is in charge, because his systems are being used to direct the aircraft to the target or deliver the weapons. Crew co-ordination, as it is called, is essential. A fighter squadron is really a connected organism, a family, a united group of like mind, in which teamwork, under strong leadership, is the essential ingredient.

SPIRIT AND AGGRESSIVENESS

The fighter pilot's will to win is symbolized by two combatants in a circle trying to get to each other's six o'clock for the kill. The first one to quit and turn tail dies. The greatest fighter pilots I have known have extended that philosophy to their personal and professional lives: they never, never quit; they go for the win. Without driving, intense spirit and aggressiveness, it is impossible to do this.

Over my 35 years of teaching and leading young men, I have often had occasion to express something I learned and strongly felt at the beginning: *It is easier and more efficacious to temper the excess spirit and enthusiasm in an inexperienced pilot than to instil that which is lacking.* It is always a compromise – air machines, lives, our own careers and those of our superiors are precious commodities – but it can be safely said that we did not lack aggressive fighter pilots over North Vietnam, the greatest challenge fighter pilots have ever faced except that faced for those few days over Sinai and that confronting the Battle of Britain pilots. The combat leader, and the instructor pilot, keep that dichotomy always in mind. We have learned much about flying safely without degrading training and mission accomplishment. As aircraft move from $20 million to $50 million a copy, and as it costs $6 million just to train a combat-ready F-16 pilot, we must accept greater constraints on aggressive training in order to preserve the assets which will win the battle if it comes. On the other hand, of course, if your training does not enable you to defeat the enemy, you have wasted everything. And there is always the built-in struggle between the political and military objectives, where both sides may be right but unsympathetic to each other.

Unrestrained, untrained spirit is dangerous and unproductive. Spirit wins, but it also kills. I will never forget the day in Thailand when a member of our squadron, returning from the last mission of his second combat tour, began to do barrel rolls around his leader, lost control of the F-4, ejected and was killed by a seat malfunction. His wife, who lived in Bangkok, was waiting in his room to welcome him. And the pilots who have driven into the ground while buzzing are a stupid portion of the legend. Senseless spirit and aggressiveness.

Spirit is the fuel of the fighter pilot. Skill is half the requirement for success; attitude is the other half. Synonyms are 'courage', 'aggressiveness', 'insouciance', 'verve', 'motivation', 'audacity', 'enthusiasm', 'enterprise', 'panache'. Without these qualities and attitudes the pilot is not a fighter pilot and he will eventually fail. Flying fighters becomes a series of choices, between the bold and the cautious. The bold, entailing risk, tend to win the day. At the same time, however, the true professional knows how to calculate the odds, how far he can go before crossing the line into foolhardy territory, when bravery is nothing but stupidity. The secret is in being so skilful and knowledgeable that the calculation of risk is an accurate one. In air combat the line and the risks are always changing, and therein lies the challenge for the fast-thinking winner and survivor.

One occasionally has to tell young pilots that the man makes the aeroplane, not the other way around. Some seem to think that just sitting in the front seat of a Phantom makes one a fighter pilot, when all it does is give one the opportunity. When flying a fighter, it is easier to demonstrate that you are *not* a fighter pilot than that you are one.

After you have been a fighter pilot for some time, you realize that spirit and aggressiveness must be tempered with judgement and skill or it is nothing more than unrestrained foolishness. It must be applied to the mission, not to joyriding and foolhardiness. Properly in hand, it is the essence of being a fighter pilot – the afterburner to ability.

PROFESSIONALISM

Every officer and fighter pilot is supposed to be a professional, although some lack all the qualities. A professional is a member of a form of élite, a group of people who have certain standards and rules to live by, a body of knowledge to guide them and a philosophy of life and work that controls the way they perform. Pride in the profession motivates the members and offers a ladder to success. It is in, essence, a discipline, limiting freedom but giving opportunity.

It is no disrespect to the highly qualified professional pilots who fly other kinds of aircraft to suggest that fighter pilots are different, a separate breed as the saying goes, a brand of people with a distinct variation of spirit, self-confidence and aggressiveness. The profession requires this, in ways other flying does not, and those who lack it are weeded out. The outsider may see the fighter pilot as a motorcycle driver, dashing, even skilled, but somehow irresponsible, someone who likes to do crazy things and lacks discipline. This is wrong. It is possible for the fighter pilot to be aggressive and ride the edge of danger and fun because he has learned the limits and can handle the physical and mental challenge.

All USAF fighter pilots are forced on to a career track, required to excel as they move up the pyramid, if they want to continue flying. The RAF has a fly-only programme, in which the pilot remains in the cockpit during his career, without the staff assignments or the promotions that go with the other careers. There will always be a debate about which of these is best, but it is true that both types of officers are true professionals when they get into a fighter and make it, and themselves, perform as designed.

WORK AND PERSEVERANCE

You can't be a fighter pilot without working your tail off. There are only a limited number of slots, and only the best get them. It is hard work physically and mentally while you do it, and it is hard work in the sense of long years of preparation and training and growing. Being a good fighter pilot is no longer a simple gift of natural ability; it must be earned by assiduously developing the skills and attitudes that separate you from all the others with the same ambition. You may get your chance at being a line pilot by showing good promise early in pilot training during the selection process, but you won't get your chance to stay in fighters and fill one of the select leadership slots if you do not fight, year after year, with everything you have to stay ahead of the others.

In the modern fighter, you don't just hop in and go: you study, plan, prepare, think, co-ordinate, brief and create. You only get twenty hours a month, and each one is supported by many more hours to ensure that the air time is worth the great expense, and that it meets the ultimate objective of creating a combat-ready fighter pilot who can do the toughest job at short notice.

This goes on during all the years you fly. With thousands of hours of flying time, and the many more thousands of preparation and training, your experience enables you to become the best. But the King rarely remains on the hill: the young challengers are all around, with youthful co-ordination and zest, while you take on more ground and leadership duties. Your motivation tends to wane, and you have to concentrate intensely to keep yourself pumped up for every mission. Your pride and your experience keep you going, but there is always someone better who wants your job.

FUN

What could be more fun than flying the greatest, fastest, most beautiful aeroplane in the world? Men love machines. They love fast and flashy cars. This attachment gives them power, it gives them sex appeal, it gives them dreams and confidence and thrills that remove them from normal life and project them into another world. The machine does not make the man, although he cannot avoid thinking that it does. It is the man who makes the machine into something beautiful, and some men, however long or hard they try, cannot do it.

Flying is fun because the human body enjoys the excitement of strange sensations, the ultimate roller coaster. There is a sense of danger, not enough to create great fear, but enough to pump the adrenalin: chemicals stimulate the system, but it gradually becomes accustomed to them, and increasing amounts are required to achieve the 'high'.

Flying is fun because you see things people on the ground never see. It is not enough to be a passenger, strapped beside a window. The real fun comes from sitting up front, way up high in the bubble canopy, with the wings and the aircraft way behind you, as though you were all alone, just a body moving at will through space. From 50,000ft the world is beautiful, devoid of its problems and fools. At 100ft, at 600kt, it becomes a high-speed kaleidoscope of new visions, flashing under the nose, thrilling the mind and all the nerves connected to it.

It is fun to be in total control, to sense and manipulate all the signs of life in the cockpit, to be able to make the aeroplane move here and there with those subtle touches, to feel all its power vibrating beneath your seat, to make it an extension of your own body, all wired together with fibre optics into your heart.

When I flew as a fighter pilot, all those years, I used to have the same frequent dream in my sleep, in a hundred variations. I could fly – not in an aeroplane, but just by myself: I had to strain my mind and body but, with great concentration, I could lift myself off the Earth and move around at will, always with people watching. It was an ego trip. It was never easy: it was always a great mental effort to force myself up into the air and be Superman. I never once fell. When I left the Air Force and became a stockbroker, the dreams stopped. Life apparently wasn't so much fun anymore.

DANGER

Flying a fighter is perilous because (a) you occasionally get shot at; (b) the complicated aircraft occasionally breaks; (c) someone on the ground or in an other aircraft does something wrong; or (d) the human pilot occasionally makes a mistake. In the jet era since the Second World War the accident rate per 100,000 flying hours has dropped to a fraction of what it was as a result of improved aircraft, training, procedures and supervision.

It used to be said that a Navy carrier pilot had, during a 20-year career, a 50 per cent chance of ejecting and a 25 per cent chance of dying. Nowadays the odds are much better, and accidents are rare compared to the old days, when metal failed, pilots were not 'up to

The mighty 'Thud'. The F-105 could carry a heap of bombs, but couldn't turn or fight MiGs well with just a gun. The 'Thud' pilots of North Vietnam were the greatest heroes of air warfare. (Cradle of Aviation Museum)

speed', ejection seats were unsuccessful near the ground and we were just beginning to learn about the challenge of high-speed flight. Today every accident is pounced upon and examined, each cause determined and eliminated, and people are removed and replaced if they are guilty of some level of failure.

The fighter pilot, even in combat, does not normally feel fear, for that would be a distraction and a betrayal of the great training and even greater self-confidence that is part of him. Outsiders, even some fighter pilots, do not understand how this is done, for it is a mysterious process to force away the normal inclination to feel danger and move it back into a corner of the brain where it will not bother the mission. Sometimes it pops out at the wrong time and causes problems, or at the right time and saves a life. Sometimes being weak is the most dangerous problem of all.

Danger is healthy because it motivates the fighter pilot to be a professional, to stay alive by being the best, to believe in himself, to escape the 'golden bee-bee' because he is immortal.

GENIUS

'I saw this car coming very quickly behind me. Just at the bottom of the dip, Ayrton came through on the inside – I'd left him room. I witnessed visibly and audibly something I had not seen anyone do before in a racing car. It was as if he had four hands and four legs. He was braking, changing down, steering, pumping the throttle and the car appeared to be on that knife edge of being in control and being out of control. It lasted maybe two seconds. Once he had checked the speed of the car and he'd got the right gear, what he was trying to do was maintain boost pressure. On a turbo you lift off and the power goes away very fast. He got to the point of the track where he wanted to make his commitment to the corner. The car was pitched in with an arrogance that made my eyes open wider. Then – hard on the throttle and the thing was driving through the corner. I mean it was a master controlling the machine. I had never seen a turbo car driven like that.

'The ability of the brain to separate each component and put them back together with that rhythm and co-ordination – for me it was a remarkable experience, it was a privilege to see.

'I was so moved that I went down to the Lotus pit and I said . . . "I've just seen something." And they said, "Yes, yes, we know." '*

---

* Extracted from *Ayrton Senna: The Hard Edge of Genius*, by Christopher Hilton (Wellingborough, England: Patrick Stephens Ltd.), quoting racing driver John Watson discussing Senna, pp. 119–120.

I have seen a few fighter pilots who were in a class by themselves, better than almost all the others, because they had so many years of experience, and such skill, that they always won on the measuring grounds – the air-to-air ground weapon delivery and the air-to-air combat situation. The genius, like Senna's, was a combination of mental and physical skill which had been developed in the aircraft by years of constant self-pushing, a disciplined drive to master the machine and the mechanics and the changing dimensions of the relationships. Every time they flew, they pressed a little harder to hit the target, to find the new manoeuvre, to know the perfect moment to move, to defeat the enemy, to control their mental and muscular entity.

They built personalities to match: they were *self-confident*, not only because they were almost always the best, but because they wanted to be even better. Only the supreme faith in their own ability could give them the control over themselves and the machine which resulted in a victory over the dangers of speed and the rub of death. They normally knew just how far they could go and were able to go closer to the edge than their less-experienced comrades; but sometimes, driven by ego, or just because of human mistakes, they slipped into unfamiliar space, went too far and lost control, and some of them died.

Genius in the aircraft is knowing your exact limitations and being able to take yourself and the aircraft right up to them, where others cannot go and retain control. Genius is a bright light in the mind, illuminating the corners of danger and opportunity that others cannot see. Genius is collecting everything together in one place and totally dominating it.

COMBAT

Before I went into combat in Vietnam, I had several years to think about it. I had volunteered, I had six months of training in the F-4 with combat foremost in my mind. I was highly motivated. I was 35 years old with 2000 hours of flying time, and when I arrived in my squadron every member in it had had combat experience and was very cool about the whole thing. As a result, I had plenty of time to adjust and there was natural pressure to be cool as well. Never did I see a fighter pilot show stress while I was there. I made some mistakes, especially as a new guy, but I never felt fear and enjoyed almost every minute of the experience – despite some hairy gunfire on occasions. Everyone else was about the same as far as I could tell. We were finally doing what we had thought about doing for many years. We were well-trained. We were confident. We were real fighter pilots.

The Tornado crews who flew the exceedingly dangerous low-level, JP.233 runway suppression missions in the first nights of the Gulf War went into combat under much different conditions. Although they had the benefit of five months of adjustment to the idea, some were in their early twenties with low flight hours. They were all new to combat, they had to fly the toughest mission right from the first time, they had to fly at night at low altitude (which is always unnerving) and they had to drive directly into the bright, terrifying streams of triple-A and watch repeated missile launches on their radar warning system. Despite this shocking experience, they pressed on, while ten of their comrades disappeared around them in the first few days. They were the great heroes of the air war, much like the American F-105 pilots over North Vietnam – not the superstar MiG-killers but the more prosaic bombers. They were inspired and propelled, no doubt, by the universal Fighter Pilot panache and the same sense of duty and spirit that drove their glorious and humble predecessors over the English Channel just 50 years before. Britain produces great fighter pilots because it loves them – and they know it. They are the prime symbols of the nation's ethos.

Combat tempers the fighter pilot's steel and tests it at the same time. 'You fight like you train', they say at Top Gun, but it is never the same. You can't simulate the proximity of death. With each mission, you gain a confidence and fortitude that never leaves you. Long after it's over, you look back and examine all your behaviour in the great test of your life, inwardly ashamed of the failures, outwardly calm, but undeniably proud, about having mastered the talents and ignored the frights.

Combat is about comradeship. The bravery and the professional performance in the midst of deadly distractions are largely motivated by the need to appear admirable in the eyes of one's compatriots. The fighter squadron is built around that fact and the

F-15 formation take-off. Working successfully together in flight is a joy for fighter pilots. (USAF: 36 TFW)

Camaraderie. F-4 squadron
mates share the joy of
Terry Murphy, who was
picked up in North Vietnam
after ejecting in 1972. It is
this spirit and mutual
support that make the
Squadron a unique fighting
organization – the
emotional as well as the
operational home of the
fighter pilot. (Terry Murphy)

mission depends on it. One Tornado pilot said, describing the target run across an Iraqi airfield on his first mission: 'You are frightened of dying, you are frightened of failing.' The second is more important because fighter pilots feel omnipotent – it's part of the self-confidence. You can't let the danger distract you from getting the job done, you can't let the thought of dying tarnish your self-esteem.

When combat turns vicious, when you look into the flashing gun barrels of your enemy, when the situation turns into a bucket of worms, when the myriad impressions – the sights and sounds and thoughts and impulses – pile up until you can't process them all, and your duties and objectives bounce all over the list of jumbled priorities that keeps you going, it is training that gets you through. The machine and the tasks are so complex, the unknown challenges so sudden, the confusion of war so pervasive as compared to the normal vicissitudes and problems of life, that only intense practice in an environment (which is really a poor substitute for the real thing), a marriage of passionate physical and mental skills, enables one to persevere in combat.

Combat changes a man. There is, indeed, a postwar syndrome that perforates the future. Of course it varies, and is usually under control, but sometimes, even in the best of men, it pushes towards the surface. It is an impatience with frustration, a desire to smash, a love of conflict, a longing for an energy outlet, the narcotic of adrenalin. On the better side, it is the confidence that the world cannot defeat you, that by mastering your own soul nothing else will ever get you down, that there are causes worth fighting for.

I admitted that combat was fun, the ultimate challenge that completed my manhood, the highlight of a warrior's career, which hurts those who rightly condemn man's impulse to war. But don't condemn the soldiers, I say, who give a lifetime to practising and then do the job with the drive and the lack of self-doubt that overcome those other human urges toward peace in society and kindness toward men. Soldiers know something of the suffering they cause, the destruction they wreak, but they also know that it is the incompetent or gutless politicians, the appeasers and the unbending aggressors, who cause wars, not the soldiers who risk or sacrifice their lives and their gentleness.

In Vietnam there was a popular quotation: it was reproduced on a multitude of brass plaques, one of which used to hang in the office of General George Brown, the Commander of US Air Forces in Vietnam, where I worked for a year in between my flying tours. I used to stand and look at it, my geo-political-scientific mind and my hatred of communism and dictators telling me that we were right, even if we were rather incompetent, in trying to save this sad, leaderless little nation on the other side of the world. I came across it again last year, hanging in a place of honour on the wall of the Aggressor Squadron commander at RAF Bentwaters. It is something that the do-gooders and those with other priorities do not seem to understand. It is even more valid now than when it was written 130 years ago. The Gulf War was the perfect example, as we were surrounded by those who could find nothing for which they were willing to fight and, even worse, those who walked reluctantly alongside and finally jumped on the bandwagon just before it got away. The fighter pilot, as all military men, tries not to think of political things, but this is one that he believes in with the greatest of sincerity and understanding. As the one who gets shot at when it starts, he is entitled to believe in it:

The Morality of War

War is an ugly thing, but not the ugliest of things; the decayed and degraded state of moral and patriotic feeling which thinks that nothing is worth war is much worse.

A man who has nothing for which he is willing to fight, nothing he cares about more that his own personal safety, is a miserable creature who has no chance of being free, unless made and kept so by the exertions of better men than himself.

John Stuart Mill, 1861

XI

FIGHTER PILOTS

W E HAVE OUTLINED the building blocks of fighter aviation – a brief and selective look at the aircraft, the weapons, the employment concepts and the background. With these in mind, perhaps we can now look at some of the individuals, some of the exceptional people who have distinguished themselves in this distinguished profession. Fighter pilots, by having exceptional skills when chance presents itself, sometimes have the opportunity to become heroes. Some work hard at it because they have big egos, other because it is part of the profession – a way to earn the respect of peers and superiors, and self – and others simply do the job expected of them with maximum performance and live with the consequences.

Eddie Rickenbacker. A motorcycle racer who later became president of Eastern Airlines, Rickenbacker shot down 22 German aircraft and four balloons. His favourite aeroplane was the Spad XIII, flown by the 94th 'Hat-in-the-Ring' Squadron. (US National Archives)

But wars do not occur very often, and the dedicated fighter pilot may practise his craft for a career and never fire a shot in anger. For some, like Robin Olds, who shot down the enemy in the Second World War and again in Vietnam, or Tom Lennon, who flew two combat tours in Vietnam and then led his F-111 Wing in the Gulf, the twenty years in between seemed like a brief hiatus between the major events in their lives. The fighter pilot measures his life in terms of aeroplanes and events: he retains friends, but he moves through the system alone, an individual, from base to base, aircraft to aircraft, always trying to stay in the cockpit, to learn, to attain command of other fighter pilots. When war comes, it is almost by accident, and some pilots are in the perfect position, perfect condition, with the drive and confidence to press on, press on, press on. If war does not come, they press on anyway, so that they will be ready if it does.

PORTRAIT OF A FIGHTER PILOT: DAVID ROTHENANGER

David Rothenanger* is one of those pilots who love to fly aeroplanes, and he has done nothing but that since entering the Air Force with a BS degree in Aerospace Engineering from Auburn University in 1980. He learned aviation maintenance, got a lot of flying time and was on his way to a successful commercial career when he decided to try USAF pilot training. He's been flying fighters ever since. As only a junior major, he has 2,500 hours of fighter time, with another 1,100 hours in 25 different kinds of aircraft. He attended the junior and intermediate-level professional Air Force schools, but only by correspondence and local seminar rather than in residence at Air University in Montgomery, Alabama. One of these days the Air Force is going to stick him behind a desk whether he likes it or not, but his job will be flying-related: he is too competent, so his future progression will tend to follow that path. These are the kinds of men who end up as Fighter Squadron Commanders, with too much flying time and experience to ignore; then the Air Force looks at them to see if they have the other qualities for promotion, even though they may have missed a little staff work and some of the normal stepping stones along the way. Some can make it to the top this way, but it is much more difficult. Rothenanger, articulate and personable, with an easy-going self-confidence, has always been advanced to important positions in his flying duties.

---

* Major David 'R-10' Rothenanger, Flight Commander, F-16C Instructor Pilot, 58th Tactical Training Wing, Luke Air Force Base, Arizona.

He began as an F-4E pilot at Moody AFB, Georgia, quickly becoming a four-ship Flight Leader, maintenance check pilot and manager of the Squadron Standardization/Evaluation programme. Because of his personality and skill, he was then assigned to the Lead-In Fighter Training (LIFT) programme at Holloman AFB, New Mexico, as an Instructor Pilot. Here he was responsible for training new fighter pilots in tactical weapons employment in the AT-38. He then moved on to the F-16C in one of Europe's top squadrons, the 526th Tactical Fighter Squadron at Ramstein Air Base, Germany, which has a primary air-to-air role in NATO. He quickly became an Instructor Pilot, was the Wing's Top Gun in several areas a few times and finally was assigned as the Wing's Assistant Chief of Stan/Eval. The last was an important move as it showed that, although only a captain, he had the special ability and the confidence of the Wing's leaders to evaluate all the other fighter pilots in the Wing on their regular and no-notice flight checks.

In 1990, 'R-10' and his wife, Sid, moved to Luke, where he became a Flight Commander in the F-16C Replacement Training Unit. From this position, he will look around, perhaps at the Thunderbirds, where he has all the qualifications, perhaps at the maintenance field, where he has a solid background and which will keep him close to his beloved aeroplanes. He is one of those special people in the Air Force – the ones who know how to use the weapon system confidently to its maximum capability, who can teach and lead and who create the force that operates with maximum safety and efficiency and then wins wars when called upon. A lot of fighter pilots have been shifted aside by this time in their careers – the jobs are getting fewer – but David Rothenanger is moving toward an important position in tactical fighters.

PORTRAIT OF A FIGHTER PILOT: 'DOC' PENTLAND

Modern fighter pilots could be said to have a PhD in air combat. 'Doc' Pentland* got his nickname because he also has a PhD in History from the University of Idaho, the state where he was born in 1949. Until recently, he was the Operations Officer of a proud unit, the 92nd Tactical Fighter Squadron at RAF Bentwaters, England; he then became a Squadron Commander in the 510th, the sister-squadron at the same base. Doc has been flying the A-10 since he graduated from pilot training in 1977, shortly after the aircraft was introduced to the USAF inventory. He is, therefore, one of the most highly experienced A-10 pilots in the Air Force.

---

* Lt. Col. Pat 'Doc' Pentland, Commander, 510th Tactical Fighter Squadron, RAF Bentwaters, Suffolk.

'Doc' Pentland. (Author)

After flying the 'Hog' at Myrtle Beach AFB, South Carolina, he was selected to join the 92nd at Bentwaters, the first A-10 squadron in Europe, in 1979. There he became an Instructor Pilot and attended the élite Tactical Fighter Weapons School at Nellis AFB, Nevada. After more flying at Bentwaters, he returned to the Weapons School – a place reserved for only the best – as an instructor. In 1984 he became the Course Manager at the school for the A-10.

Along the way, he also filled two coveted and important career squares by attending the select Armed Forces Staff College and serving in Fighter Plans and Requirements on the Air Staff in the Pentagon. Returning to Bentwaters, he served as the Wing Flying Safety Officer before becoming the Squadron Operations Officer in 1990. Every fighter pilot dreams of being the Operations Officer and Commander of a fighter squadron where he can lead and fly. After that, regardless of rank achieved, it's all downhill in terms of hands-on contact with line pilots and aircraft: the desk and broader duties take over. 'Doc' Pentland, with his unique and accomplished combination of education, staff experience and flying skill, is likely to move rapidly to higher rank and responsibility. But he will never have a better job than the one he now holds and cherishes.

'Doc' recently took me around the Squadron, showing me all the improvements that had been made since I was around. He talked about the A-10 and the mission:

'When I started flying the A-10 in 1977, a lot of people thought of it as a step backwards – straight-wing, slow – but others saw it rightly as a single-mission airplane that could do a good job, what it was designed to do, in certain circumstances, such as, for example, the missions in South Vietnam that the A-1 flew. Now, whether we ever see those again in combat is another question, but the A-10 certainly proved itself in the Gulf in both the FAC and strike role. If there was ever a war designed for the A-10, we have just seen it –

long loiter time, heavy bomb load, ideal targets, good weather. It did a magnificent job. I have never known a pilot who converted to the A-10 who did not fall in love with it. You can master your trade in this airplane. Every man in this Squadron, in the context of having families of course, wanted to go to the Gulf and fly his airplane. The status of the A-10 in the Air Force is going to change drastically in the next couple of years, but whatever happens, it can be said that the airplane certainly did its job well, we got our money's worth in terms of deterrent and combat capability, and the airplane will be in demand, in some capacity, in some part of the world, for years to come.'

PORTRAIT OF A FIGHTER PILOT: MAL PRISSICK

Mal Prissick* brings a wealth of experience to the process of training new Tornado crews to deliver weapons. He joined the RAF in 1966 as a craft apprentice in ground radar, then transferred to aircraft technician training. From there, he was awarded a cadetship to RAF Cranwell in 1969, then the RAF Academy. On graduation as a pilot in 1972, he went to advanced training in the Gnat and tactical weapons training in the Hunter. He was then posted to operational duty in the Buccaneer with No. 15 Squadron at RAF Laarbruch, Germany, flying the overland strike/attack mission for NATO. Returning to Honington where he had checked out in the Bucc, Prissick flew a tour with No. 12 Squadron in the maritime attack roll, and then a two-year tour as an instructor pilot in the Buccaneer Operational Conversion Unit. He completed the Qualified Weapons Instructor Course in 1981, which included participation in a Red Flag exercise at Nellis AFB, Nevada.

In 1982 he converted to the Tornado and served as a Flight Commander (Weapons) at RAF Marham in No. 27 Squadron. During this tour he was sent to the United States several times to plan and participate in Green Flag exercises and then as part of the team which won the 1985 Strategic Air Command Navigation and Bombing Competition – a result which shocked a lot of professional SAC crews who always thought they were the world's best. The fighter pilots showed them how that year.

Prissick then served a staff tour at Headquarters, No. 1 Group, where he was responsible for Tornado training. In July 1988 he was promoted to Wing Commander while on the Advanced Staff Course at the RAF Staff College, Bracknell. Following Tornado refresher

* Wg Cdr Mal Prissick, Officer Commanding, Tornado Weapons Conversion Unit, RAF Honington, Suffolk.

training, he assumed his present position as Officer Commanding the TWCU at Honington. This also places him in command of the 'shadow' squadron, No. 45, should it be required for operational duty. By the end of 1991, he will have moved on to new responsibilities, and will undoubtedly play an important role in RAF fighter operations in the years ahead.

He is married to Liz, and they have three young sons. His brother Howard flies the Tornado F.3 with No. 5 Squadron at RAF Coningsby, which undoubtedly makes for interesting conversations at family reunions. Howard also flew an exchange tour in F/A-18s with the US Marine Corps.

Prissick has strong opinions on the value of intensive training to the quality of the fighter force and the way the Tornado is the key aircraft in RAF strategy. And, of course, he also believes in the values of the fighter pilot that he expressed in the Foreword of this book. Speaking near the end of the Gulf War, he expressed great disappointment that he and his highly experienced Tornado instructors had not been called on to fight while inexperienced, young crews were flying the most difficult and dangerous missions of the war. 'But,' he said, 'the fact that they performed in such splendid fashion shows that our training job is just as important.' Mal Prissick is a great fighter pilot.

PORTRAIT OF A FIGHTER PILOT: JOHN ROBERTS

John Roberts* and I have the same name, so we enjoyed talking about the fighter pilot profession in our different generations when I paid a visit to his training squadron. John had spent his entire career in the F-111 before being selected as an Exchange Officer. After his childhood and school in Phoenix, Arizona, he was nominated to attend the US Naval Academy at Annapolis, Maryland, graduating in 1982. He elected to take an Air Force commission. After pilot training at Laughlin AFB, Texas, he checked out in the F-111 at Cannon AFB, New Mexico, in 1983. His first tour was flown at RAF Lakenheath from 1984 to 1987. He then returned to Cannon to be an Instructor Pilot in the F-111 Replacement Training Unit, where all crews learn to fly the aircraft. During that tour, he earned one of the coveted slots at the USAF Fighter Weapons School at Nellis AFB, Nevada. He then returned to Cannon until his assignment to Honington and the Tornado. Before becoming an instructor, he proceeded through the full

---

* Capt. John Roberts, Instructor Pilot and USAF Exchange Officer, Tornado Weapons Conversion Unit, RAF Honington, Suffolk.

SOME GREAT FIGHTER PILOTS

Eddie Rickenbacker (USA)	26 kills. Medal of Honor. Highest US ace in WWI.
Manfred von Richthofen (Germany)	80 kills. 'The Red Baron'. Most famous fighter pilot in history.
Oswald Boelcke (Germany)	40 kills. Greatest fighter pilot of WWI, and great leader.
Albert Ball (Britain)	44 kills. Victoria Cross. The great British loner.
Georges Guynemer (France)	54 kills. Second to Fonck in score, but not popularity.
Mick Mannock (Britain)	50 (68?) kills. Victoria Cross. The greatest British ace of WWI.
Dick Bong (USA)	40 kills. Medal of Honor. Highest US ace in WWII.
'Johnnie' Johnson (Britain)	38 kills. Highest-scoring British and Commonwealth pilot. Rose later to high rank and wrote two very successful books.
Adolf Galland (Germany)	104 kills. Perhaps the greatest fighter pilot of all time, by virtue of his accomplishments both in the air and on the ground.
Douglas Bader (Britain)	26 kills. Greatest fighter leader and tactician of the war. Of great courage – flew combat after having his legs amputated.
Joe McConnell (USA)	16 kills. Highest US ace in Korea. Movie made of his life.
Steve Richie (USA)	5 kills. The only USAF pilot ace in Vietnam.
Randy Cunningham (USA)	5 kills. The only USN pilot ace in Vietnam, and also the first. Now a United States Congressman.
Robin Olds (USA)	12 (WWII) + 4 (Vietnam) kills. The greatest fighter pilot of the jet era.

And let us not forget the F-4 back-seater aces in Vietnam who were part of the team: Chuck DeBellevue (6 kills), Jeff Feinstein (5) and Bill Driscoll (5).

Tornado training course. He enjoys flying the Tornado GR.1 because it has so many similarities to the F-111. He and his wife, Jeanie, also enjoy the pleasure of getting to know the British pilots and their families and living once again in England.

I asked him what being a fighter pilot meant to him, and he said: 'I feel the term "fighter pilot" relates to an attitude of a person. Many individuals may have this attitude and not just a pilot of a military fast jet. My definition of a fighter pilot would be a professional who has the confidence and willingness to do a difficult job regardless of the danger. This person could be an AC-130 pilot, an F-111 WSO or

John Roberts (not the author!). (Author)

a flight surgeon on a rescue helicopter. The confidence of a fast jet pilot comes from training. The training must be realistic and demanding but with practical rules. It should institute a set of learning objectives and, once these are met, new ones must be established in the proper sequence. Limits are used to task the individual and help prevent losses. The confidence of a fighter pilot is continually built up by further training throughout a career. It is interesting to see that, even though we have different methods in some ways, the results of USAF and RAF training are the same – a professional fighter crew.'

John Roberts, the younger, is a perfect example of the young, motivated and well-trained fighter pilot who is the backbone of the United States' Tactical Air Forces.

PORTRAIT OF A FIGHTER PILOT: CHUCK SIMPSON

Chuck Simpson,* 39, became the leader of the Thunderbirds during the 1990 season. A Texan, he earned his degree and commission at the US Air Force Academy in 1972. He then received his master's degree in Business Administration from the University of California. He received his Silver Wings in 1974 at Webb AFB, Texas. Following F-4 Phantom training at Luke AFB, Arizona, he was assigned to Kunsan Air Base, Korea. In 1976 he moved to the 4th Tactical Fighter Wing at Seymour-Johnson AFB, North Carolina, where he was selected to attend the USAF Fighter Weapons School at Nellis in 1978. He then returned to Seymour-Johnson to serve as both Squadron and Wing Weapons Officer.

After a tour at Hahn Air Base, Germany, in the F-4, he upgraded

---

* Lt. Col. Chuck Simpson, Commander/Leader, United States Air Force Thunderbirds, Nellis Air Force Base, Nevada.

at Hill AFB, Utah, in the F-16 and returned to Hahn to serve as the Wing Weapons Officer and Flight Commander for the first operational F-16 Wing in Europe. In 1984 he reported to Nellis as the 57th Fighter Weapons Wing Director of Tactics and Test; there he also served as an F-16 project manager and as Chief, F-16 Project Office, and then Assistant Director, Tactics and Test Operations. He then moved to the Fighter Weapons School as both Operations Officer and Commander of the F-16 division.

Lt. Col. Simpson then became 'Thunderbird One'. He has 3,700 hours of fighter time in his 17 years of service. He is married to Christine, and they have two daughters.

THE COMPLETE FIGHTER PILOT

Captain John C. Meyer, the fourth-ranking ace in the Second World War and later the four-star Commander of Strategic Air Command, was the Squadron Commander of Major George Preddy for more than a year. He wrote: 'George was small and slight. He was soft-spoken, without even a hint of braggadocio. I have never met a man of . . . such intense desire to excel . . . George Preddy was the complete fighter pilot.'

After flying the P-47, Preddy converted to the P-51 in the 352nd Fighter Group. John Frisbee, of *Air Force Magazine*, picks up the story:*

'Major Preddy was scheduled to lead the entire group on an August 6 escort mission. The mission was scrubbed due to forecast bad weather, and – with a free day ahead – a big party was inevitable. Shortly after midnight, the mission was on again. At briefing, the group commander judged that Preddy was not in shape to lead, but John Meyer assured him that George would be ready by takeoff time.

'A few hours later, from his perch at 30,000 feet, Preddy spotted more than thirty Me-109s coming in on the third box of B-17s. He led his flight into the midst of the -109s, shooting down three in rapid succession.

'At that point, four other P-51s joined the fight. Preddy shot down two more -109s, then followed the formation down to 5,000 feet, where he found himself alone with the enemy. One of them broke to the left, followed by Preddy in his *Cripes A' Mighty*. After a hot duel, George shot down his sixth of the day. On landing, a slightly green Preddy vowed never again to fly with a hangover. That mission

---

* Quoted, with permission, from *Air Force Magazine*, John L. Frisbee, Contributing Editor, December 1987.

earned him the Distinguished Service Cross and an unsought leave in the States.

'Major Preddy returned to the ETO in October 1944 as commander of the group's 328th Squadron. During the Battle of the Bulge in December, elements of the group were moved to a fighter strip in Belgium. On Christmas Day, Preddy led ten of his P-51s on a patrol. They were vectored to a formation of enemy planes, and in the ensuing fight, though the squadron became scattered, Preddy downed two more -109s. He and his wingman, Lt. James Cartee, were then vectored to an unknown number of bandits near Liège. Preddy saw an FW-190 on the deck and went after him at treetop height. As they roared over American ground troops, George Preddy – at war's end the third-ranking American ace of the European war with 26.83 victories – was hit by friendly ground fire and crashed to his death.

'His letters home showed Preddy to be a true believer with a philosophy of life that seemed beyond his twenty-five years. General Meyer wrote that he was a man with a "core of steel in a largely sentimental soul." Among other virtues, Major Preddy showed boundless loyalty to the men with whom he flew and a typically American attitude toward air-to-air fighting. He once said, "I'm sure as hell not a killer, but combat flying is like a game, and a guy likes to come out on top."

'Almost certainly, he would also have come out as top American ace in Europe had it not been for the tragic error on Christmas Day in 1944.'

THE GREATEST ACE: GENERAL ADOLF GALLAND

Who was the greatest of them all? In the First World War it was certainly either Richthofen or Boelcke, but they were killed in action. In the Second World War I believe it was Galland, because he was both an ace and a great leader. In Vietnam, it was Robin Olds, for the same reasons. Of the three, I must say that Galland was the greatest. Even though he was on the losing side, the circumstances of the war gave him the opportunity to demonstrate greatness in flight and on the ground. Olds, an ace in the Second World War, tried valiantly but was unable to kill the fifth MiG in Vietnam before being sent home. He was, nevertheless, a truly great combat leader, inspiring his pilots and creating innovative tactics.

Galland began with a big advantage: he flew nearly 300 missions of ground attack in Spain before becoming a fighter ace in Germany. He then survived 400 more missions, although, like some other leading aces, he was shot down several times. His

Lieutenant-General Adolf Galland, here depicted at a fighter conference, was one of the Luftwaffe's greatest fighter aces. He had victories dating from the Spanish Civil War, and his flying skills made him Germany's youngest general, but his uncompromising views and determination always to get the best available for his pilots led to confrontations with Hitler and Goering.

operational flying encompassed nearly the entire war on the Western Front, and he shot down more aircraft exclusively there than any other pilot — 104 — despite much time in staff and command positions away from the cockpit. The majority of Hartmann's victories were on the Russian Front, the majority of Marseille's in Africa. Seven of Galland's victories were in the Me 262 jet, and he was the commander of JV 44, the jet squadron composed of a majority of aces formed in February 1945.

Along with his flying accomplishments, Galland distinguished himself by his leadership of fellow fighter pilots, teaching them, gaining their respect and protecting them against the more foolish orders from above. He was well known for speaking his mind to Göring at the risk of his own career. On one famous occasion, he offered to turn in his medals after the Luftwaffe chief had criticized the courage of the fighter pilots.

At the age of 30, he became the youngest general in the German armed forces, as Inspector General of Fighters in November 1941. By 1943 his frustration with Göring led him to return to flying in an attempt to solve the growing difficulties of dealing with the long-range Allied fighters over Germany. His vocal struggle finally resulted in his demotion (for him it was a delight) as commander of the jet squadron, despite his high rank. It is clear, as told in his autobiography *The First and the Last*, that he had a superb

> *Only the spirit of attack borne in a brave heart will bring success to any fighter aircraft, no matter how highly developed it may be.*
>
> General Adolf Galland

understanding of tactical air power, learned in battle and combined with courage and common sense. It was fortunate for the Allies that Göring and not Galland commanded the Luftwaffe.

After the war Galland spent some years training the Argentine Air Force – and made an impact which showed up many years later in the courage of the Argentines in the Falklands War. He then served in the new Luftwaffe and became a respected friend of many Allied airmen in NATO and Europe.

So, yes, there are aces who killed more of the enemy, were more famous for their development of tactics, rose later to higher rank and had a greater charisma, but, taken together, none of them combined as much accomplishment. Galland was not only respected by his own pilots, but by his enemy as well. Despite his losing battle with Göring and the German Air Staff, no ace was more influential or rose to higher position in the same war in which he flew to victory.

THE GREATEST ACE: A SECOND OPINION*

Who is the greatest fighter pilot of all time? This is a very difficult question to answer. Picking the top fifty would have been hard enough. Everything depends on the criteria adopted. Success in combat, flying ability, marksmanship, leadership and charisma, tactical ability and innovation, and situational awareness are all factors to be considered. Let's have a look, pulling a few names out of the hat as we go.

Firstly we have success in air combat. Manfred von Richthofen led the field in WW1 with 80 victories; Erich Hartmann in WW2 with 352. Heinz-Wolfgang Schnaufer was the top scoring night fighter ace with 121. By comparison the Allied top scorers came nowhere, Dick Bong scoring 40 in the Pacific theatre and Johnnie Johnson 38 over occupied Europe. In the jet age, Mac McConnell knocked down 16 MiG-15s in Korea; the top scoring Israeli pilot is credited with 17 victories, while in Vietnam Steve Ritchie and Randy Cunningham got five each.

Flying ability is a completely subjective judgement. Georges Guynemer, Werner Voss, Billy Bishop, Jim Lacey, Hans-Joachim Marseille and Chuck Yeager are names that spring immediately to mind as outstanding, although there are many others in contention.

Marksmanship. Most successful air fighters adopted the 'stick

---

* By Mike Spick, author of such books as *The Ace Factor, Fighter Pilot Tactics* and *Jet Fighter Performance*.

Far left: Manfred von Richthofen – the most famous ace of all time, but not the greatest. A nobleman of great courage, he shot down 80 enemy aircraft, the highest total of the war, but was killed in combat. (US National Archives)
Left: Oswald Boelcke. A great leader and tactician, he found and trained Richthofen. After achieving 40 victories, he was killed in a mid-air collision caused by one of his own pilots. (US National Archives)

your nose in the enemy cockpit and you can't miss' approach. Few ever mastered the art of deflection or long range shooting. Notable marksmen include Rene Fonck, Richthofen himself, James McCudden, Sailor Malan, Werner Moelders, Johnnie Johnson, George Beurling, and David McCampbell.

Leadership is another completely subjective area. Some of the acknowledged great fighter leaders failed to achieve outstanding personal scores, for example Eduard Neumann and Don Blakeslee. Then there is charisma, which is an inspirational quality, and here a few names stand supreme; Oswald Boelcke; Adolf Galland; the incomparable Douglas Bader, Gregory Boyington, and Robin Olds.

In terms of tactical ability and innovation, one man stands head and shoulders above the rest. Oswald Boelcke developed fighter tactics from scratch, and his methods have stood the test of time almost unchanged to the present day. His closest rivals are Mannock, Moelders, Malan, Bader, and John S. Thach.

Situational awareness is a rare faculty possessed by only about five percent of the fighter community. The dominant factor in air fighting is surprise. A high level of SA allows its possessor to avoid being surprised, while enabling him to keep track of a fast moving fluid situation. While exceptional eyesight helps. SA seems to be at least partly intuitive, in the same way that a few men are naturally gifted marksmen. Here we have Boelcke, Voss, Mannock and Guynemer from the first war; Bader, Brendan Finucane, Don Blakeslee and Heinz Baer from the second, Asher Snir from Israel, and Robin Olds in both WW2 and South East Asia. Erich Hartmann's ability to keep the situation controllable was outstanding, although it should be recorded that he did not always succeed, and was shot down 17 times in all.

It is not practicable to go through the various attributes of the great fighter pilots, and assign points to each, the contender with the greatest points total being the winner. The choice has to be made taking all factors together. The question now becomes, which pilot made the greatest contribution to air fighting? There can only be one answer to this – Oswald Boelcke. The reasons are as follows.

His score of 40 victories, while low by later standards, was exceptional at the time. He died as the result of a collision with one of his own men; had this not been the case his score would almost certainly have gone far higher. Victories were certainly not easy to achieve in Boelcke's era. Had they been, this would have been reflected in the scores of others. But this notwithstanding, Boelcke's greatest achievement was in formalising the tactics of battle and putting them into practice. Many others tried; only Boelcke succeeded. He saw what needed to be done more clearly than any man before or since, and was obviously destined for high command had he lived. His situational awareness was of a high order; as his star pupil Manfred von Richthofen commented on one occasion, 'he saw more than most men!' While his SA seems to have deserted him at the end, this was probably due to fatigue. He had scored 21 victories in the previous eight weeks, and his final flight was the sixth of the day.

Boelcke's leadership quality is evidenced by the number of aces among his pupils in Jagdstaffel 2, who included Richthofen (80), Max Muller (36). Erwin Boehme (24) and Stephan Kirmaier (11). Blessed with an infinite capacity for taking pains that amounted to

---

THE AIR COMBAT RULES OF OSWALD BOELCKE*

German Air Service, World War I (40 victories)

1. Try to secure advantages before attacking. If possible, keep the sun behind you.
2. Always carry through an attack when you have started it.
3. Fire only at close range and only when your opponent is properly in your sights.
4. Always keep your eye on your opponent and never let yourself be deceived by ruses.
5. In any form of attack it is essential to assail your opponent from behind.
6. If your opponent dives on you, do not try to evade his onslaught, but fly to meet it.
7. When over the enemy's lines, never forget your own line of retreat.
8. Attack on principle in groups of four or six. When the fight breaks up into a series of single combats, take care that several do not go for one opponent.

---

* From *Fighter Combat*, p. 274.

> *In air fights it is absolutely essential to fly in such a way that your adversary cannot shoot at you, if you can manage it.*
>
> Captain Oswald Boelcke

genius, he was the first to introduce dissimilar air combat training, using captured enemy aeroplanes, thus anticipating Top Gun by some fifty years. That he was also a very charistmatic personality there can be no doubt. Richthofen also commented, 'It is strange that everyone who came to know Boelcke imagined that he was his one true friend . . . a strange phenomenon that I have observed only with Boelcke.'

In many ways, the choice of Boelcke was inevitable. Many of the contenders of all periods who survived their conflicts, failed to achieve high rank in peacetime, while yet more who did not survive, clearly would not have done so, whereas Boelcke certainly would. Few of those who followed were tactical innovators, and even they were left with little to do except build on the foundations laid by the young German pilot, to suit their own unique scenarios.

One final question must be posed. If Oswald Boelcke is the greatest fighter pilot of all time, why isn't he the most famous? In times of war, nations need living heroes. Boelcke died too early in the war, and his fame was eclipsed by the living, in particular by Richthofen. The Red Baron is a phenomenon, in that his fame has transcended national boundaries to the extent that he has become the most famous fighter pilot of all time. Why then has he been passed over for the title of the greatest? There are several reasons. Firstly he made virtually no contribution to the development of tactics: as a protégé of Boelcke, he learned all that he knew from the master. A first class marksman, he jealously hoarded his victories, unlike Mannock who gave several away to encourage new boys. He was also concerned that his score might be overtaken by his younger brother Lothar. By contrast Boelcke maintained that a victory was a score for the Staffel rather than the individual. The Red Baron was great, but not the greatest!

ROBIN OLDS: THE GREATEST FIGHTER PILOT OF THE JET ERA

When Robin Olds returned from Vietnam to become the Commandant of Cadets at the Air Force Academy, I was assigned to fly with him while he travelled around the country to give some rip-roaring speeches to Air Force groups. During those hours in flight in a T-33, and in some late-night conversations over a bottle of scotch, he sought my advice on matters at the Academy and gave me in return his invaluable wisdom on combat which I took to the F-4 in Vietnam a few months later. No other colonel or general I ever met treated me with such camaraderie and kindness. That simple example, a general communicating openly with a relatively naïve young captain, only on the verge of being a fighter pilot, shows what a great combat leader he was. It was the way he worked with and motivated the young pilots in the his Wolfpack at Ubon. I would have done anything for him.

I suggested to him the obvious, that it must have hurt to fail to get his fifth MiG, and he admitted that it had been the greatest disappointment of his career. He had been locked up in the stateside Air Defense Command during Korea, despite his twelve victories in the Second World War. Although he went hunting for victories in Vietnam, his greater accomplishment was the training and development of the 8th Tac Fighter Wing which dominated MiG-killing until the 432nd Wing at Udorn created the first aces several years later.

The foremost example of his innovative thinking was Operation 'Bolo' in January 1967: F-4s from the 8th Tactical Fighter Wing, commanded by Olds, pretended to be more vulnerable, bomb-heavy F-105s by flying their typical flight patch and using their call-signs. When the MiGs arrived, they found a swarm of missile-loaded F-4s with Olds in the lead. He shot down one MiG-21 and other members

Robin Olds. With 12 victories in the Second World War and four MiGs in Vietnam, he set an example of personal leadership, flying skill and tactical ability which placed him above all other jet pilots. (US National Archives)

> *Don't go getting your ass shot off: you and that Phantom are worth more than a two-ton lorry.* – Letter from Robin Olds to the author in Vietnam

of the force shot down an additional six enemy fighters, with no US losses. A very successful mission!

At the Air Force Academy, Olds, the West Pointer, was a dynamic leader, expecting his cadets to be soldiers as well as scholars. His outspoken opinions about the political restrictions in Vietnam got him into some hot water with his superiors, and he retired as a Brigadier General to Steamboat Springs, Colorado, where he still attacks the ski slopes with the same fighter pilot's spirit and aggressiveness. No fighter pilot of his era will ever forget his strength, common sense, honesty, charisma, heart and example.

THE FIGHTER PILOT HEROES OF VIETNAM

By virute of his charisma, personal leadership and flying accomplishments, Robin Olds was a great, overall hero of the Vietnam War. But even he would admit that the greatest heroes were the F-105 'Thud' drivers who braved the flak and missiles and MiGs again and again over Thud Ridge. And of those, the greatest heroes were those who took hits and ended up spending years under torture and deprivation in the 'Hanoi Hilton'. Tough, hard-nosed Robbie Risner and Jim Kasler, both aces in Korea, and many of their comrades, set an example of courage and indomitable spirit in flight over the North and in prison that earns more respect than any number of air-to-air victories. With rare exceptions, the POWs of North Vietnam, almost all of them fighter pilots, demonstrated how man at his best can survive with self-respect in the hands of man at his worst.

In the Vietnam War, 238 Medals of Honor were awarded, twelve to members of the Air Force, 155 to Army personnel 14 to the Navy and 57 to the Marines. Of the Navy total, three were fighter pilots in North Vietnam:

Captain James B. Stockdale (POW; later Rear-Admiral)
Lt. Cdr. Michael J. Estocin (posthumous)
Lt. (j.g.) Clyde E. Lassen

Of the 12 USAF recipients, not all were fighter pilots, but each one of them demonstrated fighter pilot determination and selfless courage:

Captain Steven L. Bennett (posthumous). Forward Air Controller, OV-10, South Vietnam. Died in intentional crash-landing to save back-seater, who was unable to eject.

Major George E. Day. F-100 FAC, North Vietnam. Escape and maximum resistance as POW.

Captain Merlyn H. Dethlefsen. F-105, North Vietnam. Despite battle damage and heavy AAA, SAM and MiG attacks, pressed attack repeatedly against gun targets in advance of bomber flights.

Major Bernard F. Fisher. A-1E, South Vietnam. Landed at airstrip surrounded by enemy to pick up crashed comrade despite littered runway and intense gunfire. Took nineteen hits but flew out.

1st Lt. James P. Fleming. UH-1F helicopter, South Vietnam. Successfully rescued patrol despite heavy gunfire, exposed position and low fuel.

THE BALLAD OF BERNIE FISHER

TUNE: *The Wabash Cannonball*

Listen to the small arms,
Hear the 20 mike mike roar,
The A-1Es are bouncing,
Off the A Shau Valley floor.
Hear the mighty roar of engines,
Hear the lonesome Hobo call,
'I'll get you home to mother,
When the work's all done this fall.'

'Listen, A Shau Tower,
This is Hobo fifty-one,
I want to use your runway,
Although it's overrun.
A friend of mine is down there,
A-hiding in a ditch,
I want to make a passenger stop,
And save that son-of-a-bitch.'

Listen to the small arms,
Hear the 20 mike mike roar,
The A-1Es are bouncing,
Off the A Shau Valley floor.
Hear the mighty roar of engines,
Hear the lonesome Hobo call,
'I'll get you home to mother,
When the work's all done this fall.'

Vietnam Medal of Honor winner Bernie Fisher. Landing his slow A-1E 'Spad' on an enemy-controlled airstrip in heavy gunfire to pick up a downed comrade was one of the most selfless acts of bravery in aviation history. (US National Archives)

Colonel Joe M. Jackson. C-123, South Vietnam. Landed big, slow aircraft to pick up surrounded team despite heavy gunfire, damaged and short runway, bad weather and eight previous aircraft losses.

Colonel William A. Jones III. A-1E, North Vietnam. Ignored heavy gunfire, radio loss, severe aircraft damage and fire and serious wounds to make firing passes and fly home to deliver location of downed pilot.

Sergeant John L. Levitow. AC-47 Loadmaster, South Vietnam. Despite 40 serious fragment wounds and pitching aircraft, captured and threw out burning flare before it exploded, saving aircraft and crew.

Captain Lance P. Sijan (posthumous). F-4C, POW. Evaded capture for six weeks, escaped despite conditions, resisted heroically until death from serious untreated wounds and torture. Hero of Air Force Academy, where a building is named after him.

Major Leo K. Thorsness. F-105 Weasel, North Vietnam. Pressed on against heavy gunfire and MiG attacks to support rescue attempt of wingman crew. Gave way to other aircraft on tanker despite low fuel.

Captain Hillard A. Wilbanks (posthumous). O-1E FAC, South Vietnam. Made repeated low passes, shooting at enemy force with rifle, to save Ranger force under attack. Mortally wounded and crashed.

TOP ACES OF THE MAJOR WARS*

WORLD WAR I

Highest British ace	Edward Mannock	68
Highest German ace	Manfred von Richthofen	80
Highest American ace	Eddie Rickenbacker	26
Highest French and Allied ace	Réné Fonck	75
Highest Canadian ace	Billy Bishop	72
Highest Italian ace	Francesco Baracca	34
Total German aces		363
Total British Empire aces		Nearly 800
Total French aces		158
Total US aces		111
Total Italian aces		43

WORLD WAR II

Highest US ace (USAF, Pacific)	Richard Bong	40
Highest US ace (Navy, Pacific)	David McCampbell	34
Highest US ace (Marine, Pacific)	Pappy Boyington	28
Highest American ace (Europe)	Frank Gabreski	28
	plus 6½ in Korea	34½
Highest British ace	'Johnnie' Johnson	38
	Tom Pattle (South Africa)	Over 40†
Highest German ace (East)	Erich Hartmann	352
Highest German ace (West)	Hans-Joachim Marseille	158
Highest German night-fighter ace	Heinz Schnaufer	121
Highest Japanese ace (AF)	Satoshi Anabuki	51
Highest Japanese ace (Navy)	Hiroyoshi Nishizawa	87

KOREAN WAR

Highest US ace	Joe McConnell	16
Second	Jim Jabara	15
	plus 1½ in WWII	16½
Third	Manuel Fernandez	14½
Fourth	George Davis	14
	plus 7 in WWII	21
Fifth	Royal Baker	13
	plus 3½ in WWII	16½

VIETNAM

	Randy Cunningham (USN pilot)	5
	Willy Driscoll (USN WSO)	5
	Steve Ritchie (USAF pilot)	5
	Chuck Debellevue (USAF WSO)	6
	Jeff Feinstein (USAF WSO)	5
	Robin Olds (USAF pilot)	4
	plus 12 in WWII	16
	Nguyen Toon (Vietnamese)‡	13

* Source: *Air Aces*, by Christopher Shores (California: *Presidio Press*, 1983).
† Lost: uncertain records.
‡ Toon was Cunningham's/Driscoll's last kill.

Captain Gerald O. Young. HH-3E Jolly Green rescue helicopter commander, South Vietnam. Shot down attempting difficult night rescue of trapped team. Despite wounds from crash, aided crewman and declined rescue under heavy gunfire.

NAVIGATORS AND WOMEN IN FIGHTERS

Until the F-4 Phantom, most fighters were single-seat aircraft. The extra weight of a second crew member, larger fuselage and assorted support items had always been a sacrifice to performance. 'Besides,' said the fighter pilot, 'I can do it myself, and it's a distraction to have to talk and work with someone else.' He had an ego, an individualism, a pride in himself that did not leave room for sharing or dependency. But with more powerful engines, the complex demands of the new black boxes and more complex missions, the US Navy and McDonnell Aircraft decided to put a second man in the Phantom. He was an RIO, Radar Intercept Officer, and he didn't have a stick in his cockpit. At first, the Navy, and then the Air Force when it bought the aircraft, had a hard time finding qualified people. The Air Force put a stick and bitter young pilots fresh out of pilot training in the back seat. Many pilots flew two tours in Vietnam, one in the back and one in the front. But the navigator force built up, as SAC and other services provided experienced people, and these highly motivated and qualified people began to make the systems hum. Especially in the demanding combat environment, the extra eyes, hands and brain made a difference. The pilots in the front, even the 'old heads', began to trust and depend on the GIB, and three of them became aces over North Vietnam. Two-seat F-105s were used for the demanding Wild Weasel, anti-radar missions over the North; and the F-111, with its side-by-side cockpit, became an effective long-range fighter-bomber. In the RAF, even more than the USAF, the navigator in the F-4 became almost an equal member of the team in the air-to-air mission. After all, he was the one who was able to observe the radar and warning systems and to look around and advise the pilot on the best thing to do in an air battle. So he became an expert on air combat and even led the ground briefings before air combat tactics training flights. Finally, however, the wheel turned: aircraft performance became all-important again, new technology enabled the pilot better to manage his cockpit alone, and the Advanced Tactical Fighter for the next century returned to the single cockpit. But for 25 years the navigator was a fighter pilot.

The US Air Force had long ago put women through pilot training, but they could only go on to become instructors or transport pilots.

Congress decided that combat aircraft were inappropriate for women, despite a number of highly qualified volunteers with, for example, thousands of hours of T-38 IP time. Canada put a couple of women into F-18 fighter training. In 1990 the RAF accepted its first women into pilot training, but not into fighters. Women want their chance, especially since some of them went into combat in Panama and the Gulf on the ground, and many of them serve as fighter crew chiefs in the USAF. I think they should be given their chance. I have known some very tough and strong-minded women, and I do not think that they lost their feminity or compassion in being so. Women in fighters certainly cannot do any worse than some men I have seen, so why not give them the opportunity if they want it? We might be surprised, as we have so often been in other areas that women have finally entered. In should be up to them, not to some man who thinks he knows what is best for them.

NAVIGATORS IN THE RAF

The RAF has a different attitude towards navigators, especially in the Fighter Groups. As compared to the USAF, the navigator is much more an equal member of the crew. In fact, although the pilot legally signs and accepts responsibility for the aircraft before he flies – he is the captain of the ship, as it were – it may be the navigator who is the *de facto* commander of the mission by virtue of his experience or instructor status. He often plans, briefs and leads the mission, telling his front-seater and the rest of the flight what to do. In the USAF, this is simply, as they say in Britain, 'not on'. On top of this, in a policy instituted in the 1970s, the RAF also promotes navigators to high command positions over pilots: they may become fighter squadron commanders or even higher.

In the USAF, in contrast, the philosophy holds that navigators should not command pilots, at least not in flying jobs. The attitude, to put it in blunt terms, is that the pilot feels superior to a navigator, knows things that navigator could not know by virtue of his past experience, and would not respect him as a leader. Not all pilots feel that way, but many do.

The USAF philosophy has always been that the navigator is placed in the aircraft to help the pilot and do as he is told: 'Just give me the heading, and I'll make the tough decisions.' The RAF accepts that the navigator is as intelligent as the pilot and is not a second-class citizen, lacking a special experience. The USAF has moved along this road, but it has a long way to go. All you have to do is spend more time in an RAF fighter squadron and you will know what I mean.

F/A-18 carrier operations. Perfect communication, often by means of hand signals, is required on a busy flight deck. Every person must know his duties and position for complete safety during aircraft movements, take-offs and landings. (McDonnell Douglas)

HOW TO BECOME A FIGHTER PILOT

With the decline of the major threat and the defence budgets, it becomes even more difficult to become a fighter pilot. The USAF is undertaking radical changes, placing fighter pilots in training positions instead of training new instructors and seeking other ways to reduce the pilot force while still maintaining combat capabilities. The number of fighter Wings declines, and more pilots will fly fighters in the Air National Guard, staying current in a 747 and an F-16 at the same time. Guard units were sent to Vietnam, Panama and the Gulf to demonstrate that they could perform the mission as well as active-duty pilots. They did well, but, in general, a highly trained, full-time USAF pilot is bound to be better at his job in these complex aircraft. Nevertheless, it is an efficient saving to maintain a reserve force able step in when it is needed.

In the United States, the surest way to get a pilot training slot is to attend the US Air Force Academy in Colorado and participate actively in the flying programme there. There are still other routes, for example by gaining an officer's commission through the AFROTC or Officer Training School, but these are limited.

In Britain, the University Flying Squadrons or direct entry into the service after other forms of preliminary flying training will help you to attain one of the treasured slots. As in America, the best way to convince the selectors is to get flying time and show the potential for a good education and being a good officer. The services want career-minded people who are highly motivated towards overall military service, not just keen on hot-dogging around in a fast aeroplane because it is fun and you want to impress the ladies. Being a fighter pilot means being a professional soldier.

XII

FIGHTER FUTURE

IT IS OBVIOUS that technology drives onwards and that new weapons and aircraft will improve our ability to perform the air force missions. At the same time, leaders must learn from the past and apply the technology properly, with the correct strategy and tactics for the situation. In another book for this publisher, I have analysed the relationship between technology and strategy and the lessons of air power since the Second Word War. The Gulf War was, of course, the primary example in modern history of technology and strategy properly applied in concert. The generals and the politicians learned the major mistakes of the Vietnam era and made a grand and successful effort to avoid them. This time they had overwhelming, superior weapons, superior leadership, the ideal environment for their application and six months to design the perfect plan against a stupid enemy which was incapable of motivating its forces or using its weapons.

With that behind us, and with big budget cuts still necessary, we move on to a smaller force, but one able to apply advanced technology with professional skill anywhere in the world. The new enemies may be smaller but dangerous, but the Russian generals are still able to generate superb aircraft like the MiG-29 and Su-27, and the West must maintain its effort to stay in the race. The Eurofighter and the American Advanced Tactical Fighter will be the

The French Rafale. The Dassault-Breguet advanced fighter flies sooner, but is less capable, than the planned Eurofighter and the American Advanced Tactical Fighter. (Dassault Aviation)

centrepieces of the new technology. The development lead time is so great that we can see what weapons we will have for the next ten years. What is more in doubt is whether our leaders will have the strength and foresight to create a flexible strategy and maintain the force necessary to oppose the unknown, high-technology threats of a rapidly changing, multi-polar world.

EUROFIGHTER*

Recent developments in East/West détente will not eliminate entirely the threat in NATO. The Soviet Union will still have formidable conventional forces, including an air force equipped with derivatives of the MiG-29 'Fulcrum' and Su-27 'Flanker'. This threat must be matched to provide credible air defence; this is the design core for EFA.

By the late 1990s the current air superiority fighters – F-4, F-104 and Mirage F.1 – will be life-expired and replacements needed. EFA has been evaluated against the alternatives – Rafale, F-15, F-16 and F-18 – and is identified as the only aircraft capable of meeting the defence requirements of the four member nations to the next century.

The European Staff Requirement for Development was issued in December 1985, defining in detail the parameters for combat performance for EFA, maintenance ease and ability for all-weather operation from short runways with minimum support. This definition will result in a single-seat high-performance agile combat aircraft, capable of air superiority, close air combat and air-to-surface attacks. To achieve this, special emphasis has been placed on low wing loading, high thrust-to-weight ratio, all-round vision and 'carefree handling'. Performance is matched by attack, identification and defence systems including long-range radar and air-to-air missiles, and ECW capabilities to increase weapon system effectiveness and survivability. The extensive use of carbon fibre composites confers strength and durability with low weight, and ensures a smooth finish to minimize drag.

The unstable flight configuration of EFA could not be controlled by conventional pilot-operated controls and so artificial stability is provided by full-authority, digital and quadruplex fly-by-wire control systems. This automated system contains self-monitoring and test features with auto-reversion through four back-up modes. There is no mechanical system. Pitch and roll control is via the all-moving foreplanes and inboard/outboard full-span flaperons, and

---

* Text by British Aerospace.

BAe EAP, technology demonstrator for Eurofighter, a joint development by several nations. The Eurofighter will compete with the French Rafale, Swedish Gripen and derivatives of Soviet MiG-29s and Su-27s as the world's foremost fighter until the F-22 and a new Soviet fighter become operational several years later. (British Aerospace)

yaw control is via a conventional rudder. Leading-edge slats are fully automatic, to provide optimum wing camber for all angles of attack, and the whole flight control system is integrated with all of EFA's other systems.

The cockpit features HOTAS, allowing the pilot to carry out complex tasks with relative ease. The stick and throttle tops house around two dozen finger-tip functions, all of which are related to sensor and weapons control, defence aids management and in-flight handling. A helmet-mounted sight, together with the head up display (HUD), will include flight data, weapon aiming and cueing modes, and FLIR (forward-looking infra-red) imagery. The helmet also incorporates night vision aids, and three multi-function displays (MFDs) will present a wide range of information including overall tactical situation, system status and checks, map displays and air traffic procedures. Any MFD can show any information and is called up through soft keys arranged around each display.

Thirteen weapon carriage points are available on EFA, four on each wing and five on the fuselage. The optimum air-to-air load is four AMRAAM on the fuselage and two ASRAAM on outboard pylons. AIM-9L are available for interchange with the ASRAAM and up to ten missiles can be carried. EFA also has large air-to-ground potential via laser designators and a 27mm cannon as well as wet points for extra fuel tankage. A new feature is that all ECM are within the airframe so that there are no external pods to be fitted. The Defensive Aids Sub System (DASS) provides all-round priori-tized threat assessment, with automatic or manual responses to multiple threats. DASS includes ECM/ESM, front and rear threat warnings, decoys and chaff/flare dispensers and well complements a design that minimizes radar signature.

Eurofighter is thus a well researched and designed aircraft that has been created to thrive and survive in the high threat environ-ment of the European front line against the very best of contem-porary Soviet designs.

ADVANCED TECHNOLOGY

There is no room in this volume for a detailed look at the new aircraft, weapons and systems that lie in the decade between the F-15E and the ATF. But, we should at least mention some of the trends and think a little about the future.

The big thing is the new generation of fighters – stealth, the new weapons, the even better electronics, the advance in air-combat capability, the super-fighters. The ATF is capable of super-cruise – that is, it can sustain supersonic flight without using afterburner. This gives it extended, high-speed range that wins air battles, for the fighter that must turn tail and head for home and fuel may never get there. The other crucial aspect of this new aircraft is its ability to engage and dominate advanced Soviet fighters which at this moment are slightly superior to those of the West: the MiG-29 and Su-27 can outperform an F-15 or F-16 in slower, close-in dogfighting. The Soviets, as is their habit, will watch to see what kind of ATF we produce, and then try to develop something slightly superior a few years later, giving them an edge until the next generation. We will see an engine with vectored thrust, which can direct the exhaust in order to change the flight path of the aircraft over and above the effect of the flight control surfaces. This gives an aircraft the edge in air combat turning performance.

The avoinics of the new fighters will be more of the same – faster, more accurate, all-embracing computers that reduce the pilot's load and give him a greater extension of his offensive and defensive capability. Most importantly, we will see a rapid development of the battlefield command, control and intelligence functions that enable our weapons systems to function with greater accuracy and efficiency in the confusing bucket of worms known as an air battle.

The weapons will be more accurate, and they will be delivered from a greater distance, protecting the pilot and his expensive aircraft from the great dangers of enemy aircraft, guns and missiles. The new cockpit will amaze people, featuring voice

F-15 Maneuver Technology Demonstrator. This experimental fighter has forward control surfaces, vectored-thrust engines and other advanced features. Fighter aircraft must always be on the leading edge of technology. (McDonnell Douglas)

The F-22, thanks to the Pratt and Whitney F-119 engine design, is the first fighter capable of sustained supersonic cruise without the use of afterburner. Maintaining energy, or high speed, is essential for success in fighter combat. Huge vertical stabilisers are necessary for control during high angle-of-attack flight when lower portions are blocked out by the wings and fuselage. (Lockheed)

control, helmet sights and advanced optics, high-speed chips, computer graphics, artificial intelligence – an extension of the pilot's brain.

But, in the centre of it all, dominating everything, will be the fighter pilot – a highly educated athlete who can tie together all the elements of his job, who can think and act under 10g, who can train for decades and perform at a few minutes' notice, who can operate his computers and controls with precision and intelligence, who can sustain it all with inimitable motivation and spirit and who never, never quits. The technology has changed him in a thousand ways since 1914, but he is still the same young man – a prince, a charmer, a killer, a tough guy for all to see and in much of what he does, but a decent sort, a kid who had a dream, a man who turned into granite, a guy who gets the job done, a dreamer of skies and loneliness, a man who loves, a comrade, a winner, a spirit, a . . . Fighter Pilot.

XII

FIGHTER PILOT

Between the amateur and the professional there is a
difference not only in degree but in kind. – USAF Fighter
Weapons School

IT IS DIFFICULT to define a profession in a few words, but there
is evidence about what kind of person becomes, and succeeds as,
a fighter pilot, what he is and does – his history, his qualities, his
wars, his missions, his tactics, his aircraft, his weapons, his
operational concepts and the nature of his life. The fighter pilot,
since he first flew in combat in 1914, in an era of bloody, bitter and
total warfare, has embodied honourable concepts of chivalry,
bravery and individual accomplishment. We should not make too
many heroes out of our warriors, but in this case we make an
exception.

I am still a fighter pilot, although I have't flown a fighter for 16
years, because it is, above all, a matter of attitude. In essence, a
fighter pilot is a self-confident, spirited, dedicated professional who
never, never quits. Symbolically, life is an air battle; if you lose your
courage and stamina and your intense will to survive and win, the
enemy will get behind you and shoot you down. Apply what it takes
to be a fighter pilot to everything you do in life, and success will fly
with you. I have known people in various walks of life who were real
fighter pilots, and I have known some who happened to sit in the
front seat of a fighter who were not. Attitude makes the difference.

Although they share many things in common, it is also true that
many different kinds of men become fighter pilots. (Let us also note
with pride that there are now some women – Canadian F-18 fighter
pilots among others.) We often think of the bold, aggressive,
outgoing, athletic type who charges at the world with self-
confidence and daring. That kind of man was likely to come out a
victor after flinging himself into a gaggle of enemy fighters in the
dogfights of the First and Second World Wars.

But it was undoubtedly true then, as it is now, that there are also
quiet, introspective men, whose steel is less visible, buried in
character, who possess the same will to win. In these men it may be
their analytical skill, their self-discipline, their need to excel, which

rewards them with victory. They may be unassuming on the ground where the might of their personality is unseen and unneeded, but the fight to survive, to defeat the enemy, to do the absolute best that they are capable of, changes them into something intense and wonderful.

And let us also admit that there are other men who have come to the profession as a way of making themselves better, of improving themselves by facing their fears and training hard to overcome their mediocrity. At their best, they are as admirable as the first two men described; at their worst, they prove that it is not the aeroplane which makes the man, but the man which makes the aeroplane. A famous climber, reaching the summit of a great mountain, was asked by his companion what they had conquered. He replied, 'Nothing but ourselves.'

When Vietnam and the one-year combat tour came along, the United States ran out of experienced, career fighter pilots. So the authorities started retreading bomber pilots and pilot training instructors who had skills that could be transferred. Most of them did just fine, although certainly not with the finesse that comes only from many years on the gunnery and air-to-air ranges, and the self-confidence that comes only from years of intense development. And now university graduates are taken and, after two years and £4 million, turned into combat-ready fighter pilots.

The modern fighter pilot, flying a supersonic £20 million aeroplane with incredible computers and weapons, is more likely to be successful if he is the intelligent, analytical type than if he is a fellow who gets by on personality and brashness. The aeroplane and the mission call for too much to tolerate those who 'wing it'.

The successful modern fighter pilot is the one who knows his flight manuals and aircraft switches backwards and forwards, who spends hours thinking of the changing relationships of the dive bomb pass and the three-dimensional air-to-air manoeuvres, who conditions his body so that he can pull more 'gs' and think clearly. These things take more than instinct and natural ability and uncalculated aggressiveness.

In reality, the best fighter pilot in the air is the one who performs best on the ground, spending dozens of hours in training and preparation for each precious hour of expensive flying time.

It is true that there are special men, somehow born with unusual capabilities of reaction time, mind and hand co-ordination and perception of spatial relationships. They seem to think more quickly and know just what to do in the midst of a whirling chaos of speed, myriad instruments and variable challenges. Sometimes the pressure builds up, danger increases, alternatives dwindle, systems fail and the enemy attacks, and the great fighter pilot

Chuck Debellevue, one of the two navigator aces in Vietnam. After Ritchie went home, Chuck (right) got his fifth and sixth kills with John Madden (left) on 9 September 1972. (Terry Murphy)

survives and wins because he did just the right thing with his mind and hands in the few moments given him.

There is another kind of fighter pilot, perhaps the one we love the most. He is the child who built the models and read all the stories of his honoured and brave predecessors. He was always a scrambler, with lots of spirit and enthusiasm, and he hated to lose. He believed in himself and his self-confidence was apparent in everything he did. He could laugh off an injury and whenever life got a little tough, he got tougher. And somehow he found his way through all the pitfalls and alternatives and became an Air Force officer, and he breezed through pilot training and the check rides and made it to combat-readiness training in one of the world's high-performance fighters. Or, perhaps later, when life seemed a little dull and he saw a fighter in the blue sky, he said, 'Hey, I can do that.' And so he did.

That was me. I decided, when I was 15 years old, in just that way. Twenty years later I led flights of Phantoms in combat, and later they gave me a hundred million dollars worth of aircraft and 60 fighter pilots to manage. I was not the greatest and I did not spend a lifetime at it, but, by God, I was a fighter pilot. I had reached the very top of one of the world's most cherished professions, surviving narrowing stages of elimination along the way. No matter what else happens to me, it was the highlight of my life because of what it took to get there and what that process created in me. I'm still struggling with life, but the enemy is in my sights in front of me, not behind. Being a fighter pilot still defines what I do and what I am – not a bad way to go for a shy little kid who feared the world but had an unthinkable dream.

APPENDIX

FIGHTER TERMS

Every profession has its jargon, the technical, operational and slang terms which it uses. To outsiders these are sometimes mystifying, but to insiders they are often a vital means of communication. Some of the terms are, of course, totally unnecessary, but they gradually become part of the language because they are useful or descriptive or humorous. In a profession which operates complicated machinery, it is inevitable that words based on that technology will become part of the professional's language. Many are acronyms, shorthand for frequently used equipment, organizations, procedures, etc. In time, many of them move into the common vocabulary. There are entire dictionaries full of words dealing with flying and aviation. Here is just a flavour of the language of the fighter pilot:

AAA	Anti-Aircraft Artillery. Ground Fire. Called 'Triple-A'.
Aardvark	An F-111.
AB	Afterburner. The extension on the rear of a turbojet engine which injects raw fuel into the exhaust, causing additional thrust; also AB thrust, AB fuel flow. Most pilots would say 'burners' or 'afterburners' in common usage, as in 'Light the burners'. The RAF term is 'reheat'.
ABCCC	Airborne Command and Control Center. Called 'A-B-Triple-C'. Cargo aircraft with computers and additional communications for controlling an air battle. No radar as in AWACS.

A great shot of an RAF Tornado GR Mk.1 of No. 27 Squadron, based at RAF Marham, Extra fuel tanks are visible, as in the power of full twin reheat. (Davis Gibson Advertising)

AC	Aircraft Commander. Front-seater in a two-seater.
ACT	Air Combat Tactics. The training and manoeuvres of air-to-air combat, as in 'ACT mission', 'ACT manoeuvres', 'fly ACT'.
Active	The primary runway currently in use. 'Take the Active', 'the Active is 23 left'.
Aileron roll	A roll around the longitudinal axis of the aircraft using the ailerons. Moving the stick causes one aileron on the trailing edge of the wing to go up and the other to go down, causing the aircraft to roll.
AIM	Air Intercept Missile, such as AIM-9 Sidewinder, as opposed to AGM, or air-to-ground missile. 'Fire an AIM missile', 'an AIM attack', 'AIM tactics', 'Load the AIMs'.
All-aspect	Air-to-air situation or type of missile, meaning 360 degrees. An all-aspect missile can home on the target from all directions, not just from the tail as with the original Sidewinders.
Angels	'Angels 30' equals 30,000ft, etc.
Auger in	Crash. 'Buy the farm', 'Buy it', die with the airplane.
Back-seater	The person sitting in the rear of a two-seat aircraft such as the F 4 or Tornado, normally a navigator instead of a pilot. Also known as WSO or 'Wizzo' (Weapon Systems Officer), 'GIB' (guy-in-back), 'Pitter' (sitting in the pit), and 'Bear' (in a Wild Weasel fighter, being led around on a leash).
Bandit	A known hostile or unfriendly aircraft, as in 'Bandits at 2 o'clock low'.
Barrel	The location for taking your turn in the barrel; performing a less than desirable duty, such as alert duty or desk duty. Also refers to a barrel-shaped section of airspace for training, in order to separate aircraft and prevent collisions.
BDA	Bomb Damage Assessment. A verbal or written evaluation of bombing or strike results, usually quantitative, given after the attack by a FAC (q.v.) or range officer to the pilot, or by the pilot back to headquarters. 'Here is BDA', a BDA report.
BFM	Basic Flight Manoeuvres. The basic manoeuvres of air-to-air tactics; the basic training which serves as the foundation of advanced ACT (q.v.).
Bingo	'Bingo fuel' is the amount needed to RTB (Return to Base), usually computed for target area. 'Red 2 is Bingo', 'Call your Bingo', 'Raise your Bingo for bad weather'. Also used for bullets, bombs, chaff, etc.
Blind	I do not have the friendly aircraft in sight.
Boards	Speed brakes. Panels extended hydraulically to cause drag and slow the aircraft.
Bogey	An unknown aircraft. 'Red Lead, you have bogeys at Ten High'. Become bandits when identified hostile.

Bogey dope	Information on the bogey, e.g. from an AWACS.
Break	A maximum-g turn to avoid a missile or aircraft.
Brick	A hand-held radio. Usually carried by field people who need to keep in touch with others, or by senior officers so that they can always be reached by the command post while in their car, on the flight line or at the club for lunch. 'Bricktown' is a headquarters base with a lot of colonels and generals carrying 'bricks'.
Bucc	RAF Buccaneer fighter.
Buff	Big Ugly Fat Fella. A B-52 or a C-5.
Bull	Bull's-eye. A perfect hit on target range.
Burner	Afterburner.
Button	'Go Button 12' means 'go Channel 12' on radio.
Buzzer X	Select a jamming mode on the ECM (q.v.) pod.
BVR	Beyond Visual Range. A BVR missile. Radar ID.
CAP	Combat Air Patrol. Fighters flying a course or orbit which provides protection to other aircraft or ground areas.
CBU	Cluster Bomb Unit. Various kinds of small air-to-ground weapons carried in pods in large numbers. When the pod opens the CBU bomblets are spread over a large area, for use against personnel, vehicles, runways. A CBU attack, carrying CBUs.
Crud	A game played in the Officer's Club on a snooker table between teams of fighter pilots involving two balls, body contact and significant skill and good humour.
DACT	Dissimilar Air Combat Tactics. Practice ACT (q.v.) with a different kind of aircraft instead of the usual practice with one's similar squadron mates.
Deadbug	A silly game played by fighter pilots. A pilot who had flown a mission north of the Red River in North Vietnam, the dangerous part, was entitled to call 'deadbug!' in a bar, and the last man to hit the floor on his back had to buy the bar. A way of getting 'new guys' or uninitiated non-combat types to buy drinks. A way of acting a little crazily and keeping the spirit up in Vietnam after getting shot at. Still heard, 20 years later.
DefCon	Defense Condition. A series of alert conditions set by the Pentagon which cause world-wide forces to establish escalating levels of readiness and security, e.g. 'DefCon 2'.
Deuce	The F-102. Only outsiders call it the Delta Dagger.
DM	Deputy for Maintenance. The Wing Commander's assistant responsible for aircraft maintenance and readiness. Would be DCS (Deputy Chief of Staff) Maintenance at higher levels such as a numbered Air Force. Also Davis-Monthan Air Force Base.
DO	Deputy for Operations. The Wing Commander's assistant responsible for aircraft operations. Would be

	DCS (Deputy Chief of Staff) Operations at higher levels such as a numbered Air Force.
Duster	A dud. A released bomb that does not explode.
Eagle Driver	An F-15 pilot. The term 'driver' is sometimes used in other expressions, e.g. a tanker driver, a truck driver (cargo).
ECM	Electronic countermeasures.
Energy	Altitude and airspeed which can be exchanged in an air battle to gain position. Low and slow is dangerous, limiting manoeuvrability against a faster or higher opponent.
FAC	Forward Air Controller.
FEBA	Forward Edge of the Battle Area. The line of contact with enemy forces. Up to the FEBA, FEBA forces, across the
Feet-Wet	Flying over water. 'Going Feet-Wet' (crossing the coast).
Fence	Fence in. Turn armament on, get ready for battle.
FIGMO	Forget it, I got my orders. No longer caring, thinking about the next assignment.
Firewall	Fireproof wall between cockpit and prop engine in front. Now used as slang in jet fighters, as in 'firewall it' or 'firewall the throttles', meaning 'go full power by pushing throttles towards firewall'.
Flameout	When the engine stops. Used to happen all the time, causing problems in single-engine aircraft. Fortunately now very rare with reliable engines.
FMC	Fully Mission Capable. Aircraft (or, in slang, the pilot) status in which all systems are up and the plane can perform all possible missions.
FNG	A new guy. Someone who doesn't know everything yet.
Four-ship	Four aircraft in formation, a flight under one leader which works together. Also two-ship, three-ship, etc.
Fox Mike	FM radio.
Fox One	I have fired a radar missile.
Fox Two	I have fired a heat missile.
Fox Three	I have fired the gun.
Frag Order	Headquarters directive specifying missions to fly. In the RAF an Air Tasking Message.
GCA	Ground Controlled Approach. Radar with voice direction for final approach.
GCI	Ground Controlled Intercept. Ground radar station which vectors fighter to target.
GIB	Guy-in-Back, the back-seater in a fighter. Mostly used with F-4. Now 'Wizzo' is common.
Gomer	Enemy fighter pilot.
HAS	Hardened Aircraft Shelter, protected from air attack, such as TAB-V (q.v.) in NATO.
Heater	A heat-seeking missile, such as Sidewinder.
Hog	The A-10 (actually 'Warthog'). Hardly ever called the Thunderbolt II by the somewhat irreverent pilots.

Hot	In firing weapons, 'Cleared Hot', 'Trigger is Hot'.
HOTAS	Hands on Throttle and Stick. A concept whereby a pilot in a modern fighter, such as an F-16, controls all major combat and flight systems with switches on the throttle and stick. Thus, with HUD (q.v.), he can fight without moving his eyes or hands into the cockpit.
Hound Dog	To leave the formation temporarily to seize the opportunity to shoot down a passing bandit or to strike a target of opportunity.
HSI	Horizontal Situation Indicator. Major composite flight instrument.
HUD	Head-Up Display. Flight, navigation and weapon information is displayed on wide glass in front of the pilot so that he does not have to look into the cockpit while flying the aircraft and looking out visually.
Hun	The F-100. Also 'Sled' or 'Silver Dollar'.
IFF	Identification Friend or Foe. Electronic system which allows other radar sets to receive special codes of friendly aircraft.
IG	Inspector General. Conducts inspections of units.
INS	Inertial Navigation System. Gyro system which tells where an aircraft or ship is located on Earth. Very accurate and self-contained. Always updating.
IP	Instructor Pilot. Also Initial Point, a place to begin the target run-in.
Jink	To fly a fighter aggressively through an unpredictable flight path to avoid gunfire. Thus 'Let's jink over to the Squadron'.
Judy	Pilot takes control of his own intercept from GCI.
Junk	To dispense chaff/flares while manoeuvring a fighter defensively, to throw off enemy radar or a missile.
Lawn Dart	An F-16. Also called The Electric Jet and the Viper, but not the Fighting Falcon, which is for FNGs (q.v.) and civilians.
LOX	Liquid oxygen.
Mark 82	A standard 500lb bomb.
Maverick	An anti-tank rocket weapon.
Mickey	Coded message sent between jam-resistant radios.
Mike-Mike	'20 Mike-Mike' is 20mm gunfire.
Mil	Military power, i.e. 100 per cent without afterburner. Also milliradian, i.e. 17.5 degrees of arc (used in setting mechanical gun/bomb sights for specific weapon or delivery, as in 'set 40 mils').
Mud Hen	F-15E Strike Eagle, the one with air-to-ground capability. 'Mud' means ground, as in 'mud fighter', 'mud mover' and 'air-to-mud', as opposed to dogfighter.
No joy	I do not have the aircraft in sight that you just told me about.
NOTAM	Notice to Airmen. The latest information for flight

221

	planning – routes, airfields, restricted areas, warnings, – etc.
Nose gunner	A front-seat pilot.
OB	Order of Battle. A list or summary of the enemy's forces. GOB = Ground, AOB = Air.
OPR	Officer Performance Report. Regular evaluation by superior officer, important for promotion and future jobs. Usually exaggerated to compete with everyone else because of inflation in system.
OR	Operationally Ready or Operational Readiness. Refers to the capability of an aircraft or unit. Also called Mission Capable.
ORI	Operational Readiness Inspection. The dreaded, realistic and tiresome evaluation of a unit's combat capability. If you bust your ORI, the Commander and others may get fired and you have to practise, practise, practise for the remake. A USAF term. NATO calls it a TAC EVAL (q.v.), a Tactical Evaluation carried out by a multinational team.
Pipper	The point on the HUD (q.v.) or gunsight which is placed on the target.
Playtime	How long you can stay according to the fuel remaining.
Puzzle Palace	The Pentagon. Also a headquarters.
Pickle	Dropping weapons by pushing the pickle button, placing them accurately in the pickle barrel. Back-seaters say, 'Ready, Ready Gherkin'. A lot of slang is merely an attempt to be different or not trite.
Pistol	The gun carried by a fighter.
Pond	The Ocean. 'Crossing the Pond'.
Popeye	IFR, Instrument Flight Rules – flying in the clouds, unable to see visually. Also called IMC, for Instrument Meteorological Conditions. VFR and VMC are Visual Conditions.
Punch out	Eject.
Ramp	The concrete or tarmac where fighters are parked.
Raven	The EF-111, an ECM (q.v.) aircraft. Originally the call-sign of the great FACs of Laos during the Vietnam War.
Recce	Reconnaissance. 'A recce bird', 'To do recce'.
Red Flag	Major, realistic, high-tech fighter pilot wargame at Nellis Air Force Base, Nevada.
RHAW	Radar Homing and Warning. A cockpit indicator which tells the direction, strength and type of radar energy. 'I have a launch light on my RAW gear.' Also RWR, for Radar Warning Receiver.
ROE	Rules of Engagement. Predetermined headquarters control over a fighter pilot covering various contingencies.
RTB	Return to Base. Go home.
SA	Situational Awareness. Knowing all the conditions

	around you in order to be able to make the right decisions.
SAC	Strategic Air Command. The last place in the world a fighter pilot wants to be.
SAM	Surface-to-Air Missile, usually the Russian variety, such as a SAM-7. A SAM-break is a hard manoeuvre to avoid the missile.
SAR	Search and Rescue. 'A SAR helicopter', 'A SAR is in progress'.
Scramble	A hasty take-off, sometimes from Ground Alert, to meet an immediate requirement.
Sierra Hotel	Phonetic of 'shit hot', a slang phrase meaning 'out-standing!'
Shack	An accurate bomb, right on the target of a small shack or building. Also an accurate statement.
Shooter	A member of the flight who is designated to fire at the enemy.
Six	The F-106. 'He's flying Sixes'.
Smash	High speed, with the implication of force and power. 'I had a lot of smash'.
Snakeye	A high-drag bomb, usually 500lb with mechanical fins which open after release to slow the bomb. This allows a lower and more accurate delivery without frag-mentation damage to the aircraft. In Vietnam, a common load was 'Snake and Nape', a mixture of bombs and napalm for a variety of ground targets.
SUU-21	A practice bomb dispenser carrying six bomblets. It is embarrassing to fail to drop a practice bomb (i.e., to make a dry pass) in front of everyone because you forgot to open the SUU doors.
TAB-V	A NATO bomb-proof aircraft shelter. The RAF term is HAS (q.v.).
TAC	Tactical Air Command, the fighter organization in the US used as an adjective, as in TAC Air, TAC fighters, and TAC-type, or as shorthand for 'tactical'.
TAC EVAL	The NATO version of an ORI, given to NATO fighter units. Also any evaluation of a tactical unit.
Tactical	Your current situation, as in 'What's your Tactical?'
Tally Ho	I have it/them in sight. 'Red Lead, bogeys at 10 level.' 'Tally.'
TDY	Temporary Duty. A temporary trip on official business, as opposed to PCS, a permanent change of station.
TFR	Terrain-following radar. Usually connected to the auto-pilot, which flies aircraft at fixed low altitude over the ground in any weather.
Thud	An F-105 (because so many thudded into the ground in North Vietnam). Soon became a term of affection and pride. 'Thud Ridge' was a prominent landmark near Hanoi.

T-38 Talon – 'The White Rocket'. The supersonic toy by Northrop has been around for nearly 30 years, preparing students for the move into high-performance fighters. The inexpensive, easy-to-maintain F-5 fighter version is still flown by air forces around the world. (US National Archives)

TOT	Time-on-Target. When you are supposed to be there!
Trash Hauler	A cargo aircraft or cargo pilot.
Training Rules	Safety limitations on flight conditions and manoeuvres during practice sessions (as opposed to serious combat rules or Rules of Engagement).
Tweet	A Tweety Bird, the Cessna T-37 jet trainer (from its small size and high-pitched engine noise).
Victor	VHF radio.
Visual	I have it in sight. I have a visual.
Weapons Tight	Operational, ready to fire.
White Rocket	T-38 Talon.
Winchester	Out of ammunition. 'Lead, Two is Winchester'.
Wire	The correct flight path for weapon delivery, on the proper wire. To be successful, to have it made, is to have it wired.
Wizzo	WSO. Weapons Systems Operator, back-seater.
YGBSM	You gotta be shittin' me.
Zoomie	Air Force Academy graduate.